TEACHER'S TREASURY
OF STORIES
FOR EVERY OCCASION

TEACHER'S TREASURY OF STORIES FOR EVERY OCCASION

Compiled
by

M. DALE BAUGHMAN

Englewood Cliffs, N.J.

PRENTICE-HALL, INC.

CONTENTS

TEACHER'S TREASURY
OF STORIES
FOR EVERY OCCASION

INTRODUCTION

Our modern schools are just as much superior to the old-fashioned one-room variety as the modern jet plane is to the Wright Brothers' first creation. The majority of today's teachers are far superior to the schoolmaster and the schoolmarm of an earlier day. How, then, do we account for the current emphasis on the needless waste of human talent in our schools? I refer to the many youths who possess a hundred acres of possibilities but who keep only about one acre under cultivation. Yes, teacher preparation, professional standards, school buildings, facilities, equipment and quality of instruction have improved, but what about the issue of inspiration?

Caleb Mills, noted Hoosier educator of years past, is said to have remarked, "Teachers must inspire as well as instruct!" The author annually interviews two or three hundred teachers and prospective teachers, nearly all of whom concur with the above statement; yet today there is much evidence pointing to the ineptitudes of too many teachers in overcoming pupil inertia. We have to face up to reality—some pupils are like what the farmer said about the mule, "Awfully backward about going forward."

What's the difference between "instruct" and "inspire"? To instruct is to impart knowledge, give information, cause to learn; to inspire is to stimulate, motivate, enliven, energize, impel to action. Our high schools and colleges grind out by the thousands graduates who have an ample supply of knowledge and information, but who lack the ability to stir the emotions, which is basic for creativity, or planned action.

Too few youngsters in our classrooms today are impelled to action. When asked to recall teachers who inspired them, interviewees in the Office of Teacher Placement, University of Illinois, where the author is a placement consultant, usually remark, "Well, I do

1

remember one, two or three teachers who stirred my emotions and motivated me." This is not an especially optimistic situation, especially when we remember that children by nature are creative—some more than others, it is true.

One wise old school superintendent admonished his youthful successor, "Look for teachers who are green at the top; anything green at the top is alive!" To meet this qualification a great many of today's teachers ought to pray earnestly the prayer of the old Scot who mostly feared decay from the chin up: "Lord, keep me alive while I'm still living." If this implies lack of enthusiasm by many teachers, good! It was intended to do so. Junius said, "Be not afraid of a jest! If one throws salt at thee, thou wilt receive no harm, unless thou art raw."

As one teacher talking to another, I'm quick to admit that there is so much good in the worst of us and so much bad in the best of us that it's hard to tell which of us ought to reform the rest of us—but you can be sure of *one* thing: the day-by-day work of an inspirational teacher is like an underground stream of water which flows quietly along unobserved, but which makes green everything growing above it.

The sponsors of the radio program featuring the Quiz Kids, who were popular not too long ago, conducted a contest in which many thousands of letters were written by pupils describing "the teacher who helped me most." "Sense of humor" was one of the most frequently mentioned traits. One pupil wrote, "I think Miss X likes to teach; she makes everyone laugh sometime during the day." Another pupil wrote, "She laughs with us and says a day is lost without a joke."

Quaint expressions, forceful delivery and a touch of dramatics all are helpful to the teacher who would inspire. One teacher, bent on impressing his pupils with an important rule of grammar, stood on his desk and crowed like a rooster immediately after stating a well-known rule. "Now," he said, "you will never forget this rule." Years later he ran into one of his former students who reminisced, "I'll never forget the day you stood on your desk and crowed like a rooster. But, say, what was that rule we were supposed to remember?" Teachers, like salesmen, should electrify their prospects, not merely gas them.

Mark Twain frequently indulged in profanity. His wife, it seems, was quite the opposite, a rather refined lady free from such deplorable habits. She once planned an experiment to change Mark's habit of swearing. She met him at the door of their home and immediately uttered a string of oaths. Her husband was momentarily stunned but quickly regained his composure and remained calm throughout his wife's outburst. When she had finished, he said softly, "My dear, you have the words but not the music." It is not outside the realm of possibility for teachers to acquire both the "words" and the "music" to motivate more pupils.

In a nationwide survey taken by the Gilbert Youth Research Council of what high school students think of education at their level, it was revealed that 77 per cent of both boys and girls are satisfied with *what* they are required to learn but have plenty of gripes about *how* subjects are being taught. Many teachers, they complain, lack enthusiasm for their subject matter, present it in a dull and uninteresting fashion, and fail to keep pace with recent developments. They had more than just complaints; they also had some interesting and constructive criticisms: "Have teachers, instead of just lecturers," "Turn away from the obvious," "Provoke more thought," "Teach more, talk less," and "Encourage, not discourage."

Many of us recognize Jesus as the greatest teacher the world ever had, yet very little was written about his pedagogical principles. "His words were stimuli that appealed to the deeper active tendencies of his hearers; stimuli to the will," wrote William Burnham in his book, *Great Teachers and Mental Health*. He rarely, if ever, used words that merely aroused emotion without opportunity to follow through with action of some kind. How did He accomplish this? Through appeal to the imagination by concrete illustrations. His Sermon on the Mount was one metaphor after another; He was master of the parable and habitually used practical experiments and suggestion by means of actual demonstrations. He freely used simple illustrations, simple comparisons, fables, similes and allegories.

What is teaching? I believe it is the ability to inspire, encourage, and guide learning. Yes, this process is repetitious in spots, but so is housekeeping and hog-raising. We make a living from what we get, but we make a life from what we give. Teachers must find challenge in doing some of the routine things that must be done. Rossini said, "Give me a laundry list and I'll set it to music." Surely, there is more appeal in a roomful of children than in a laundry list.

There is much satisfaction in being satisfied with our identity as teachers. A good teacher is someone who can *understand* those not very good at *explaining* and *explain* it to those not very good at *understanding*. That's why a teacher can never truly teach unless he is still learning himself. One candle can hardly light another unless it continues to flame. The mere repeater of lessons can only load children's minds; he never quickens them.

Teachers, like other human beings, can live without air for a short while, without water for several days, without food for several weeks, and without a new idea for who knows how long? The village idler was approached by a curious observer, "Must be pretty dull to sit here all day and do nothin' but whittle." "Well," said Uncle Billy, "I'm thinkin', mostly." "Do you mean you can sit and do nothing but think—and not get bored?" asked the stranger. The old native of the Sassafras and the Sumac spat a brown stream. "That's right," he answered, "thinkin' is a heap like sin; them that don't is scairt of it; them that do it enough finally git so they like it."

The teacher's job is to make pupils and other listeners think often enough so that they learn to like it. The pages of this book abound with similes, illustrations, quips, clever remarks, anecdotes and other thought-provoking expressions that will help you to accomplish this goal, once you learn to use them often.

Why This Book Can Be as Handy as Your Latin "Pony"

Quoted in *Phoenix Flame*, Professor Dexter Williams stated, "Talk is the principal product of the world. It is divided into plain, loud, big, back, double, idle, and just. It is said in every language known to man, and of course, to woman. It comes out of loudspeakers, professional speakers, after-dinner speakers and plain windbags. It is a means of communication, expression, exaggeration and prevarication. . . ."

Teachers also talk—in a variety of places: formally—in the classroom, at PTA, at local service clubs and women's clubs, at professional meetings; and informally—on the athletic field, in school corridors, in pupils' homes and on downtown corners. You can't poke a hole through a board with a soda straw. You need a sharp, pointed object. You can't use abstractions for injecting ideas; you need concrete illustrations and expressions with cutting edges.

According to most sources, we are in short supply of people who can speak effectively and sway men's minds. Effective speaking is a prerequisite to effective leadership and teachers, like bullets, go farthest when they are smoothest. There are three things difficult to do with words: make people laugh, make people think, and make people cry. The collection of uncommon, though attention-getting, scraps of sunshine, humor, philosophy, and miscellaneous quotes in this book is intended to help the teacher who has a yen to do only the first two: make people laugh and make people think.

I began collecting word-tools for provoking both laughter and thought during my first year of teaching, at the age of 19. Somewhere in this compilation are examples of wordplay that I have used successfully in classroom teaching at all levels, ranging from grade one through graduate classes in college, in speeches of introduction, in toastmaster assignments, in discussions, and in major addresses before parent groups, at educational conferences, at athletic banquets, in commencement programs, in teachers' institutes, and at service club programs.

Teaching is largely, if not wholly, communication and inspiration. It follows, then, that the teacher who would be a lamplighter, not merely the funnel for filling the lamp, must turn to speech and dramatics. The well is deep, and one must have something to draw with. Prepare for that speech! Don't make your listeners drink from the bucket or chew on the rope.

How Can You Best Use This Book?

Horace Binney, American lawyer, writer, and public speaker, writing to a friend in 1868, included this passage on books: "I certainly think the best book in the world would owe the most to a good index, and the worst book, if it had but a single good thought in it, might be kept alive by it." Since I am sympathetic with the above view, a topical index has been included at the back of the book. Although the topic items are arranged alphabetically and there is an index, you will, no doubt, at times want to pick up this book and read through parts of it just for enjoyment and entertainment. Remember this—in this volume there is help for you if you are to deliver a major address, make an introduction, serve as toastmaster, act as panel moderator, or just teach a class of normal students.

In the "Speech" category there are "openers," "closers," and other pertinent squibs which can skillfully be woven into your remarks. There are in addition a few tried and tested "relief devices" which serve as recoveries in case your story falls flat, and which sometimes can serve as transition techniques. For example, when a particular story evokes only mild response, you can add, "I told that story to my secretary the other day; she laughed so hard, she fell off my lap!" When the joke is not well received at all, you might comment, "Well, you may not like my jokes, but you will have to admire my nerve."

Elementary teachers will find appropriate materials, for example, under "children-parents," "pupils," and "teachers." Junior high school and high school teachers will immediately find helpful new expressions listed under "youth," "adolescents," "school," and "education." School administrators will want to familiarize themselves with the above categories plus the special topics of "principal" and "school administrators."

Athletic coaches, too, can use materials very effectively from the various headings as well as from the broad category "sports."

Although the topical index and the alphabetical categorization of items will suffice as aids to finding what you want, I have an additional technique to recommend. At those times when you sit down to browse through the book, keep in the back of your mind the idea that one day you may be in a position to use some of the inspiring or humorous items you come across. When you read a story, anecdote, or illustration that especially appeals to you, write down on a sheet of paper the item number, the page number and what the item is about. Keep the sheet of paper in the book just for this purpose.

If you have to give a formal address before a large audience, or simply an informal talk to a smaller group, you're sure to find material here as helpful to you as the back of your eighth grade arithmetic book. When the subject of your remarks is established, write down all the topics related to it. Then look through the index to find items on these topics. You will discover some that are humorous and entertaining, some that provoke thought and meditation, and others that make an intellectual or emotional appeal.

You can, if you wish, make an entirely serious speech or an entirely humorous speech. Uusally, however, most successful talks by teachers contain both humor and intellectual appeal.

After deciding on some definite response to the introduction, you will be wise to select some clever "openers" for purposes of intrigue and attention-getting. The body of the speech should be punctuated with some sparklers here and there. A little practice will enable you to weave them in naturally.

You must have terminal facilities—that is, your close should be a planned close. Some effective "closers" appear in the section on "speech."

It will be obvious to you that much of this material will need to be adapted to fit specific purposes. Therefore, some language changes will be necessary. Fortunately, most of the items are easily adapted for different purposes and different situations. Telling stories in which you, your relatives or your friends play some of the roles, is often more successful than merely using random names.

Why Don't You Start Your Own Card File Collection?

A card file collection of items bearing on some subject of your own special interest could prove to be both a productive and satisfying hobby. At first, my scraps clipped from here and there were kept in labeled envelopes. Later, I tried scrapbooks, and finally, adopted the card file system which I strongly recommend. I use 4 x 6 unlined cards on which I either paste or write new materials. Most shoeboxes work quite well as the card container.

To do this kind of collecting successfully, one must have the zeal and attitude of the hunter who relentlessly stalks his prey; in this case, the hunter's weapons are scissors, sharp pen-knife or whatever can be used, and the prey is the pointed phrase, the simile, the humorous poem, and the anecdote lurking in the back of some magazine, house organ, or newspaper.

INTRODUCTION

Long ago I formed the habit of always carrying some 4 x 6 file cards in my coat pocket. After all, you shoudn't let cliptomania get the best of you—in some instances you would refrain from clipping articles; in such cases you can write them on your 4 x 6 cards and the prey is not lost for lack of ammunition.

How Can You Make Yourself Wanted as a Speaker?

1. Learn how to prepare your speech material and yourself for the occasion. Making a speech is like "going to the dentist." No matter what the dentist's reputation, the occasion is seldom, if ever, painless.

PREPARATION OF MATERIAL. Spend some preliminary time in concentrating on the theme or subject of your speech. Provide handy places for writing down ideas as they come to you days before the speech—pocket, bedside, office desk, auto. Divide the anatomy of your speech into five parts: (1) getting started, (2) picking up steam, (3) the body of the message, (4) slowing down or summing up, and (5) the close. List all the topics you can think of which are significantly related to the theme of your speech. Search this book and others of your choice for items which seem to be appropriate. You will discover that most of the selected items can easily be included in one of the rough divisions of your speech mentioned above. The items you have selected from this book and others, plus your own written ideas, are now ready to be thrown into the master pool. You are now ready to write the rough draft of your speech. As you string together the various items and ideas, in no circumstances negate your own ability to throw in thoughts, ideas and expressions from your own experiences. In general, it's a good idea to include "something old, something new, something borrowed, but never blue." Lastly, select two or three good "openers" and one good "closer" from this book.

For major addresses it is wise to have a written manuscript and one or two carbon copies. One never knows when the speech text will be needed for various purposes. As to your using the manuscript in giving your speech, that's your choice. Some effective speakers use notes, a few speakers use neither notes nor manuscript, and still others have the manuscript before them. I am firmly convinced that the speech, short or long, which does the most for both the giver and his hearers is the one which has been carefully prepared, carefully studied, and then presented as studied, using the manuscript as an emergency device only.

It must be admitted that giving a speech with a manuscript is like making love to a girl through a picket fence; everything that's said can be heard, but there isn't likely to be much contact. It is so often true, however, that speakers who neither prepare nor use a manuscript actually have three speeches and usually give the third, the three being, what he has in mind to say, what he actually says, and what he wishes he had said after it is all over.

I like to prepare a manuscript as described above, refine it and then study it. Finally, I put it on tape and play it back with the manuscript in my hands. I may do this two or three times. I have found that the reading of the speech for the recording and the subsequent listening makes me so familiar with the manuscript that I seldom have to rely on it any more than I would rely on notes. One might ask, "Then why do you use it when giving the speech?" My answer is another question, "Why take a chance?" The human mind is a wonderful mechanism; it starts working the minute you're born and doesn't stop until you stand up to speak in public.

Remember this: When you build a speech, you are also building yourself. Speeches that are neither carefully prepared, nor systematically presented, too often turn out to be twin-cylinder exhausts of one-cylinder motors. To do the best job, diligently prepare a manuscript, study it and put it on tape if possible, and then give the speech as nonchalantly as if it were not carefully prepared. Most teachers are good readers and good readers can do this easily. The good reader who has studied his speech and is reasonably familiar with its content will seldom need to refer to his manuscript, and when he does, his eye takes in several ideas and several lines at a glance.

1. *Preparing yourself.* The beauty of careful preparation and study of a manuscript is that by so doing you have pretty thoroughly prepared yourself. You know that you have something to say and not merely that you have to say something. You have confidence, too, in your delivery, for you have practiced it and heard it. There is very little left to do in preparing oneself, other than in

indulging in some concentrated positive thinking. For example, "This is an audience, not a jury; they will like my humor"; "Laughing is good medicine and the members of my audience know good medicine"; and "My audience will give me their attention because I have some thought-provoking ideas to present."

2. *Develop an effective and appealing delivery.* Let your voice, manner, and facial expression convey your enthusiasm while your words transmit your prepared message. First, say something at the very beginning of your talk that will capture the attention and the imagination of your hearers. Avoid like the plague the too common, "I'm happy to be here," or, "it's always a pleasure" opening remarks.

Some anonymous political office seeker advised, "First tell them what you are going to tell them; then tell them; then tell them what you have told them." This is especially necessary in an informative type presentation. Another bit of advice I picked up from an old pro is this: "Begin slow, go slow, rise higher, take fire, and sit down amid tumultuous applause." Don't drag your stories and anecdotes in by the heels! Pave the way so they march right in and are well under way before the listeners are aware of it.

Unless you are definitely instructed to talk for 40 minutes or longer, I suggest 25 to 30 minutes as the time length of your speech. With a tape recorder this can be ascertained very accurately.

If you should somehow find yourself in a situation where you carefully prepared a manuscript but then didn't have time to familiarize yourself with it, you have no alternative other than to read it. As I see it, worst has come to worst, but be not dismayed! There are some tricks to reading technique. Above all, don't apologize or try to justify your reading of the speech. In spots where indicated, read rather loudly; in others a near whisper is best. If you gesture naturally in your ordinary talk, then by all means do so now. Occasional pauses relieve the monotony of reading. Why not use such pauses for various monotony-relief devices? Some are suggested in this book under "speech." For example, stop, take a drink of water and then remark that once before when you did that, you heard someone in the front row whisper, "First time I ever saw a windmill run by water." It is not a bad idea to have some kind of relief device for each page of reading. Tell a short story, give a comic definition, or insert some wisecrack. A "read" speech with these trappings may not bring down the house; neither will it promote sleep.

Nicholas Murray Butler and Brander Matthews were discussing stories. Said Matthews, "In the case of the first man to use an anecdote, there is originality; in the case of the second, there is plagiarism; with the third, it is lack of originality; and with the fourth, it is drawing from a common stock." "Yes," broke in Butler, "and in the case of the fifth, it is research." I like to think that the poems, similes, epigrams, wisecracks, stories, illustrations, and anecdotes included here illustrate the fifth level, research.

Absent-Mindedness

1. "Let me illustrate the significance of this theory," said the absent-minded professor as he erased the blackboard.

2. "Mama," a college professor's daughter said to him, "has decided she wants to be cremated."

"All right," said the preoccupied professor, "tell her to get her hat on."

Accomplishment—Achievement

3. If you have met with repeated failure in trying to get something from life, do you try to forget your own mistakes? Why not, instead, put your fizzles out in the open on a shelf—so you can keep learning from them?

—HAL BOYLE

4. Two qualities make the difference between leaders and men of average performance. They are curiosity and discontent. I have never known an outstanding man who lacked either. And I have never known a man of small achievement who had both.

—CHARLES H. BROWER, *Town Journal*

5. In the final analysis you should not measure your success by what you *have* accomplished, but by what you *should* have accomplished with your ability.

6. Everything comes to him who hustles while he waits.

—*Supervision*

7. Everyone ought to fear to die until he has done something that will always live.

8. Man is at his best when stimulated by hope of reward, fear of failure, and the light of a star.

—PROF. ERWIN H. SCHELL, *Journal of American Trade Assn. Executives*

9. Real power has fullness and variety. It is not narrow like lightning, but broad like light. Power is a thing of solidity and wholeness.

—R. D. HITCHCOCK

13

10. Sooner or later the man with a pull bows to the man with a push.

11. It is a mistake for any person to assure himself that he can "have anything he wants or be anything he wants, providing he wants it badly enough and is willing to work hard enough." Life imposes some limitations upon us which neither hard work nor stern determination can overcome.

—*Christian Advocate*

12. A man achieves according to what he believes.

13. If history were to consider only the errors and never the accomplishments, the world would never produce any "great" men.

—*Cincinnati Enquirer*

14. Observe the teakettle with the loose lid. As steam rises, the lid shakes, accomplishing nothing except a good noise. As the lid allows steam to escape, it makes a big noise. Those people who make a big noise accompanied by little accomplishment might be described as having a "loose lid."

15. A small boy visiting the Metropolitan Museum was told by his mother that it had taken a sculptor three years to carve the statue they were looking at. "Then it took him *another* three years to make another one?" he asked. His mother nodded. "When he was six, he'd only carved two statues?" the lad demanded.

—*New Yorker*

16. A man who is contented with what he has done will never become famous for what he will do.

17. It is when we forget ourselves that we do things that are remembered.

18. An expert hunter once was asked: "How do you manage to clear your fences and take your amazing leaps?" He replied, "I put my heart over, and my horse is sure to follow."

—Edwin G. Frye, *Telescope-Messenger*

19. He who finds diamonds must grapple in mud and mire because diamonds are not found in polished stones. They are made.

—H. B. Wilson

20. The guy who cuts a wide path rarely cuts a long one.

21. After all is said and done, more is said than done.

22. What a man can imagine or conceive in his mind, he can accomplish. Impossibles are only impossibles as thinking makes them so.

—HENRY J. KAISER

23. Remember that life's length is not measured by its hours and days, but by that which we have done for our country and kind. A useless life is short if it lasts a century. We may do much in a few years, and we may do nothing in a lifetime.

—ALBERT PIKE, *Solomon Huber's Notebook*

24. The world is not interested in the storms you encountered, but whether you brought in the ship.

Action

25. I divide the world into three classes: the few who make things happen; the many who watch things happen; and the vast majority who have no idea of what happens: We need more people who make things happen.

—NICHOLAS MURRAY BUTLER

26. Formula for achievement: Congregate, coordinate, cooperate.

—GRETCHEN SCHENK, *Michigan Library News*

27. People roll up their shirtsleeves higher if they feel they are on the team and not just sitting on the sidelines.

—RALPH WALLACE, *Coronet*

28. Ideas have to be hitched as well as hatched.

—B. C. FORBES, *Forbes*

29. Pray for a good harvest, but keep on hoeing.

—Slovenian Proverb

30. Yesterday has passed; tomorrow is just a possibility; today is now.

31. In order to make a place in the sun for yourself . . . you have to be a shade better than the next fellow.

—T. HARRY THOMPSON, *Sales Management*

32. When it's finally settled that it can't be done—stand back and watch the other fellow do it.

33. One of the greatest labor saving devices of today is tomorrow.

34. Have you seen all your dreams come true? Probably not, and perhaps it is a good thing. For when you get all you wish for, you will be miserable. Alexander, having conquered the world, died of sheer boredom. To be forever reaching out, to remain unsatisfied, is the key to spiritual progress.

—N. C. Christian Advocate

35. To *look* is one thing. To *see* what you look at is another. To *understand* what you see is a third. To *learn* from what you understand is still something else. But to *act* on what you learn is all that really matters, isn't it?

36. We are not the only architects of our structures, but we must lay the bricks ourselves.

—Rev. Norman H. Schultz

37. Tomorrow will be the most wonderful day in history. That's the day when we all are going to begin doing better.

38. Actually, the word "speculation" comes from the Latin *speculare,* which means "to spy out and observe." I have defined a speculator as a man who observes the future and acts before it occurs.

To do this successfully—and it is an ability of priceless value in all human affairs, including the making of peace and war—three things are necessary:

First, one must get the facts of a situation or problem.

Second, one must form a judgment as to what those facts portend.

Third, one must act—before it is too late.

—Bernard Baruch, *Saturday Evening Post, 1957*

39. Indecision is fatal. It is better to make a wrong decision than to build up a habit of indecision. If you're wallowing in indecision, you certainly can't act—and action is the basis of success.

Copyright 1938-1944, 1954.
—From *How Never to Be Tired.* By Marie Benyon Ray, used by special permission of the publisher—The Bobbs-Merrill Co.

40. Getting an idea and sitting on a tack are much alike; both should make you rise and take action.

41. A man was hired to chop wood, at three dollars an hour, with the *back* side of the ax, not the bit. To the woodchopper the pay sounded good but the idea sounded crazy. After making like he was chopping wood for a couple of hours, the hired man went back to his employer and said, "I'm through!"

"If the wages aren't high enough, I'll pay you more," answered the employer.

"No, sir, the pay is sufficient; but when I chop wood I've got to see the chips fly!"

42. An old man bought some apples of a new variety and found them so pleasing that he asked his son to plant a tree for him. The son objected on the grounds that it would take too long for the tree to start bearing fruit. The grandson objected for a similar reason. The grandfather, bent on having a tree of the apples, planted it himself and lived to eat the fruit for some time. Such is life. It's impossible to enjoy fruit from trees that are never planted. If you have a secret yen, no matter what, begin now to work on it.

Adolescence—Adolescents

43. They're neither fish nor beast; therefore, they must be fowl.

44. Growth-wise, up to age 12 boys are about one year behind girls: during the ages 12 to 17 the boys are gradually catching up and from 17 on it's neck and neck.

45. Typically, the adolescent mind is like the basement on wash day, temporarily cluttered up.

46. Seventh graders come in assorted sizes, weights, and colors. They may be either boys or girls and will likely be found scuffling with, shouting at, running to, or whispering about. Their pockets and purses bulge with puzzles, bits of plastic, bean shooters, bedraggled lipsticks, pictures, and rubber bands—*but no pencils.* . . .
—HELEN P. CHAPMAN, *It Starts in the Classroom*

47. A mother, annoyed because her 14-year-old daughter had been calling her boyfriend too frequently, took a tip from a former wartime advertisement and posted a sign over the telephone: IS THIS CALL NECESSARY?

17

Next day there appeared, pencilled on the card, a brief but logical reply: HOW CAN I TELL 'TIL I'VE MADE IT?

—*Long Lines*

48. Giving the adolescent child advice is like pouring hot water on delicate glasses; it can be done . . . after a warming up period.

—MARCELINE COX, *Ladies' Home Journal*

49. A high school girl has the energy of a miniature atomic bomb, the lungs of an auctioneer, the curiosity of a cat, the imagination of Edgar A. Poe, the fault-finding ability of a bookkeeper, the irresponsibility of a butterfly, and the friendliness of a bus driver.

—JOYCE BASS, *Chatterbox*, George Washington High School, Danville, Va.

50. A boy becomes a man when he stops asking his father for money and requests a loan.

51. Nowadays when they speak of a girl reaching that "awkward age" it means that she's too old for teddy bears and too young for wolves.

—PETE SIMER, *Assembler*

52.   A baffling parental problem
A sequence unforeseen,
How to get the baby to sleep,
After she's eighteen!

—*Wyandotte Pantograph*

53. *Adolescence:* The period in which the young suddenly begin to sense a tremendous responsibility about answering the telephone.

54. *Adolescence:* That period when youth feel that their parents should be informed of the facts of life.

55. An adolescent is one who is well informed about anything that wasn't given him in an assigned lesson.

56. Early adolescent: a person whom nobody loves but his mother, and sometimes she is doubtful.

57. Adolescence is when a boy goes from a Mickey Mouse watch to a Marilyn Monroe calendar.

58. *Adolescent mind:*
> A mind, yes he has one of those,
> But it sometimes comes and it sometimes goes,
> And, if sometime, you should find it gone,
> Don't fret, don't fume, don't curse the lack,
> Just wait awhile, it will be back.
>
> *—Author unknown*

59. All of the young adolescent's emotions are intense; many new interests are opening up to him and prove to be absorbing at the moment. . . . There are moments when we as educators might conclude, along with parents, that early adolescence is a period of constant problems to the older generation. But the size of the problem to elders is as nothing as compared to the size of the problems the young adolescent is to himself.
> —ELIZABETH LEE VINCENT, *Phi Delta Kappan*

60. I was asking my nephew, who was in the adolescent age bracket, what he did in the evenings. He said, "Oh, I just hack around." They do just hack around, sit around, stand around, and seem to gain a great deal of social experience during these unorthodox and unorganized get-togethers.
> —CAMILLA LOW, Prof. of Education, University of Wisconsin

61.
> The patter of those tiny feet
> Has changed to teen-age chatter;
> Our phone bill mounts, reminding us
> Now we must foot the patter!
>
> —JAN JENSEN, *American Legion Magazine*

62. After hearing his 15-year-old son discussing a forthcoming dance that was to be "formal," a father asked, "What will you wear? You don't have a tux."

"Oh, 'going formal' means wearing a tie, Dad," was the answer.

63. Two teen-age girls were discussing their problems. One said, "You shouldn't be discouraged. Today, there is a man for every girl, and a girl for every man. How can you improve on such an arrangement?"

"I don't want to improve on it," retorted the other. "I just want to get in on it."

64. A teen-ager was rambling on to her father, "And then, Dad," she said, "when Bill asked me to go to the prom I gave him the geological survey. . . ."

"You did what?" asked her father.

"Oh, Dad, you're so uninformed. I gave him a stony stare."

65. *Adolescence:* When boys begin to notice that girls notice boys who notice girls.

—S. OMAR BARKER (*Quip*)

66.   Lucky the lad whose teachers know
That it takes time for a boy to grow;
That Rome was not achieved in a day,
Nor a boy perfected the easy way;
Teachers view his falls from grace,
His strident voice, his reckless pace,
His scorn for dentrifice and soap
With an inexhaustible fund of hope.
Lucky the lad whose teachers know
That it takes time for a boy to grow.

       —MAY RICHSTONE, *N.E.A. Journal*

67. One of the newer phrases of the teenagers is F.F.F.F.T.O.Y.F.F. As any fool should know, this means Fall Fatally Flat Five Times on Your Fat Face.

Adversity

68. Pierre Mendes-France, French political leader, on vacation in Switzerland: "Skiing is the perfect exercise for French Premiers —it teaches them to fall."

       —*Quote*

69. Say not that this or that thing came to thwart you; it came only to test you.

    —MURIEL STRODE, *American School Board Journal*

Advertising

70. In a boardinghouse window near a Midwest coeducational college there is a sign reading: "Irresistible foreign accents taught here. Success inevitable. Come in and read our campus testimonials."

71. The difference between "out advertising" and "out-advertising" is just a little dash.

Age

72. Older teachers may think experience is a substitute for intelligence; younger teachers sometimes think intelligence is a substitute for experience.

73. Men of means who don't worry over lost golf balls are usually at the age where they can't hit 'em that far.

74.   I used to think that forty years
    Would make me wiser than my peers,
    But now that I have reached the age,
    I find I'm anything but sage.

75. Middle age is when a man must keep fit as a fiddle or look like a bass viol.

76. *Man's needs:* From 0 to 40: build on a strong foundation; from 40 up: a strong foundation to hold up his build.

77. The 3 R's in the school of experience: at 20 it's romance; at 30 it's rent; and at 60 it's rheumatism!

78. Men are like tacks; if they have good heads and are pointed in the right direction, they serve their purpose well.

79. A good hunter is not known by his weapons but by his aim.

80. In the words of the Mississippi river boat pilot, "Remember the channel, not the obstacles!"

Ambition

81. If you get up earlier in the morning than your neighbor, work harder and scheme more, stick closely to your job and stay up later planning how to get ahead of him while he is snoozing, not only will you leave more money behind you when you die, BUT you will leave a hell of a lot sooner.
    —*Detroiter,* Detroit Board of Commerce

82. Be first in the classroom every morning, the last to leave when the school-day is spent, never be absent, volunteer to sponsor night activities, and one day the superintendent will call you in and remark, "I've been observing you very closely, Smith. Just what the hell are you up to, anyhow?"

83. The enthusiastic young man entered the offices of the big firm and inquired, "What sort of chance is there for a young man beginning at the bottom to work his way to the top?"

"Not much chance," replied the manager. "You see, we're contractors for digging wells."

—Home Folks

84. A manufacturer of electric light bulbs was talking to the owner of a theater.

"I'd like to supply you with bulbs for your marquee," the manufacturer said, "and it won't cost you a cent. It will enable me to realize a lifelong ambition."

"If I accept the free bulbs," the curious theater owner asked, "will you tell me about this ambition of yours?"

"Of course," the man replied. "It's just that I've always dreamed of seeing my lights up in names."

85. When Horace Maynard entered Amherst College, he inscribed the letter V on a white card and placed it up over the door. This aroused curiosity and led to questions and taunts. But Maynard paid no attention to them, went about his work.

Four years later he was chosen class valedictorian and received commendations on the way he had acquitted himself. Maynard pointed to the letter V over his door, admitting that he had valedictory in mind when he placed it there.

—Joys of Life

86. The itching sensation that some people mistake for ambition is merely inflammation of the wishbone.

Banquets

87. Most banquets turn out to be full discourse dinners.

—ED WHITTAKER, *American Legion Magazine*

88. The coffee break with doughnuts is being described as "the pause that refleshes."

89. A dinner was recently given to men from different parts of the country. I was there, representing the South. The chicken was cut, giving the front, breast, and neck to those from the North, the right side to those from the East, the left side to those from the West. I said I did not want any chicken.

—Toasts and Stories for All Occasions

90. The dinner is stale and the speaker is too
The whole affair is a shame;
And it's quite clear for all to see
That the program chairman must shoulder the blame.
And it's also clear that the brawl's a bust,
A star in nobody's crown;
And that the people who roast the chairman with crust
Are the ones who turned him down.

—Author Unknown

91. Most indoor sports are either illegal, immoral or fattening.

92. Dinners without the post-prandial oratory have been called "giggle, gabble, gobble and git" affairs.

Behavior

93. No man is as important as he sounds at his alumni banquet.

94. Children may wreck the furniture and tear up the house
But they seldom cause Dad to leave his spouse.

95. A chip on the shoulder indicates that there is wood higher up.

—Life Today

96. How wonderful life would be if we could only forget our misfortunes as easily as our blessings.

97. If a particle of meat, a pat of butter, some sand, some mud, and some shavings are subjected to extreme heat, the meat fries, the butter melts, the sand dries, the mud hardens and the shavings take fire. So it is with man; although influenced by identical factors of environment and circumstance, one man may flourish, one may grow weaker and another may fade into complete obscurity.

98. A man's Sunday self and his weekly self are like two halves of a round-trip ticket; not good if detached.

99. If someone were to pay you 10¢ for every kind word you ever spoke about people, and collect 5¢ for every unkind word, would you be rich or poor?

—Friendly Chat

100. Always behave like a duck; keep calm and unruffled on the surface but paddle like the devil underneath.

101. Charles Simmons gave us a sentence sermon when he wrote, "No man has a right to do as he pleases, except when he pleases to do right."

—Church and Home

102. There's so much good in the worst of us, and so much bad in the best of us, that it's hard to tell which of us ought to reform the rest of us.

—EARL WILSON

Book—Books

103. One pupil, assigned to comment on "Books that have helped me most" replied, "My Mother's cook book and my Father's check book."

104. The following lines were found in a college textbook:
>   If there should be another flood,
>   For refuge hither fly;
>   Though all the world would be submerged,
>   This book would still be dry.

105. When they clean up all the comic books and literature that might be harmful to children, many adults will not have anything to read.

—Grit

106. Harry C. Bauer, the Seattle library director, tells of a chap who went to a library to take out a book, and took out a librarian instead. She was, Bauer concludes, a charming girl with a good sense of public relations. "Of course, she had a perfect right to be alluring," he concedes, "but no librarian has a right to be more alluring than a book."

—Quote

107. "It's a mighty good book," said a professor, speaking of one of his own publications, to a student. "Have you read it? What do you think of it?"

"There is only one thing to be said in its favor," said the student. "A friend of mine carried it through the war in his breast pocket. A bullet ricocheted against his ribs, but the book saved him. The bullet was unable to get beyond the 4th chapter."

108. Our nation was founded, and our constitution was written, by men who got their learning from reading books.
—Dr. E. G. Trotzig, *Phi Delta Kappan*

109. "How dare you recommend such a vile book for my daughter to read," cried an enraged parent to the English teacher.

The teacher, completely baffled, asked for further elucidation. "Why," said the mother indignantly, "she tells me you recommended a book called *The Vices of the Virgins!*"

"Oh," the teacher breathed a sigh of relief. "There has been a slight misunderstanding. The book I suggested was Devices for Diversions."
—M. M. Myers, *Los Angeles School Journal*

110. A book is the product of mind and yearning, spread patiently across long centuries. It is the sign and symbol of man's culture and understanding. It prevents the loss of good thinking and it expands man's highest moments into permanency. It is the carrier and distributor of the germinations of the mind. It will not permit noble visions to wither. It breathes vitality into the past and brightens the eyes that search the future . . .
—Editorial, *Peabody Journal of Education*

111.   Oh, I wish I were a Bookman with suave and gracious looks,
    With smiles for each stenographer, with lots of sample books,
    Oh, the Bookmen, the Bookmen, they greet us with a shout,
    They know when Jones is slipping; why Smithers was let out.
    They know the latest gossip; just who will "get the hook."

> They go their way; to our dismay, we've bought
> another book.
> Oh, the butterfly with golden wings; the lightning
> bugs, a flame.
> The Bookman has the gift of gab, and gets there
> just the same.
>
> —FREDERICK MOFFITT, *Nation's Schools*

112. Books are quiet; they do not suddenly stop functioning, nor are they subject to wavy lines and snowstorms. There is no pause for commercials, and for convenience in handling, they are small and compact. From a purely materialistic standpoint they are 3-dimensional-length, breadth, and thickness, but they live indefinitely in the fourth dimension of time.

Business

113. It is a well known fact that some college deans get involved in problems and projects in far-flung parts of the globe. One story tells of one such official rushing into an airport terminal and demanding: "Gimme a ticket."

"Where to, sir?" asked the ticket seller.

"Anywhere, Mister!" returned the dean. "I've got business all over."

Cause—Effect

114. I don't believe in special providences. When a mule kicks a man and knocks him anywhere from eight to twenty feet, I don't lay it on the Lord; I say to myself, "That man got a little too near the mule."

—*New Outlook*

115. All went well on the Ark until Noah discovered a big leak. He ordered the dog to hold his nose over the hole, but when the hole grew bigger, Noah sent his wife to hold her hands over the opening. Still the hole grew larger and more water poured in. Finally, Noah sat on the hole.

That's why a dog's nose is always cold.

That's why a woman's hands are always cold.
And that's why a man always stands with his back to the fire.
—LEONARD LEVINSON

116. The young prince of a small principality in central Europe was eager for definite knowledge concerning the use of tobacco and its effects. He went to the dungeon and selected five robust outlaws who were in for life, and he explained to them what each was expected to do.

No. 1 was to smoke exclusively.

No. 2 was to chew tobacco.

No. 3 was to use snuff.

No. 4 was to use all three.

No. 5 was not to touch tobacco in any form.

Upon the death of each man a post-mortem was performed.

No. 1, who smoked, had no lungs.

No. 2, who chewed, had a stomach that was in tatters.

No. 3, who used snuff, and pulled the fine, brown powder into his head, showed up with an empty skull.

No. 4, who used all in moderation, outlived the prince.

And what happened to No. 5? "Why, that fellow went crazy the second day."

Change—Changes

117. There is positive proof that Americans are getting stronger. In the early 30's as a teenage clerk in my father's store, it required two trips to carry two dollars' worth of groceries to a customer's car. Now my little five-year-old can carry that much in one load.

118. Nature knows but one cardinal sin—the failure to change.

Character

119. I must not interfere with any child, I have been told; to bend his will to mine, or try to shape him through some mold of thought. Naturally, as a flower, he must unfold. Yet flowers have the discipline of wind and rain, and though I know it gives the gardener much pain, I've seen him use his pruning shears to gain more strength and beauty for some blossoms bright. And he would do

27

whatever he thought right. I do not know—yet it seems right to me that only weeds unfold naturally.

—Author and Source Unknown

120. Character is like a rifle; it cannot shoot higher than it is aimed.

121. True character comes to the fore after one has been experi‹ enced in fixing a flat tire, in installment buying, in coaxing a stalled car in traffic, and in raising an adolescent.

122. Temperament we are born with, character we have to make; and that not in the grand moments . . . but in the dark, quiet paths of pilgrimage.

—BALDWIN BROWN

123. Man can attain extraordinary heights merely by remaining on the level.

124. Fame is a vapor, popularity an accident, riches take wings. Only one thing endures, and that is character.

—HORACE GREELEY

Children—Parents

125. Parents and teachers are linked together like a team of runners in a three-legged race. If you fail to jog-trot in harmony, you may not only fall down on the job, but perhaps you short-change a child educationally.

—Quoted in *National Parent-Teacher*

126. The telephone rang in the principal's office the other day. "Is this the high school?" asked a worried voice.

"Yes," replied the principal. "What can I do for you?"

Replied the worried one: "I'm calling up to find out if you have any classes at night that a father can attend to learn the slang of the day, so he will be able to understand what his children are talking about."

—*School Activities*

127. A child is a thing that stands halfway between an adult and a television screen.

—*Indiana Telephone News*

128. The kindergarten teacher told of an animal lover who found a wounded dog by the side of the road, apparently hit by a passing auto. He took it home wrapped in his coat and nursed it back to normal health. The teacher concluded by asking, "Do any of you children know of any such acts of kindness?"

Silence prevailed; then one little tyke said: "I didn't see this with my own eyes, but I heard Daddy say that he had put his shirt on a horse and lost it."

129. The only things that children wear out faster than shoes are Mom, Dad, and Teacher.

130. After a visit to dancing school, one mother advised her daughter that she should not just dance silently like a totem pole; talking to her partner was also a part of the social picture. On a later visit the mother saw that each time the music started, the same little boy tore across the floor, bowed to her daughter and swept her away to the music. Later the mother asked why the same lad chose her for every dance. "Oh, him!" the daughter exclaimed. "I'm telling him a continued murder mystery."
—*Des Moines Tribune*

131. Children haven't changed much in the last 40 years—that's what worries parents and teachers.

132. You might disparage, might deplore
My child, when introduced to him,
And so might I, were it not for
The fact that I am used to him.
—ANITA RASKIN

133. A four-year-old girl was heard singing "God Bless America" this way: "Stand beside her, and guide her, through the night with the light from a bulb."
—*Texas Outlook*

134. Modern children who run away from home may be looking for their parents.
—JACK HERBERT, *American Legion Magazine*

135. Yesterday I heard a prophecy that the end of the world was coming next weekend. I repeated this to a friend with three children under seven, whose maid had just left, and her only answer was, "Good!"

—The Outpost

136. When a certain youngster asked his mother where he came from, his mother replied, "The stork brought you." He received the same answer when he asked about his older brother and sister. His comment was, "Well, I guess there hasn't been a normal birth in our family."

137. My five-year-old son Bobby and his "Sand Box Gang" were busily making mud pies under our kitchen window.

Suddenly activity ceased, then: "We've run out of dirt, men," Bobby piped up. "Everyone take off their shoes and empty them."

—Mrs. ROBERT W. WALLACE, *Coronet*

138. Six-year-old James Robert, son of a prominent New Yorker, answered the phone for his absent father.

The caller asked: "Could you take a message for your father?"

Said James Robert: "Yes sir, wait till I get a pencil."

The caller waited.

James Robert returned to the telephone: "The point is broken. I'll get another one."

James Robert came back again: "I'm here, but do you know what?"

Said the caller: "No."

"I can't write."

139. Comedian and former school teacher Sam Levenson has this comment on why parental discipline is ineffective these days. "To-day, when a child disobeys his mother, he is sent to his room. When he goes to his room, he has a radio, a TV set, a 17-year-old baby-sitter—his father didn't have it so good on his honeymoon."

140. Things had not gone well for the four-year-old that morning. It seemed that he was always in trouble. After being repri-manded by his mother a time or two, she finally said to him: "Son, you go to that chair and sit on it, now!"

The little lad went to the chair, sat down, then, with meaningful words, said, "Mummy, I'm sitting down on the outside but I'm standing-up on the inside."

—OLIVER G. WILSON, *Wesleyan Methodist*

141. Three small boys were seated on the curb. One was playing with an airplane. One was playing with a fire engine. The other one was reading "Esquire." A kindly old man approached and asked them what they wanted to be when they grew up. The first replied he wanted to pilot a B-29. The second wanted to be a fireman. The third looked up from his magazine and said, "Aw, I just want to grow up."

142. Prof. Henry Johnston, counselor, Oklahoma State University, "Too many parents regard school as a kind of free and convenient baby-sitting. They should realize that they are the first, best and most important teachers of all . . ."

143. *Small boy to librarian:* "Do you have anything on the parent from 30 to 35?"

—J. Monahan in *Family Circle*

144. As mother and 10-year-old Larry trooped in, father looked up from a lapful of newspapers to ask what he'd learned at Sunday School.

"Well," said the lad, "our teacher told us about when God sent Moses behind the enemy lines to rescue the Israelites from the Egyptians. When they came to the Red Sea, Moses called for the engineers to build a pontoon bridge. After they all crossed, they looked back and saw the Egyptian tanks coming. Quick as a flash, Moses radioed headquarters on his walkie-talkie to send bombers to blow up the bridge and saved the Israelites."

"Larry," exclaimed his startled mother, "is that really the way your teacher told that story?"

"Well, not exactly," he replied, "but if I told it her way, you'd never believe it."

—*United Mine Workers Journal*

145. The other day my husband, who is with Dick Wareing, Ford dealer in North Sacramento, was demonstrating the retractable hardtop "Skyliner," to a customer accompanied by his small daughter. The girl watched the roof lift up and slide out of sight, then said, "Daddy, it's got a flip-top box."

—Mrs. Robert Danielson, *Ford Times*

146. All parents think their children are gifted and all children think their parents are retarded.

147. As any parent can tell you, mealtime is when the kids sit down to continue their eating.

—*Kiwanis Magazine*

148. Our six-year-old daughter was visiting our neighbors across the street for the first time. She had often longed to see inside the big house. When she thought she had stayed about long enough, she mentioned something to the lady about going home. When the neighbor lady asked, "What's your hurry?" she immediately called across the street, "Mommy, what's my hurry?"

149. *December:*

> While children eagerly await
> The twenty-fifth's arrival
> Parents eye the twenty-sixth
> And hope for their survival.

—HELEN LEMMON, *Farm Journal*

150. Many a child is spoiled because you can't spank two grand-mothers.

—*Elberton (Georgia) Star*

151. A small boy was dolefully practicing his piano lesson when a salesman knocked on the door. "Son, is your mother home?" "What do you think?" answered the boy.

—MARVIN J. BROCKETT, *American Legion Magazine*

152. "Well, my son, what did you learn in Sunday School today?" "We learned all about a cross-eyed bear." "About a what?" "Yes, sir, named Gladly. We learned a song about him, all about 'Gladly, the cross I'd bear.'"

153. "There are no problem children—only children with problems."

154. One child's version of the pledge to the flag:
   "I pledge allegiance to the flag of the United States of America and to the Republic for which it stands, one naked individual . . ."

155.
> If a lass or a lad,
> Simply has to be bad,
> Because of compulsions inner,
> Let it not be at school

Where the little fool
Would spoil the poor teacher's dinner.

Let it likewise not be
Where the neighbors can see
When objects are hurled and broken,
Or at church where the ear
Of the Preacher can hear
The horrible words that are spoken.

If a child must rage
At a certain age,
With hostile emotions a-tingle,
It's best that he foam
And explode at home,
Says the expert, who's probably single.
—Author Unknown

156. From the Yuma, Arizona, *Daily Sun:* "Wanted: Part-time job for 11-year-old boy for the summer. Necessary to build his $elf-e$teem . . . Experienced as a carpenter's helper. Guaranteed to put 100 nails in each board. Experienced as a painter and can be relied on to let paint dry thoroughly in brush before second coat. Has unspoken agreement with lawn mower. If mower is too tired, he won't push it. Has experience as a designer and inventor. Can give intricate details on how to build a rocket to fly to the moon. For appointment call SU 3-7649."

157. Parent to lad while browsing in the toy department: "Now, son, if you promise to be as quiet as a mouse when you get home, I'll buy you a drum."

158. A father of four boys came home to find them all engaged in something of a free-for-all. Addressing his remarks to the most aggressive of the four, he asked, "Butch, who started this?" "Well, it all started when Harold hit me back," exclaimed Butch.

159. Our six-year-old daughter, Dala Dee, was eager to enter first grade. On the day before the opening of school she heard some older neighborhood children singing, "School Days." Evidently, she misinterpreted one phrase, for after her first day at school, she came home somewhat disconsolate. Upon being questioned, she revealed the reason. "Well," she explained, "I didn't get any licorice. I heard some of the other children singing, "School days, school days, good old golden rule days, reading and writing and 'rithmetic, taught to the tune of a licorice stick."

—M. Dale Baughman

160. Young Brad Bratson, caught in mischief for the "umpteenth" time one day, was asked by his mother: "How do you expect to get into Heaven?"

The youngster meditated for a few seconds, then replied: "Well, I'll just run in and out, in and out, and keep slamming the door until the gateman says, "For Heaven's sake, Brad, come in or stay out!"

161. A young teacher, imbued with the true spirit of her profession and aware of an excellent opportunity to emphasize citizenship through service, told the members of her class that we are here in this world to help others. The statement was well taken but one bright lad piped up, "What are the others here for?"

162. About raising children, the experts' confusion
Finds some of us clinging to this old conclusion;
The kids who are healthy, with appetite fust rate,
Are gonna be hard as the dickens to frustrate!

—S. Omar Barker

163. A father of eight offered to watch the children while his wife enjoyed an evening of relaxation at the movies. He was admonished by his wife as she left the house, "Don't allow a one of them to come downstairs."

He had hardly settled down to watch his favorite television program when he heard little feet on the stair-steps. Carrying out his orders to the letter, he commanded firmly, "Go back upstairs and stay there."

He again became absorbed in his television show but this was of short duration. Hearing footsteps again, he repeated his word of warning, this time adding the threat of spanking. When the sound of muffled footsteps again invaded his privacy, he dashed from his chair in the nick of time to see a little lad pass from view over the top step. Just then a neighbor lady burst in with a look of worry on her face. "I can't find my Bobby anywhere. Have you seen him?"

"I'm up here, Mom," announced a shaky voice from upstairs. "He won't let me come down, so how could I come home?"

164. Among the passengers on the crowded bus were a mother and her small daughter, who was holding a small box, appropriately ventilated. Silence reigned as the bus stopped for a red light. Suddenly in words for all to hear, the little miss asked, "Mother, is this a man kitten or a lady kitten?"

With only slight hesitation, the mother returned, "A man kitten."

"But how can you tell?" inquired the lass.

Tense expectation was sensed in all the passengers. "That's easy," promptly explained the mother, "he has whiskers, doesn't he?"

165. *Teacher:* "What is your name, son?"

Small boy: "Jule, sir."

Teacher: "You shouldn't use a nick-name. Your name must be Julius. Next, what's your name?"

Second small boy: "Bilious, sir."

166. In questioning the logic of his parents' actions, one lad wanted to know why they insisted that he was too young and too little to stay up late at night, but the next morning tell him that he's too old and too big to stay in bed.

167. My five-year-old daughter watched intently as the service station attendant filled the gas tank, checked the oil, and filled the battery with water, using a bulb syringe. As the last service was performed, she looked up at me and asked, "Daddy, are they giving the car an enema?"

—M. DALE BAUGHMAN

168. *Teacher:* "Billy, what is a flood?"

Billy: "It's a river too big for its bridges."

169. *Teacher:* "If your mother has a package delivered C.O.D., what do the initials mean?"

Precocious Youngster: "Call On Daddy."

170. *Friendly Bus Driver:* "How old are you, little girl?"

Little Girl: "If you don't mind, big boy, I'll pay full fare and keep my statistics to myself."

171. The little first-grader was being groomed for school. Hearing the cracking noise during the hair combing procedure, the little girl asked, "Why does it make that cracking noise?"

"Because there is electricity in it," explained the mother.

"Gosh," exclaimed the bright little miss, "what a story. I've got electricity, Daddy's got gas on his stomach, and Grandpa's got water on his knee."

172. Johnny could not hold himself while the Sunday school teacher told the story of Lot and his wife. When she explained the part where Lot's wife looked back and turned into a pillar of salt, little Johnny couldn't stand it any longer. Interrupting excitedly, he expostulated with fervor, "My mother looked back once, as she was driving, and *she* turned into a fence post."

173. A modern mother is one who worries if her daughter gets in too early.

—WALT FRAMER, *Indianapolis Times*

174. Children, whose parents don't want the grass to grow under their feet, are often told to mow it.

175. She's the picture of her father and the sound track of her mother.

—*Reader's Digest*

176. He was an infant prodigy. The trouble was that he kept on being an infant long after he ceased being a prodigy.

—HAROLD ICKES, quoted by SIDNEY J. HARRIS

177. There wouldn't be so many problem children if parents would give more time to their children's problems.

—JOHN QUILL

178. Included among things that rise slowly: biscuits in a cold room, husband reading a newspaper, teenager from a warm bed.

179.   When children indulge in some pastime
         Forbidden by chapter and text,
         And their mother reproaches them, vexed,

And announces, "Now this is the last time,
I'm going to warn you about it!"
It may be the last, but I doubt it;
It's only the last till the next.
                                    —*Saturday Evening Post*

180. One twelve-year-old's views of parents: "It is useless to try to change most parents. Studies of many cases show that this can rarely be done, even by other parents. However, life can be made much happier for everybody if we understand that most adults' behavior, however odd it may seem, is normal for that age—and that they are going to behave that way anyway."
—MARGO MASON BARRETT, *The Saturday Evening Post*

181.   The alarm is set,
                         But I fear the worst;
                         Come dawn, the baby
                         Will go off first.
                                    —Author Unknown

182. Child psychology is what parents use in letting their boys and girls have their own way.
                                    —FRANKLIN P. JONES

183. You can learn many things from children. How much patience you have, for instance.
                                    —FRANKLIN P. JONES

184. Good parents today have to fulfill the 3-G requirement: grace, grit and gumption.

185. Today some parents are sowing little winds in their homes and reaping whirlwinds.

186.   The neighborhood we live in
                         Is full of dogs and kids
                         And the din is so terrific
                         That we almost flip our lids

                         But there's no point in moving,
                         For investigation shows
                         That most of the disturbance
                         Is created by our own.
                                    —Author Unknown

187. Children start to school these days with a big advantage. They already know 2 letters of the alphabet—TV.

—*Quote*

188. A letter from a parent to a teacher:
Dear Mr. Jones:
    The real reason for Mary's absence yesterday was extreme lassitude, throes of romantic fever, and excruciating lackadaisical inertia.

Sincerely yours,
(Mrs.) Margaret Bay
—*It Starts in the Classroom*

189. As a parent you may have to pull a switch if your kid gets on the wrong track.

190.   Other parents' children never seem,
Compared with ours, as clever.
We can't help feeling this is true
Of other children's parents, too.

—D. L. WINKLER, *Today's Woman*

191. Maybe the kids could do a better job of keeping on the straight and narrow if they were getting road information from someone who had traveled the route.

—D. O. FLYNN, *Catholic Digest*

192. Our mechanized age has its influence on today's youth. One father, after telling his little girl a bedtime story heard her ask, "Daddy, what's the story on the other side?"

193. *Ten Most Useful Sentences for Parents:*
    1. Where's your other shoe?
    2. Give it back to the little boy.
    3. I warned you it would break, didn't I?
    4. Shh-h-h-h-h.
    5. Why do you have to bend over your plate?
    6. Not now, I said.
    7. Who did that?
    8. Because—well, it just does, that's all.
    9. Take that out of your mouth.
    10. No—now quiet down and go to sleep.

—*Pipe Dreams*

194. Children are growing up when they start asking questions parents can answer.

195. Between my dinner and bedtime, when the kids are
Losing their power,
Comes a pause for the day's recreation that is known
As the parent's hour.

Forgive me for mocking the poet's sweet lines,
But Longfellow's children were never like mine.
—Author Unknown

196. When I was single and had no children, I had three very definite theories about child rearing; now I'm married, have three children and no theories.
—M. DALE BAUGHMAN

197. Standard operating equipment for the parent of a high-school-age youngster ought to be a shockproof constitution, limitless supply of patience, an understanding of how adolescents grow, and an ability to roll with the punches.
—MRS. GUDRIDGE, *It's High Time*, joint publication of the N.A.S.S.P., PTA Congress, and the National School Public Relations Association

198. It is just as difficult for a parent to keep up with an adolescent's whims as it is for a dog to catch up with a bounding hare.
—M. DALE BAUGHMAN

199. Let poets sing the joys of spring
Or perfect days in June;
Maternity induces me
To pipe another tune.
Instead, I'll praise September days;
Who cares if winds grow cool?
The birds depart, I'm light of heart—
My kids are back in school!
—JOYCE CARLILE, *Country Gentlemen*

200. The father of a new son put two cigar boxes on his office desk. One box was full of cigars and bore a sign reading: "It's a boy! Help yourself!" The next cigar box was empty and its accompanying sign read: "It's the 6th one. Help me! All donations gratefully received."

201. A young student of child behavior frequently delivered a lecture called "Ten Commandments for Parents." He married and became a father. The title of the lecture was altered to "Ten Hints for Parents." Another child arrived. The lecture became "Some Suggestions for Parents." A third child was born. The lecturer—so the story goes—stopped lecturing.

—Toastmasters' Manual

202.   I hear my relatives debating
Why I'm perverse and irritating
Too strict a home! I heard the murmur,
Or else his parents should be firmer!
Till they unite on how to save me,
I'll just enjoy what nature gave me.

—Woman's Day

203. Seven-year-old Horace, returning home from a birthday party, was asked by his mother, "And how was the party?"

"It was a joyful, but mad affair," he answered. His mother asked him to explain. "Well," said he, "us kids were joyful, and Mrs. Green was mad."

204. How can children have an incentive to study when they see adults miss a question and win a Cadillac?

*—*Raymond Duncan, *Coronet*

205. During "Sharing Period" at school, Johnny was telling about refurnishing their house. "We've been having arguments most every day, about our new furniture, but I guess it's all settled now," he said. "Mommy got her way about the living room, but Daddy won the bedroom deal."

"Yes?" said the teacher, encouragingly.

"Yes," replied Johnny. "Mommy wanted twin beds, but Daddy said that he commuted every day and he'd be darned if he was going to commute at night."

*—*Mrs. S. Holley, *Readers Digest*

40

Citizen

206. A citizen is a man who wants better roads, better schools, better public officers, and lower taxes.

207. The difference between a pressure group and a body of public-spirited citizens is that I disapprove the purposes of the former and applaud the aims of the latter.

—Author Unknown

College

208. The professor loaded his class down with enough problems to keep them engaged for several hours. After 15 minutes, when the instructor was settled comfortably in his swivel chair, his reverie was marred by, "Sir, do you have any more problems?"

Somewhat aghast, the instructor queried, "Do you mean you have finished all those I assigned?"

"No," answered the student, "I couldn't work any of these, so I thought I might have better luck with some others."

209. "How come you can't pay your bills on time any more?" the collector demanded of a furniture dealer.

"Because I'm helping my boy through college."

"But he's been there for the past three years, and you have always paid up promptly."

"Yes, but he had a fight with his wife and she quit her job to go home. Now I have to foot all the bills myself."

210. "Dad," said the farmer's son, who was about to begin studying at medical school, "when I get to be a doctor, I think I'll specialize in obstetrics."

Dubiously the old man shook his head. "Likely you'll be just wasting your time, son. Chances are, soon as you begin making money at it, somebody else'll find a cure for it."

211. The love-struck collegian was trying to reason with his father. "But, Dad," he persisted, "don't you believe two can live as cheaply as one?"

"Certainly," growled Dad. "Right now your mother and I are living as cheaply as you."

—*Lion*

212. The young man had flunked his history examination and was explaining his troubles to his professor. "I've always had trouble with history," he admitted. "Now in English, it's a different story. Never do I have trouble in getting good marks in English, but when it comes to history, I never can remember what was did or who done it."

213. "Are they very strict at your college?"

"Are they? You remember Smitty? Well, he died in class, and they propped him up until the lecture was over."

214. *Freshman:* "What'll we do tonight?"

Sophomore: "We'll toss a coin. If it's heads, we'll get dates; if it's tails, we'll go to the movies alone; if it stands on edge, we'll study."

215. The old farming couple had skimped and saved to send their only daughter to college. Two years later she came home for her first vacation trip.

After the heartwarming reception they gave her, she threw a pall of frigidity over the room when she candidly exclaimed, "Ma and Pa, you might as well know it. I ain't a virgin."

The silence for the next ten minutes was painful. The old fellow recovered first. He looked at his wife and said, "Don't it beat all, Ma, the things we've denied ourselves so Muriel could go on to college—and now, after two years, she still says *ain't.*"

—GOLDEN in *Tales for Salesmen*

216. To his son who was attending college, the deacon of a church wrote:

"Dear Henry: I suggest that you add penmanship to your other courses; at least long enough to learn that the small "e" and "l" are not the same height. Until your mother deciphered your last letter for me, I was sure that you and the other young man sharing your room both had coeds—colds."

217. Colleges: Institutions which sometimes lower entrance requirements with an end in view—not to mention promising tackles and backs.

—*Michigan State Normal News*

218. "What is 'college bred,' Pop?"

"College bread is a four-year loaf made from the flavor of youth, and the old man's dough."

219. Confronted with a serious situation, Sandy, a college freshman, sent her mother a special delivery airmail letter reading:

"Dear Mother: Please send me $40 for a new dress immediately. I've had six dates with Tommy and have worn each of the dresses I brought to college. Have another date next Saturday night and must have another new dress for the occasion."

Her mother replied via Western Union: "Get another boy friend and start over."

220. "What do you think of our little college town?" asked the student.

"It certainly is unique," answered the visitor.

"What do you mean by 'unique'?"

Replied the visitor: "It's from the Latin 'unus,' meaning one and 'equus,' meaning horse."

221. *College definitions:*

A meeting at the summit ... session at the Dean's office.
Massive retaliation .... the discipline applied.
At the brink .... about to flunk.
Agonizing reappraisal ..... the memory of what was
written on a final.

—Texas Outlook

222. At the end of his first semester away from home a young college boy wrote to his dad: "Made A's and B's—feather in my cap."

After the second semester, he wrote: "Made the honor roll—another feather in my cap!"

After the third semester he wired: "Sacked—send money." His dad telegraphed back: "Use feathers. Fly home."

223. During an interview with Dean Jones, Sam stated quite candidly his reason for coming to college: "According to Mother, it's to fit me for the presidency; by Uncle Jim's version it's to sow wild oats; my sister Helen says it's to get a chum for her to marry; and Dad said, 'Go to college, son, and bankrupt the family!' Are my reasons acceptable, Dean?"

—Texas Outlook

224. If all the people who go to sleep in college classes were laid end to end—they would be more comfortable.

225. A university is a place for 2,000 in the classroom and 50,-000 in the stadium.

—School Activities

226. The farmer sent his son to college, and the lad came home at the end of the first year jubilantly announcing that he stood second in his class.

"Second?" said his father. "Second? Why weren't you first? What do you think I'm sending you to school for, anyway?"

Filled with determination, the boy plowed into his books, and returned home from his sophomore year with top honors in studies. His father looked at him silently for a few minutes, then shrugged his shoulders and grumped, "At the head of the class, eh? Well, it can't be much of a college!"

227. American University of Washington, D.C. recently announced the beginning of a course in ghost writing. Purpose? To teach students to write in such a way that orators will understand what they are saying.

—Quick

Commencement

228. Commencement Days are here again, the gladdest of the year; the stage is wreathed with daisies and a festive atmosphere and in the squawking chorus confusions multiply; the signs and portents prove, at last, the Great Event is nigh.

The hall is filled with grandmas, papas, mammas, uncles, aunts, while sundry infant siblings send forth their dissonance. The stage is framed with daisies and the lights are beaming bright to honor little Bobbie who will graduate tonight.

For four long years the faculty toiled on its tedious way; though half a dozen teachers fell disabled in the fray. And the course in mathematics was kicked higher than a kite to ensure that little Bobbie will graduate tonight.

We shall miss our little Robert and the tricks he used to play, we shall miss his darling mamma who was always in the way. The zest has gone from living since the school has won its fight, for we never thought that Bobbie would graduate tonight.

O hail, thrice hail, Commencement, when babies yell and bawl; when groans and snores and lassitude creep through the yawning hall. Commencement is a time of joy—of sweetness and of light, for Bobbie hit the jackpot and will graduate tonight.

> —Items from *Chalk Dust*, a monthly feature in *National Schools*, written by Dr. FREDERICK J. MOFFITT

229. Counseling Graduating Volvanoes:

Just now I cannot speak an exhortation to thrill your class upon its graduation. I first must act as ethical advisor to 40 young volcanoes and a geyser, reprove a hurricane, while also showing the Mississippi how to do its flowing; instruct a thunderhead in lightning-making, and teach an earthquake due restraint in quaking. Thus, having calmed some waterspouts and squalls, and preached a sermon to Niagara Falls, I may feel better qualified to give advice to Youth, and how it ought to live.

> —ARTHUR GUITERMAN

230. Charles W. Eliot, famous president of Harvard University, was being honored one night by a group of well-known educators.

"Permit me to congratulate you on the miracles you have performed at the university," said one educator. "Since you became president, Harvard has become a storehouse of knowledge."

"That is true," laughed Eliot. "But I scarcely deserve the credit for that. It is simply that the freshmen bring so much and the seniors take away so little."

231. With the commencement season coming up, Representative Omar Burleson (Democrat-Texas) is reminding graduates of the fellow who just couldn't keep a job. "He spent his life," said Burleson, "trying to find a boss as smart as he was."

> —*Quote*

232. The few words Winston Churchill used to encourage the English people during World War II could be used appropriately in a commencement speech. He said: "This is not the end, this is not even the beginning of the end. This is just the end of the beginning."

45

233. A popular member of the commencement circuit, long known for his dynamic and forceful delivery, suddenly changed his style of delivery to one of scholarly intonation.

One of the old pro's in school administration asked him to explain the change. His answer was, "I always thought it was the thunder that killed people; since I have recently discovered that it is the lightning, I decided to lighten more and thunder less."

234. It is hoped that things are going well for a certain young lady in a small college town. This co-ed approached and addressed the room clerk in a hotel.

"I'd like to make a reservation for the June Commencement week-end—one room for my parents and one for my fiancé." Then, in a somewhat lower confidential tone, she continued, "I haven't a fiancé yet, but I expect to have one by then."

235. The kids started marching down the long aisle in caps and gowns, looking so much handsomer then their surrounding papas and mamas as to cast a minor doubt upon the laws of heredity.
—TONY WEITZEL, *Chicago Daily News*

236. To the graduating class, I bequeath the good advice that I gave to the students of former years. It really is as good as new, for very few have ever used it.
—RAYMOND L. NOONAN, *High Points*

237.
Graduation time draws nigh
And soon from place to place
Our commencement speakers
Will tell us what we face.

We face interplanetary travel
And how we ought to dress
We face the forked road,
One leading to success.

We face the future brightly
And withhold our pride a bit,
But in the midst of all this talking,
We sit and sit and sit.
—M. DALE BAUGHMAN

Committee

238. One reason why the Ten Commandments are so brief and so concise is the fact that they were issued in a direct manner and were not put through the process of committee action.

239. A committee is usually made up of five persons—one does the work, three give him moral support, and the fifth calls the story in to the newspaper.

—Link

240. Chairman: "In most organizations half the committee does all the work, while the other half does nothing. I am pleased to announce that in this association it is just the reverse.

241. A committee is a group that keeps minutes and wastes hours.

242. Committee: A group of the unwilling, appointed by the ineffective to do the unnecessary.

Communication

243.   The captain told the mate and— . . .
The mate told the crew.
The crew told me, so . . .
I know it must be true.

What cartloads of words we heaped and tossed
On our towering conversation.
And in this haystack of talk,
We lost the needle, communication.
    —George Starbuck Galbraith, *Saturday Evening Post*

244. Real communication between friends consists not in saying a lot, but in being able to leave a lot unsaid, although mutually understood.

Concentration

245. Different affairs are stowed away in my mind as in a chest of drawers. Whenever I wish to take up any subject I open one drawer and shut the others. This never confuses me or fatigues me; when I get tired, I shut all the drawers and go to sleep.

—Napoleon

246. One well-cultivated talent, deepened and enlarged, is worth 100 shallow faculties. The first law of success in this day, when so many things are clamoring for attention, is concentration—to bend all the energies to one point, and to go directly to that point, looking neither to the right nor to the left.

—WILLIAM MATTHEWS, *Good Business*

247. Great men have but a few hours to be "great." Like the rest of us, they must dress, bathe, and eat; and, being human, they must make visits to the dentist, doctor, barber, and have conferences with their wives about domestic and family affairs. What makes men great is their ability to decide what is important, and then focus their attention on it.

—*Salesmaker*

Conference

248. A conference without a leader is like a ship without a helmsman—it's apt to wander all over the ocean.

249. Conference: the confusion of the loudest talking character multiplied by the number present.

250. A poor conference is like a plane without a good pilot—it's likely to stay up in the clouds.

251. Conference: a meeting at which people talk about things they should be doing.

Confidence

252. Bread is said to be the staff of life, although a lot of people get by on crust.

253. It's fine to believe in yourself. Just don't be too easily convinced.

254. A lot of folks believe they have the world by the tail, until they try to swing it.

Convention

255. A convention is a succession of 2's. It consists of 2 days, which are 2 short, and afterward, you are 2 tired 2 return 2 work and 2 broke not 2.

256. As Alice and the Mad Hatter strolled down the famous Board-Walk, a curious sight met their eyes. Little groups of excited men were arguing wildly in some unknown and bewildering language. "Total Growth," the leader would yell in a loud voice, to which the chorus would respond in unison, "group processes," "life adjustment program," "frame of reference," "federal aid." At the mention of "federal aid" they would all bow reverently.

"Whatever is the matter with them?" asked Alice.

The Mad Hatter grinned. "It's the annual convention of school administrators," he said. "They have escaped from their schools for a few days."

—FREDERICK MOFFITT, *Nation's Schools*

257. There is an old saying that when educators assemble for a convention, they bring a copy of the Ten Commandments and a $10 bill, and the poor souls can't afford to break either of them.

Conversation

258. Even the experts in the art of holding a conversation know when to turn it loose.

259. Take a lesson from the whale: The only time he gets harpooned is when he comes up to spout.

260. He's a fine talker—the best I've escaped from; when you ask him a question, it's like pulling your finger out of a hole in a dike.

261.
His hosts were bored as usual
No need to tell you why
He was me—deep in conversation
With no twinkle in his I.
—ERNEST HOLBROOK in *Empire Magazine*

262. Perhaps he does talk too much, but he does have occasional flashes of silence that make his conversation absolutely enjoyable.

Cooperation

263. The second fiddle is a respectable instrument and can be very important if the orchestra is trying to play a symphony.

—Indiana Teacher

264. If you don't believe in cooperation, just observe what happens to a wagon when one wheel comes off.

265. The W.P.A. worker called back to the foreman, "We forgot our shovels." The foreman admonished, "Just lean on each other."

266. Cooperation, as practiced by some, resembles this story. A little boy wandered out into the yard and was asked by a neighbor where his brother was. "Oh," answered the lad airily, "he's in the house playing a duet. I finished first."

267. People who play a part in life are much better off than those playing apart.

—Ken Shively

268. Once upon a time a man had seven sons and as part of their training the father called them together out in the back yard. The father had each of the sons cut two sticks of equal length and thickness. Then the father asked each son to hold one stick and place the other stick in a pile of seven sticks on the ground. The father then asked each son in turn to break the stick in his hands. The father then asked each son in turn to pick up the pile of sticks and to break them as a unit. None of the sons could break the unit of seven sticks. The lesson is obvious.

Courage

269. If everyone who got seasick, or frightened by a hurricane, could have turned the ship back to port, the Indians would still own this country.

—Edwin H. Stuart, *Buck Bits*

270. The world has always been a bad world for the cowardly, the tired, the weak; always a good world for the brave.

271. The essence of courage is not that your heart should not quake but that nobody else should know that it does.

—E. F. Benson, *Cincinnati Enquirer*

272. I have great respect for the woman who started out during the war with a poker. She heard that the enemy were coming and went out to resist them.

Asked what she thought she could do with a poker, she said she could at least let them know what side she was on.

—Origin Unknown

273. There is a calculated risk in everything. There has been a calculated risk in every stage of American development. The nation was built by men who took risks—pioneers who were not afraid of the wilderness, brave men who were not afraid of failure, scientists who were not afraid of truth, thinkers who were not afraid of progress, dreamers who were not afraid of action.

—Brooks Atkinson

Courses

274. Odd courses offered in colleges:
Wine-making; University of California
Gunsmith; Lassen Junior College, California
Taxidermy; Iowa
Cartooning; University of Kansas
Drugstore Management; Michigan
Piano Tuning and Repair; Indiana University.

—*Daily Student,* Indiana University

275. The University of Minnesota's general extension division lists two evening classes in this order:
Efficient listening.
Preparation for Marriage.

—Paul Light in St. Paul *Pioneer Press*

Courtesy

276. There is nothing in politeness but wind. Neither is there in pneumatic tires, yet it eases the jolts along life's highway.

277. Three major advertising media are radio, direct mail, and courtesy. The first two cost you real money. The third is free, but it's the most effective one of all.

Critics—Criticism

278. This took place at Boston College during a lecture by a young priest. The professor, after a long discourse, asked for questions. A student arose and demanded documentary proof of various statements made in the lecture. The professor admitted he had no proof with him, although it was easily obtainable. Unabashed, the show-off replied, "Well, sir, until you can produce documentary evidence, do you mind if, for the time being, I call you a liar?"

The stunned audience waited for the professor to find his voice. Then he quietly asked the student for his parents' marriage certificate. Unable to produce, the student sat dumbfounded as the professor said, "Well, sir, until you can produce the documentary evidence, would you mind if I called you an impertinent young bastard?"

—RICHARD K. MALCOLM, *True*

279. Those who have free seats at the play hiss first.

—Chinese proverb

280. The difference between coaching and criticizing is your attitude.

—FRED SMITH

281. Mullah Nasr-Ed-Din, ancient Persian humorist, and his son were walking along a country road behind their donkey, who was contentedly nibbling grass along the way. A man, seeing Mullah and his son sweating profusely, remarked, "Look how foolish they are, walking instead of riding." Hearing the remark, Mullah and his son climbed on the donkey and rode through the next village where they heard an old man exclaim, "They ought to be ashamed, making that poor old donkey carry two riders." Mullah dismounted and walked while the son rode the donkey to the next village. There Mullah heard this commentary, "Poor old man! That boy should be ashamed, making his poor old Dad walk!" Then Mullah got on the donkey, while his son dismounted and walked for some distance. Finally, another villager made this observation, "Look at that old man riding, while his son has to walk. How cruel!"

Mullah rubbed his beard, shook his head and said to himself, "You can't please any of the people any of the time."

282. Nothing is easier than fault-finding; no talent, no self-denial, no brains, no character are required to set up in the grumbling business.

—ROBERT WEST, *Grit*

283.   A little seed lay on the ground
              And soon began to sprout.
          "Now which of all the flowers around,"
              It mused, "shall I come out?"
          The lily's face is fair and proud,
              But just a trifle cold;
          The rose, I think, is rather loud,
              And then its fashion's old.
          The violet is all very well,
              But not a flower I'd choose;
          Nor yet the Canterbury bell—
              I never cared for blues."
          And so it criticized each flower,
              This supercilious seed,
          Until it woke one summer hour,
              And found itself—a weed!

—Author Unknown

284. I do the very best I know how; the very best I can; and I mean to keep on doing it to the end. If the end brings me out all right, what is said against me will not amount to anything. If the end brings me out all wrong, then a legion of angels swearing I was right will make no difference.

—ABRAHAM LINCOLN

285. It is the great tree that attracts the wind.

—Chinese proverb

286. Oh, great Father, never let me judge another man until I have walked in his moccasins for two weeks.

—Indian Prayer

287. A principal kept for ready use a special notebook with the label, "Complaints of teachers against other teachers." When a member of the faculty began to talk of the faults of fellow teachers, he would say, "Here's my complaint book. I'll write down what you say, and you can sign it. Then when I handle the matter officially,

53

I shall know at a glance what you will be ready to testify to." Complainers usually refused to sign such statements and so no entries were made. The principal says he kept the book for 40 years, opened it many, many times, and never wrote a line in it.

288. Said the sieve to the darning needle, "You have a big hole right through the middle." The needle replied, "Well, you must have a hundred yourself."

289. Be not afraid of a joke. If one throws salt at thee, thou wilt receive no harm, unless thou art raw.

—Junius

Curriculum

290. You can lead teachers to curriculum planning but you can't make them think.

291. Our curriculum has a two-fold purpose—to help the pupil achieve personal and social integration; neither goal can be achieved without the other. Both are especially vital at the junior high school level, when pupils, like butterflies, achieve new forms and become aware of a world beyond the cabbage patch.

—Author Unknown

Dating

292. A college senior dated a young lady from a nearby girls' school a few times. Then some weeks passed, and when she hadn't heard from him, she sent a telegram reading: DEAD, DELAYED, OR DISINTERESTED?

To which the young man promptly wired back: HUNTING, FISHING, OR TRAPPING?

293. Did you hear about the young college boy who tried and tried with no success to date a popular and pretty coed? He finally did make it, though, after he had bought a new car and became so safety conscious that he always fastened his safety belt. His curiosity prevailed and he finally asked, "Why did you finally consent to go out with me?" "Well," she returned, "I like to go out with nice young men like yourself when you're strapped down."

—M. Dale Baughman

Decision

294. I'm a Little League umpire and I have to call 'em as I see 'em.

295. There would be fewer arguments if we tried to determine what's right, instead of who's right.

296. A farmer hired a hand and set him to chopping wood. When he checked in the middle of the morning, he was amazed to find the wood all chopped. Next day he told the hand to stack the wood in the shed; he figured this would keep him busy, but by noon the job was done. On the third day, the farmer decided to give him a light job. He told him to sort out the potatoes in the bin, putting the good ones in one pile, the doubtful in another and to throw out the rotten ones. An hour or so later the farmer went back to see how the job was coming. He found the hired man passed out cold, with virtually nothing done. After throwing cold water in the man's face and bringing him around, the farmer demanded an explanation.

"Damn," the man said, wearily. "It's makin' them decisions that's killin' me."

Degrees

297. New degree in college: ABD—all but the dissertation.

298. The grave professor wagged his beard and grinned in owlish glee. "Young man," he said, "the time has come to give you your degree. For umpty years I've kidded you and kicked you 'round the place, 'til I'm sick and tired of seeing your bright and shining face. I've had you rate my papers and stoke my furnace, too. You've done the thousand chores that every candidate must do. I approve your dissertation in its ponderosity, so hustle to the office now and get your Ph.D. APRIL FOOL!

—Frederick Moffitt, *Nations Schools*

299. Two Ph.D.'s were discussing the money value of their new degrees. As they talked, it was "Doctor this," and "Doctor that." They ordered nickel drinks, cherry phosphates. When they finished and started to pay the fountain clerk, he shook his head. "No charge," he said. "In this drugstore we make it a practice never to charge doctors for cold drinks."

Somewhat self-satisfied, the two walked outside. "Well," said one, "there's the answer. Our Ph.D. degrees are worth just exactly one 5¢ cold drink."

—C. C. SPRINGFIELD, *Quote*

Delinquent—Delinquency

300. Last year some 18 million boys and girls between the ages of 10 and 17 were *not* picked up by the police for any crime whatsoever.

301. One man proposes to whip juvenile delinquency by bringing into captivity every teen-ager and assigning him to two adults, preferably a man and a woman who would be given full authority over the youth. These adults and youth would live together on a very friendly basis as a kind of unit (not greatly unlike the old-time family). Teen-agers would be made to feel at home since special education would show the adults how to accomplish this.

302. The trouble with present-day manners and morals is that the children who used to learn their lessons at their mothers' knees are now at other joints, and the adolescents who once associated respectfully with the Edisons and Victors are now playing around with the Jukes.

—*Nations Schools*

303. Billy Graham, evangelist, speaking in Madison Square Garden, offered parents six suggestions on how to curb juvenile delinquency: 1. Take time with your children. 2. Set your children a good example. 3. Give your children ideals for living. 4. Have a lot of activities planned. 5. Discipline your children. 6. Teach them about God.

—United Press

304. A country preacher said this: "Most of the naughty things I hear about our youngsters are the same things I watched their parents outgrow."

305. One reason so many children are seen on the streets at night is that they're afraid to stay home alone.

306. He started out as an unwanted child, but he overcame the handicap. By the time he was 19 he was wanted in 24 states.

—Champaign-Urbana *News-Gazette*

Determination

307. A determined man can do more with a rusty wrench than a loafer with all the tools in a machine shop.

—*Healthways*

308. Give the best you've got today. That's a recipe for a better tomorrow.

309. During a heavy wind a railroad crew foreman, leaning into the icy gale, walked up to a motionless locomotive on the main tracks. Spying but one crew member standing beside the huge engine, he yelled out: "Hey, George, where's your fireman?"

The engineer of the train turned, hesitated and then yelled, "Up in the cab. He was knocked down by a hunk of flying ice."

"Flying ice?" echoed the foreman.

"Yeah, sure enough," shouted the engineer. "He tried to spit against the wind."

Diplomacy—Diplomat

310. Five-year-old Tommy was given a parental warning before going to lunch at the home of a nursery-school friend.

"Be sure to thank your hostess," his mother warned, "and if there's any food you don't like, don't discuss it."

He was a perfect little gentleman. Before leaving, he told his hostess, "Thank you very much for the peanut-butter-and-jelly sandwich. We won't discuss the rest."

—R. KIEHL, *Louisville Courier-Journal*

311. A diplomat is one who can put in his oar without rocking the boat.

—FRANKLIN P. JONES

312. A 14-year-old high school principal's son asked his father what was meant by diplomatic phraseology. "My son," he said, "if you tell a girl that time stands still when you gaze into her eyes, that's diplomatic phraseology. But if you tell her that her face would stop a clock, look out boy, you're in for it."

313. Elsa Maxwell credits three simple words for making guests at her parties feel welcome and at home. "When they arrive," says Miss Maxwell, "I murmur 'at last' and when they depart, I protest 'already'?"

314. A diplomat is one who can tell you where to go in such a way that you look forward to going there.

—*Illinois Central Magazine*

315. Obviously, members of the women's club strongly disapproved of the principal speaker's habit of smoking cigars, chain fashion. Although several ladies coughed and sputtered while others cast disapproving glances at the prominent guest, he simply ignored them and continued to smoke one cigar after another as he awaited his turn to speak.

When he received his check in the mail, he found also a note from the program chairman stating, "I suggest that you smoke fewer stogies when you are in the midst of ladies."

The speaker's written reply was, "Where there are angels, clouds are near by." He was asked to come back next year for twice the fee.

Direction

316. A cowboy was saddling his horse one morning when a dude came up and said: "Aren't you putting that saddle on backwards?"

"You don't even know which way I'm going," returned the cowboy.

—Ann M. Marrer, Penfield, New York

317. The trouble with so many of us is that we keep ourselves direction-minded instead of enjoying the trip.

Discipline

318. I don't disbelieve in corporal punishment for children, but I don't think it is very good for teachers. What we need is a good impersonal machine that will whack the little blighters.

—John Brophy, *Scottish Educational Journal*

319. A pat on the back develops character, if administered young enough, often enough and low enough.

320.
> Every time I begin
> To show some hearty discipline
> A roguish tot will pout a bit—
> And all the heart goes out of it!

321.
> When Junior's hopefully
> Asked by his dad
> If he will consent
> To do the work of a lad,
> Refusal is quickly reinforced
> By enumerating the things of much greater
> Significance he's contemplating,
> But when he commands with
> Obvious sharpness
> He's quick to sense
> The tone of definiteness,
> And expecting an end to his
> Royal evasion
> Gives in to Dad's will
> In the name of persuasion.
> Amazing to be sure, the amount
> Of his knowledge in the interesting
> Subject of parent psychology!

322.
> When the board of education
> Is applied with emphasis
> To the pantied seat of learning
> Of junior lad or miss,
>
> You'll get results psychologists
> Only dream of getting,
> With much less time expended, and
> The minimum of fretting!
> —Elizabeth Ellen Long

323. Give a pig and a boy everything they want and you'll get a good pig and a bad boy.

324. Boys will be boys, but, as someone said, they don't have to be the James Boys.

—T. Harry Thompson, *Sales Management*

325.   Our children are as good as gold,
            And always do just as they're told!
            Psychology we've used for years,
            Then, too, we've spanked their little rears!

—Dorothy B. Francis, *Farm Journal*

326. Remember Bob Benchley's little Spurgeon, the lad who blushed every time he stole a police car, or little Fletcher, who helped his aunt off with her mink coat and then hung it up in the nearest pawn shop?

327. The first step in discipline is taken before the child takes his.

328. "Don't cry, little boy. You'll get your reward in the end."
"I suppose so. That's where I always get it."

329. In the old days when a youth started sowing wild oats, Father started the thrashing machine.

—Tama (Iowa) *News-Herald*

330. About the best advice I ever received was from my father, a high school principal. Saying goodbye to my mother one morning, he added, "Tell Harry that he can cut the grass today, if he feels like it."

Going down the walk he called back in a tone loud enough for me to hear: "He'd better feel like it."

—Harry Emerson Fosdick

331.   When he's been deaf to an assortment
            Of tips on changing his deportment
            How much better Junior hears
            After I've pinned back his ears!

—Thomas Usk

332. The time to start correcting the children is before they start correcting you.

—Homer Phillips

333. There is a mistaken notion prevailing among some parents that discipline is the same thing as punishment. It is not. *Discipline*

comes from a Latin word meaning "to teach." The best discipline is that which teaches, not the kind that hurts.
—JOHN CHARLES WYNN, *How Christian Parents Face Family Problems*

334. No problem in education is more important than discipline. No other single factor so vitally affects a teacher's success or failure. If a teacher is poor in what is generally called "discipline," he is almost certain to fail; if he is skillful in his relations with students, he is equally certain to be effective in other aspects of teaching.
—E. V. PULLIAS, *The High School Journal*

335. The teacher gave Sammy a warming with a hickory stick for turning an owl loose in the schoolroom. The next day Sammy's mother came to protest.

"Madam," she said in cultured manner, "I am quite disturbed by your severe treatment of my boy. Don't you think a mother's tears and prayers would have been far more effective than punishment?"
"I didn't have any mother's tears, so I used what I had," replied the impatient teacher.

336. Everything else in the modern home is now controlled by the flick of a switch. Why not the children?

337. Neither unfettered freedom and limitless opportunity for independent action, nor stern domination by adults is the satisfactory course to pursue. In the first instance, chaos is the likely result, and, in the second, open rebellion or broken spirits will be the likely consequence.
—ARNO BELLACK and LELAND JACOBS, *N.E.A. Journal*

Discontent

338. There are two kinds of discontent—the discontent that works and the discontent that wrings its hands. The first gets what it wants; the second loses what it has. There is no cure for the first but success; there is no cure for the second.

339. If you want to be discontented, think upon yourself, about what you want, what you like, what respect people ought to pay you, and what people think of you.

340. The farmer's old mule fell into a deep pit from which it seemed impossible to extricate him. The farmer, perfectly aware that the ole mule was no longer useful and wishing to fill up the hole anyway, gave up any hopes of getting him out.

He began shoveling in dirt but as he did so the mule quickly shook it off and kept treading on the dirt underfoot. The pit, of course, finally filled up and the mule rose up and up until he was able to step out and walk away.

There is a moral. None of us have to be buried under adversity and calamity unless we are willing for it to happen.

Discouragement

341. Discouraged? Abraham Lincoln was defeated badly when he ran for the Legislature in Illinois. Abe and a business partner failed in a venture and Lincoln spent the next 17 years paying off the debts. He was defeated in his race for congress and the United States Senate, and even when he finally reached the presidency he found frustration and obstacles at every turn. But the final triumph was his, according to history.

342. There is an old fable which tells how the devil decided to make some money and spread more evil throughout the world by selling some of the tools he had designed to increase iniquity and unhappiness. So he laid out his favorite tools—greed, jealousy, selfishness, hate, lust, fear, self-pity, disloyalty, deceit, ingratitude and covetousness—each labeled with a different price indicating the devil's idea of their effectiveness. A prospective buyer, looking over the labels and prices of the whole assortment, came upon a wedge-shaped tool with no label as to its use, but marked with a much higher price than the others. He asked the devil the price and the purpose of this particular tool. The devil answered that this particular tool was the most effective of the whole assortment—the wedge of discouragement.

"I have found," explained the devil, "after thousands of years of using my various tools, that once I got this wedge of discouragement inserted in a human mind, I can do nearly anything I wish with my victim. Once successfully implanted, discouragement festers in the subconscious, and if not completely eliminated becomes more and more weakening and destructive until the victim is easy game for me. In fact," said the devil, "I am prouder of the wedge of discouragement than of any other devilish tool I ever invented."

Nearly all of us occasionally find this wedge blocking some of our cherished and long-hoped-for accomplishments, for the devil has succeeded in distributing an infinite number of his most devilish tool.

—EDGAR J. BUTTENHEIM

343. "Aren't you the fellow who sold me this car a few weeks ago?" inquired a man who stopped at a used-car lot.

"I sure am," smiled the salesman.

"Well, tell me about it again," said the buyer. "I get so discouraged."

Duty

344. Duties are the tasks we look forward to with distaste, perform with reluctance, and brag about ever after.

—PATSY TRAFLINGER, *Louisville Courier-Journal Magazine*

345. There are three classes of people: Those who do not do all their duty; those who do full duty; those who do more than their duty. The first lose their positions; the second hold them, and the third are promoted.

—*Foundation Stones*

Education

346. "Suppose," said the professor to the incoming freshmen, "that by paying a modest sum, you could get a permit to go into the largest store and help yourself to everything—diamonds, precious stones, watches, sporting goods, expensive clothing—the only limit being what you could carry away. Only a fool would say, 'Guess I'll take a paper of pins and a shoe string.' Consider the imbecility of the youth who pays for a college education which entitles him, to the limit of his capacity, to absorb the accumulated wisdom of the ages, to intimate acquaintance with the geniuses of all time, to a knowledge of the universe; and who then says, 'Guess I'll take a snap course, ride a pony over the hard places, and be content to keep an eyelash above the flunking point!'"

—*Advance*

347. A college degree and education are not synonymous. Possibly they never will be but a good deal could be done to bring them into closer harmony.

—Origin unknown

348. Says B. Gordon Funk, Industrial Arts Supervisor for the Los Angeles Board of Education: "Boys and their parents are made to believe in the social necessity of a university education, even though we know that an IQ of 110 is necessary to succeed in college, and many of those who have it would be happier, and often earn more, in a trade or a technical job."

349. At one extreme is the popular writer who said recently that the only thing he learned at Yale was how to sleep sitting up. At the other extreme would be Harvard's famous Chaucerian scholar, George Lyman Kittridge. When asked why he did not study for a Ph.D., he replied, "There was no one around who knew enough to examine me."

350. When James A. Garfield was President of Hiram College, a parent inquired about the work. "Can't you simplify these courses? My son never could learn all this." To which Garfield replied: "It just depends upon what you want. When God wants an oak, it takes him one hundred years; but when he wants a pumpkin, it takes only three months."

351. I fail to see the reason for panic, and I cannot understand why we should allow ourselves to be scared into radical emergency measures which will rob some of our children of the best possible education of which they are capable and to which, in conformity with our American philosophy, they are entitled. The education of our children must not be shortchanged for administrative or financial expediency.

—HERMAN B. WELLS, President, Indiana University

352.   She talks for hours of Edgar Poe
And tells me stuff I oughta know.
She tries to make my grammar good,
To use them pronouns as I should.
Sometimes we have a spelling meet
And I'm the first guy to his seat.

And when she calls me to recite,
Them things I learnt jes' don't seem right,
And when she thinks I'm awful dumb
And after school she makes me come
Into her room where I recite
Them words until it's almost night.
And then next day she gives a test
And I'm the guy what flunks the best.

But supposin' things should change a wee
And for a spell I might teach she.
I'd open class down by the brook,
And teach her how to bait a hook.
"Ya take the worm like this," I'd say,
"Now, put it on the hook this way."
(I think she'd probably squirm with fright
Like me, when she'd make me recite.)
And when we'd both get on my boat,
And soon as all was calm and quiet
We'd catch a frog and learn his diet.
She'd sure pick up a fact or three
If she'd but take a course from me.
I may be dumb 'bout punctuation,
But there's lotsa kinds of education!
— PRUDENCE PLATT, Student, North (Kansas City, Mo.)
High School, in *Nea Journal*

353. Recipe for education: take a cup of thinking, 2 cups of dreams, from 2 to 4 years of youth (depending on how strong), 3½ cups of persistence, 3 teaspoons of ability, 1 cup of cooperation, a teaspoon of borrowing, 1 cup of good books and lectures and teachers, 1 cup of health, and 1 cup of plans made and followed through.

Cream the thinking and the dreams. Add the years and beat until creamy. Sift persistence and ability together and add alternately, with cooperation, to the first mixture.

Add borrowing, books, lectures, teachers, health and plans. Fold in the years of youth, beaten stiff. Bake in any moderately good college or university. Time in college, 4 or more years, depending on how you like your cake. Temperature, plenty hot. Servings will last for life.

354. Education can't make us all leaders, but it can teach us which leader to follow.

—National Safety News

355. Education is a thing of infinite usury. Money devoted to it yields a singular increase to which there is no calculable end, an increase of knowledge, and therefore of intelligence and efficiency . . .

—WOODROW WILSON

356. Education makes people easy to lead, but difficult to drive; easy to govern, but impossible to enslave.

—LORD BROUGHMAN

357. It now costs more to amuse a child than it once did to educate his father.

358. Education which is simply intellectual taxidermy—the scooping out of the mind and the stuffing in of facts—is worthless. The human mind is not a deep-freeze for storage but a forge for production; it must be supplied with fuel, fired, and properly shaped.

—FATHER WM. A. DONAGHY, President,
Holy Cross College (Mass.)

359. Spoon feeding in the long run teaches us nothing but the shape of the spoon.

—E. M. FORSTER

360. Education has no terminus and he who is willing to serve through teaching will never lack pupils.

—AHMED BOKHARI, United Nations

361. A teacher, skeptical of the effectiveness of the common learnings program, commonly called CORE, asks, "Why is it that all dirty words are four-lettered?"

362. The object of progressive education is to make infancy as interesting to infants as adultery is to adults.

—*Quote*

363. The task of our educational system is to take a lot of live wires and see that they are well grounded.

—PAULINE GLENN

364. Good education is not so much one which prepares a man to succeed in the world as one which enables him to sustain failure.

—Canon Bernard Iddings Bell

365. My education made me conscious of differences but not of compassion.

—Norman Cousins

366. Education should be as gradual as the moonrise, perceptible not in progress but in result.

—George T. Whyte-Melville, *Journal of Education*

367. Anybody who thinks education is compulsory in this country hasn't talked to many high-school graduates.

368. It is not only the *I.Q.* but the *I Will* which is important in education.

369. From tasting we get ½₂ of all we learn,
Smelling gives us 2 per cent whichever way we turn,
The ears give only 7 per cent however large they be,
But eyes, the windows of the soul, percentum 83.

—Origin Unknown

370. An educational fanatic is one who redoubles his efforts when he loses sight of his objective.

371. How can you expect our youngsters to get an education in college if they can't find a place to park their cars?

372. . . . "I don't buy 'life adjustment' education either. This is supposed to mean that I want everyone to grow up unhappy, frustrated and delinquent. Not at all. My objection is that the surest way to *increase* frustration is to dethrone intellectual training and substitute the aimlessness of 'life adjustment.'"

—Arthur Bestor, Symposium on U.S. schools today,
U.S. News and World Report, June 7, 1957

373. Young Rip wanted to beat his father's record of twenty years' sleep, so in 1907 he entered a fur-lined cave in the mountains. He awoke in 1957, arose, walked to the door of his cave, stepped outside and stretched. Being hungry, he thought of his old home in the town at the foot of the mountain.

He walked to the old gravel road, but lo and behold, there was a

67

double ribbon of solid stone in its place. Being curious, he stepped on it to try it and as he did so, a monster machine with two glass eyes, and pink in color came up the hard road at him at 70 miles per hour. He jumped to safety behind some trees as others came roaring by; black, red, yellow, and green.

Still seeking refuge, he ran to the nearest cornfield, entered it and crouched low to hide. At that moment he heard and saw a great snorting beast with one front wheel and two great back wheels lunging down the row upon him. He could see that it wasn't husking corn—it was eating up the cornfield—whole.

Realizing that he was not safe there, he scurried for the highest level for safety from such dangers. He sat down, caught his breath and started to plan his next action. While in deep meditation five huge arrows came at him out of the blue, with the speed of light. Scared by this sudden noise, he hugged the ground as they went by. As he lay prone, they came at him from the opposite direction, and behold, they were gone almost before he heard them.

Desperately, he sought a place of safety. Suddenly, he spied a little red brick schoolhouse down the mountainside and ran for it as fast as he could go. When safely inside, he looked around and sighed to himself, "I'll be safe here! They've made no changes here in the last 50 years."

374. My two nephews were wrestling with the meaning of "Doctor," as applied to my Ed.D. degree. Whispered one, "He's not really a doctor, is he?" "Yes," was the answer, "but not the kind who can do you much good."

—M. Dale Baughman

375. The main difference between an educated person and an ignorant one is that the former knows more things he can't understand.

—Grit

376. The two basic processes of education are *knowing* and *valuing*.

—Robert J. Havighurst, Journal of National
Association of Deans of Women

377. A Chicago professor told his pupils they were not really educated unless they could say "yes" to these qualities:

Have you learned how to make friends and keep them?
Do you know what it is to be a friend yourself?
Do you see anything to love in a little girl?
Will a lonely dog follow you down the street?
Are you good for anything, yourself?
Can you be happy alone?
Can you look out on the world and see anything but dollars and cents?
Can you look into a mud puddle and see anything in the puddle but mud?

—Leaves of Gold

378. Somehow we are not getting the (educational) results we expect. Aldous Huxley points up that when he says, "We have improved means toward unimproved ends."

—AARON M. MECKEL, *Watchman-Examiner*

379. Education fails unless the three R's at one end of the school spectrum lead ultimately to the four P's at the other—Preparation for Earning, Preparation for Living, Preparation for Understanding, and Preparation for Participation in the problems involved in the making of a better world.

—NORMAN COUSINS, *Clearing House*

380. A nation-wide survey of new activities by state and public agencies for the aged shows educators agree that learning knows no age limits. "It is utterly false and cruelly arbitrary," says famed anthropologist Margaret Mead, "to put all the play and learning into childhood, all the work into middle age, and all the regrets into old age."

—THOMAS C. DESMOND, *Today's Health*

381. Education in its deepest sense is the improvement of man so that he will be a thinking individual, not afraid of the validity of his conclusions even though they may deviate from what may be acceptable and safe at the moment.

—HENRY T. HEALD, President, Ford Foundation

382. The education of the young child takes place through the quality of his living rather than through words we say, techniques we use, or the deeds we demand of him.

—JAMES L. HYMES

383. An educator is not one who lectures and gives examinations. An educator lights up dark places.

384. Education is both a personal interest and a national asset. For education enlarges life—not only for each of us as a person, but for all of us as a nation.

—MARION B. FOLSOM, Secretary of Health, Education and Welfare, *National Parent-Teacher*

385. There are many more objectives of education that are command assignments. In short, the aim of modern education is to produce mature, competent, conscientious, and loyal citizens. Illiterate, inadequate, unethical citizens are liabilities. The most dangerous people in the United States of America are those whose powers of influence are adult, but whose motives and responses are infantile.

—WILLARD E. GIVENS, Speech, Third General Session, A.A.S.A., 1952

386. Like many another speaker it is difficult for me to avoid occasional comment on education. When I recall the political illiteracy of our young troops at the start of the war, I am moved to charge education with gross dereliction in its responsibility to teach knowledge of the human values at issue in the world . . . Unlike too many critics of education, however, I cannot lay the blame on the doorstep of education alone. . . .

—OMAR BRADLEY

387. Lay-professional cooperation is not a novel idea, nor is it romantically idealistic. On the contrary it has been tried out here and there throughout the country. The success of these attempts warrants our extending them. I should hope we might do so, not as an expedient, not as a clever defensive measure to quell criticism, but as the right thing to do in any circumstances for the improvement of education in our society.

—WILLIAM A. BROWNELL, Speech, Third General Session, A.A.S.A., 1952

388. He cheerfully pays the tax which is necessary to support and punish convicts but loudly complains of that which goes to prevent his fellow-being from becoming a criminal.

Let us so cast our votes that the blessings of education shall be conferred on every son of Pennsylvania . . . shall be carried home to the poorest child of the poorest inhabitant of the meanest hut of your mountains, so that even he may be prepared to act well his part in this land of free men.

—THADDEUS STEVENS

389. Promote, then, as an object of primary importance, institutions for the general diffusion of knowledge.

—GEORGE WASHINGTON

390. The commonwealth requires the education of her people as the safeguard of order and liberty.

—THOMAS JEFFERSON

391. I view education as the most important subject which we as a people are engaged in. . . .

—ABRAHAM LINCOLN

392. Without popular education, moreover, no government which rests upon popular action can long endure.

—WOODROW WILSON

393. Education is good only as it helps people to enrich and fulfill their lives, both in leading towards personal joy and in leading towards the extension of one's talents into modes of helping other people.

—HAROLD TAYLOR, President, Sarah Lawrence
College, *School and Society*

394. The common school is the greatest discovery ever made by man. It is supereminent in its universality and in the timeliness of the aid it proffers. The common school can train up children in the elements of all good knowledge and of virtue.

—HORACE MANN

395. When we listen to the radio, look at television and read the newspapers, we wonder whether universal education has been the great boon that its supporters have always claimed it would be.

—ROBERT M. HUTCHINS

396. Mass education, because of its universality, has a new and unequalled chance to spot the real elite, to discover talent and further it where it can be found.

—FRED HECHINGER

397. Dr. Nathan M. Pusey, President of Harvard University, comments on the fact that many parents consider an automobile more valuable than their children's education. Autos have increased in price almost threefold since 1940, while the cost of education has been much less. Yet, when a father goes to pay college tuition, he exclaims, "How the cost of education has risen!" When he buys the new car, he merely mumbles, "Labor and materials have gone up. I suppose the increase is natural."

—REVEREND A. PURNELL BAILEY, *Grit*

398. An educated man is one who has finally discovered that there are some questions to which nobody has the answers.

—*Texas Outlook*

399. Neither mossbacks nor theoretical twitterers should dominate education today.

—Author Unknown

400. Once upon a time we used to read in the obituary column that so-and-so "completed his education, at such-and-such a college." But the phrase, I am glad to say, has about gone out of use. We now know that if a man's education is finished, he is finished.

401. In the struggle for free public education of all youth, spokesmen cannot be neutral. They cannot both run with the hare and hunt with the hound.

402. Your education has been a failure, no matter how much it has done for your mind, if it has failed to *open* your heart.

403. The highest personal satisfactions are made available chiefly through education. Beyond the mere physiological requirements for adequate food, clothing, shelter and other more or less "animal" drives are a wide range of aesthetic satisfactions which can be obtained through education.

—JOHN DALE RUSSELL

404. To be a good educational surveyor—or any kind of social analyst, for that matter—you must have a sharp eye for foreign motes but a dull one for domestic beams.

—MARTEN TEN HOOR

405. But it is a point worth making—that education, in the deepest sense, is continuous and lifelong and in essence unfinishable; and it is true also that what we think we already know is often less helpful than the desire to learn.

—JAMES HILTON

406. Education is not something done *to* but something done *by* an individual which is actually self-educational. It is a slow, subtle growth entailing a life-time of self-discipline and an unquenchable passion to learn and to grow up to the full stature of one's abilities. The outcome should be competent, self-active, responsible, and socially minded citizens whose lives are predicated on faith, courage, integrity, intelligence and the will to achieve.

—F. EARL WILLIAMS, Bulletin, *National Association of Secondary School Principals*

407. The modern school is as superior to the little red schoolhouse as the modern automobile is to the Model T Ford. Today's teachers are far superior to those of the so-called "Good old days."

—LAWRENCE C. DERTHICK, U.S. Commissioner of Education

408. What would a hen be called if a teacher brought one into the classroom for educational purposes? At the turn of the century the hen would have been merely a hen. In ten years, however, the hen would have been called a "problem." By 1915 it would have been proper to refer to the hen as a "project." By 1920 the "project" would have become a "unit of work." By 1925 it would have been referred to as an "activity."

Five years later the educational hen had become the "basis of an integrated program." From that the next step to becoming a "frame of reference" was easy. During World War II the hen would have found itself "implemented" into an area in a "workshop." Soon after that it would have been "calibrated as a part of the orchestration of school and community affairs."

By 1945 the hen would have realized that she had a definite status as a "dynamic in the group process." She might even have served as a "resource person." By 1950 with the new emphasis on the mental health approach the hen hardly would have recognized herself as a "scapegoat in the frustration-aggression process."

—*Newman Review*

409. If educators . . . are to take their place along with religious and political leaders . . . education (must be) brought to the general public with a small part of the vigor and salesmanship that took chlorophyll out of biology and put it into everything in the drugstore.

—F. J. VAN BORTEL, *Education Digest*

410. The acceptance of the principle that everyone should be able to go as far in his schooling as his talents permit is one of the moral achievements of the present century.

—PROFESSOR CHARLES FRANKEL, *Phi Delta Kappan*

411. The great danger in public education today is that we have failed to see the difference between knowledge and wisdom. We train the head and let the heart run hog-wild. We allow culture and character to walk miles apart, stuffing the head with mathematics and languages—leaving manners and morals out of the picture.

—DR. THEO. H. PALMQUISTS

Enthusiasm

412. Enthusiasm is the greatest asset in the world. It beats money and power and influence. Singlehanded, the enthusiast convinces and dominates where wealth, accumulated by a small army of workers, would scarcely raise a tremor of interest. Enthusiasm tramples over prejudices and opposition, spurns inaction, storms the citadel for its object; like an avalanche, overwhelms and engulfs all obstacles. It is nothing more or less than faith in action.

—HENRY CHESTER

413. Fires can't be made with dead embers, nor can enthusiasm be stirred by spiritless men. Enthusiasm in our daily work lightens effort, and turns even labor into pleasant tasks.

—BALDWIN

414. A tiny ant stood looking helplessly at the carcass of a dead horse, wondering if she could nibble some of it to take home. A truck filled with cases of whiskey passed by, and a bottle fell out near the ant and broke. The ant took a sip, and then another, and pretty soon began to feel revitalized. Grabbing the horse by the tail, she shouted, "Come on, big boy, we're going home!"

415. Enthusiasm is the most convincing orator; it is like the infallible law of nature. The simplest man, fired with enthusiasm, is more persuasive than the most eloquent man without it.

416. The best shortening for any job—enthusiasm—makes heavy work lighter.

417. In the village where I grew up, the blacksmith shop was often the center of a group of curious youth. The smithy, a religious man with brawny arms, sometimes taught some of the boys how to hold the tongs, how to lift the sledge, how to smite the anvil, how to bend the shoe, and how to blow fire with the bellows. But he always explained, "It's a lot easier to handle the tools than it is to light the spark."

Ethics

418. Nobody ever got hurt on the corners of a square deal.

419. No amount of principal should be able to buy principle.

420. Ethics is something a man talks about when he thinks it will benefit him.

—*Miami Herald*

421. Right is right if nobody is right, and wrong is wrong if everybody is wrong.

—BISHOP FULTON J. SHEEN

422. Cowardice asks, "Is it safe?" Expedience asks, "Is is politic?" Vanity asks, "Is it popular?" But Conscience asks, "Is it right?"

423. Historians may refer to the present as the "Age of Chiselry."

424. The greatest want of the world is the want of men—men who will not be bought or sold; men who in their inmost souls are true and honest. . . .

—E. G. WHITE, *Signs of the Times*

Examination

425. Being completely baffled by a particular question in an astronomy mid-term exam, a college student finally inserted this notation below the question: "This rings no bell."

When the papers were returned, the student found that the professor had written a note of his own. It read: "Ding-Dong—page 117."

426. College student before final examination:

> Backward, turn backward,
> O time in your flight;
> And tell me just one thing
> I studied last night.

> —Jo HISEL, Lexington, Ky.

427. The Dean of Admissions had dark circles under his eyes and his colorless face bore a worried expression.

"You don't look well," said his wife. "Is something wrong, dear?"

"Nothing, really," he replied. "But—I had a disturbing dream last night."

"What was the nature of the dream?" asked his wife.

"Well, I dreamed that a new requirement by the Board of Trustees demanded that I should pass the freshman examination for admission!" sighed the dean.

428. A youngster was asked by his history teacher to name the principal cultural contribution of the Phoenicians. The answer? "Blinds"!

429. Grade school exam question: "What kind of sports take place at the Olympics?" Answer: "Jumping, running, hurling biscuits and throwing the java."

> —ROBERT T. GRUMMAN, *Cincinnati Enquirer*

430. As colleges contemplate courses on problems of travel in outer space, it is interesting to guess what some of the exam questions might be:

1. How would you brush your teeth while wearing a space suit?

2 If the menu called for boiled eggs, how would you prepare them if you were standing upside down in the space ship?

3. If Pluto is your destination would you take along your golf clubs and bathing suit? Explain your answer.

4. It is believed that the inhabitants of one planet have three eyes. If you visit them, you should take along a gift as a good will gesture. Which of the following do you consider as the most ap-

propriate gift? (a) a package of cigarettes (b) a pair of tailor-made sun glasses (c) an air-conditioner.

5. It is estimated that your trip of 1,500,000,000 miles will be made at a cruising speed of 5,000 miles per hour. If you leave on January 1, 1958 on what day should you instruct your paper boy to start leaving the paper again?

431. An American history instructor asked his class for a list of the eleven greatest Americans. As the students wrote, the professor strolled around the room. Finally, he asked one student if he had finished his list.

"Not yet," said the student, "I can't decide on the fullback."

432. This note appeared on a high school exam paper, "Views expressed in this paper are my own and not necessarily those of the textbook."

433. An ill-prepared college student taking an economics exam just before Christmas vacation wrote on his paper, "Only God knows the answers to these questions. Merry Christmas!"

The professor graded the papers and wrote this note: "God gets 100, you get 0. Happy New Year!"

434. A fifth grade boy brought home a dreary report card for which he felt neither apologetic nor chastened. However, he sought vengeance on the teacher by listing some questions which he would like to ask her. He added, "I'll bet she doesn't know the answers to some of these." The list included:

How can you tell a Ford Station wagon from a Studebaker station wagon from the rear?

Where is the best place in the neighborhood to seine for minnows?

What is the horsepower of a Caterpillar bulldozer, Model D-8?

How do you feed a pet snapping turtle?

How long does it take to dismantle and reassemble an alarm clock?

What is a Phelps screwdriver?

What is the best way to start a car when the starter is stuck?

When does the infield fly rule in baseball apply?

The youth added, "There are some questions that are easy for me to answer."

Example

435. A young man recently said, "I'd rather see a sermon than hear one."

—Indiana Freemason

436.   Who stands in the limelight for the young
To mark, and does not bear him well,
Has loosened with a careless hand,
Some stone within their citadel.

—ADELAIDE LOVE, Chicago Tribune

437. Coming upon a football the farmer's son had brought into the yard, the rooster called his hens around him. "Now, ladies, I don't want to appear ungrateful, but I do want you to see what's being done in the other yards."

438. Be careful how you live; *you* may be the only Bible some people ever read. Be careful how you teach; *you* may be the only lesson some pupils ever learn.

439. I can't figure out why so many of my pupils "lithp" said the worried teacher.

440.   A careful man I ought to be;
A little fellow follows me;
I do not dare to go astray
For fear he'll go the self-same way.
I cannot once escape his eyes
Whate'er he sees me do he tries,
Like me he says he's going to be
The little chap who follows me.
He thinks that I am good and fine,
Believes in every word of mine.
The base in me he must not see,
That little chap who follows me.
I must remember as I go

Through summer's sun and winter's snow
I am building for the years to be
That little chap who follows me.
—Author Unknown, *Illinois Parent-Teacher*

441. The fourth grade boy persisted in swearing in school. As a last resort the teacher called in the boy's father. "I know it," he said. "My boy does swear, but I don't know where the hell he gets it from."

Experience

442. "Pardon me," said the speaker, "for using for illustrations so many personal experiences but they're the only kind I've ever had."

443. Training means learning the rules. Experience means learning the exceptions.
—*Indianapolis Times*

444. Experience may be gained painlessly by doing and painfully by being done.
—Martin Vanlee

445. You can't bathe twice in the same river.
—Hindu proverb

446. In the school of experience, class colors are black and blue, the school yell is "Ouch" and tuition rates have been raised.

447. A well known educator, making a high school commencement address, presented a strong case for higher education. After the ceremony, one of the graduates asked, "How can you really prove to me what it is like to be college bred? I want definite proof."
    The speaker asked for a banana, peeled it and ate it as everyone watched. On finishing, he asked the young graduate, "Do you know what the banana tasted like?"
    "Certainly not," came the reply. "Only the one who ate it can tell that."
    "So it is with a college education," concluded the educator. "You must taste it yourself."

Expert

448. An expert is an ordinary man who happens to be a long way from home.

449. An expert is one who creeps slowly and tediously toward the same goals that you and I reach satisfactorily in one jump, and when he arrives, isn't sure he's there.

450. An expert is like the bottom half of a double boiler. It lets off a lot of steam, but it really doesn't know what's cooking.
    —DR. HOWARD MEYERHOFF, *Automotive Service Digest*

451. An expert is a person who avoids all the small errors as he sweeps forward to the grand fallacy.

452. Expert: "X" is the unknown quantity; "spert" is a drip under pressure.

453. A prominent businessman was asked to describe an expert. "An expert," he said, "is a man wearing a tie and an important look on his face, who knows how to complicate simplicity."

Facts

454. In the broad sense there is no such thing as a trivial fact. A chain is no stronger than its weakest link and all facts fit somewhere into the great scheme of things. An apparently unimportant fact may turn out to be important in the hands of a scholar or scientist.

    —GEORGE STIMPSON

455. A fresh-out-of-school reporter was instructed by an editor never to state anything as a fact that he could not verify from personal knowledge.

Sent out to cover an important social event soon afterward, he submitted the following article: "A woman giving the name Mrs. Elmer Astorfeller, who is said to be one of the society leaders in our city, is reported to have given what was purported to be a tea yesterday to a group of alleged ladies. The hostess claims that she is the wife of a reputed financier."

Family—Family Life

456. There is just as much authority in the family today as there ever was—only now the children exercise it.
—Rev. Harold C. Phillips, First Baptist Church, Cleveland Heights, Ohio

457. Some families are really and truly operatic; daughter likes the grand opera, the son prefers horse opera, the wife adores the soap operas and Dad can't tear himself away from the comic operas.

458. "We have two shifts in our household," reports Jim Owens, head of a big family. "The night shift takes out of the refrigerator what the day shift puts in."

459. There has been too much talk of what children owe their parents, too much talk of the tremendous gift we give them when we bring them to life. Life is a pretty terrific gift for those of us who get a reasonable number of breaks, but it is a gift only if it is a free gift. Yet most of us parents have an irresistible impulse, as soon as we have given a child the gift of life, to start tying strings to it.
—Hannah Lees, *Saturday Evening Post*

460. "Never waste household scraps," says an economy hint. Agreed. Open the windows and let the neighbors hear.

461. Some families can trace their ancestry back 300 years but can't tell you where their children were last night.
—*Changing Times*

462. The family is a storehouse in which the world's finest treasures are kept. Yet the only gold you'll find is golden laughter. The only silver is in the hair of Dad and Mom. The family's only real diamond is on Mother's left hand; yet can it sparkle like children's eyes at Christmas, or shine half as bright as the candles on a birthday cake?
—Alan Beck, *Good Housekeeping*

463. Starting research for a book in which he planned to show the misery resulting from large families, a sociologist interviewed the mother of 13 children. After taking down information about children's ages, family income, and such he asked, "Do you think all

81

children deserve the full, impartial love and attention of a mother?"

"Of course," she said.

"Well, which of your children do you love the most?" he asked, hoping to catch her in a contradiction.

"The one who is sick until he gets well," she answered, "and the one who is away until he gets home."

464. I finally hit a jackpot last night, something I've been trying to do for weeks. I was just lucky, I guess. There was no meeting to attend, so I stayed home. For those who aren't so fortunate, I can report that it's a great experience. You get to play with the children, listen to the radio, talk with your wife, read, and fall asleep in your favorite chair. I repeat, "It's great." Sometime I hope to have enough time to take up membership in the organization known as the HOME.

—*Lena* (Illinois) *Star*

465. "I wasn't born in a log cabin," declared the candidate, "but my folks moved into one as soon as they could afford it."

—*Anderson* (South Carolina) *Independent*

466. The doctor, driving up to a homestead to deliver the family's 11th child, said to the father when he opened the door, "I almost ran over a duck out there—is it yours?" "That's no duck," sighed the man. "It's the stork with its legs worn down."

—Harold Helfer, *American Legion Magazine*

Fear

467. The highway of fear is the shortest route to defeat.

468. If every black cloud had a cyclone in it, the world would have been blown into toothpicks long ago.

—*Baptist Beacon*

469. Here's how one mother solved the problem of her children's fear of thunder. During a storm she seated her five children in a circle on the kitchen floor. Then she distributed her pots and lids to them, one set to each child.

She instructed them to try and make more noise than the thunder. "Go on," said she, "be as noisy as you can and scare the thunder away."

Her children reported that it worked and they forgot to be afraid.

Flattery

470. Flattery is the thinnest thing in the world—and the hardest thing to see through.

471. Fools swallow flattery at one mouthful but drink truth drop by drop.

Follower

472.
We hear about the clever man,
The man who leads the line,
But seldom do we hear about
The other ninety-nine;
The men who bravely battle in
A world of enterprise,
Who form the steppingstones on which
The clever man may rise.

The wheel of life is not cast
That issues from the mould;
On each small part depends the heart
Which hath the greater hold;
The outer pinions may revolve
And glisten in the sun,
But it's the oil-stained cogs beneath
On which those pinions run.

Cooperation is the word
That's worthy of a thought;
By that alone can all men gain
The brotherhood long sought;
Each man has got his part to play,
Each man can hope to shine,
But he who leads, most surely needs
The other ninety-nine.

—Author Unknown

473.
> You can follow the crowd,
> But there's not much cheer
> In always looking
> At someone's rear!
>
> —JACK TINKER, Addressing Art
> Director's Club of Chicago

Food—Diet

474. When dessert was served, young Jimmy finally reached what threatened to be his limit of expansion. He reached for his belt buckle and explained, "Guess I'll have to move the decimal point two places."

—*Senior Scholastic*

475. And then there was the professor who is dieting—he wants to win the nobelley prize.

476. A corpulent gentleman, famed for his abundant appetite, was one asked, "How do you know when you've had enough?"

"Very simple," replied the roly-poly one. "When sitting down, I always leave six inches between my stomach and the table. When the two meet, I figure it's time to quit."

477. Someone asked a happy friend if he hadn't been putting on a little weight and he explained beautifully: "I'm a calorie fighter, and recently I've spent too much time fraternizing with the enemy."

—OREN ARNOLD, *Presbyterian Life*

478. It happened that I had not gone shopping with my wife for the past two or three years. When I demanded to know where all the grocery money was going, she curtly asked, "Have you stood sideways in front of the mirror lately?"

Freedom

479. There are two freedoms—the false, where a man is free to do what he likes; the true, where a man is free to do what he ought.

—CHARLES KINGSLEY

480. The greatest glory of a freeborn people is to transmit that freedom to their children.

—WILLIAM HARVARD

481. If a man does only what is required of him, he is a slave. If a man does more than is required of him, he is a free man.

—A. W. Robertson, *School Board Journal*

482. Freedom is a man at the lathe, or at the desk, doing the job he likes to do, and speaking up for himself. It is a man in the pulpit, or on the corner, speaking his mind. It is a man puttering in his garden in the evening, and swapping talk with his neighbor over the fence. It is the unafraid faces of men and women and children at the beach, or looking out of the car windows speeding along a four-lane highway. It is a man saying "Howdy, stranger," without looking cautiously over his shoulder. It is the people of the country making up their own minds. It is a soprano singing "The Star Spangled Banner" off-key and meaning every word of it.

Freedom is the air you breathe and the sweat you sweat. It is you, and 150 million people like you, with your chins up daring anybody to take it away from you.

—Origin Unknown

Friendship

483.
If it costs you a dollar
To make a friend,
Keep the dollar.
If it costs you a friend,
To make a dollar,
Keep the friend.

—*Midland* (Michigan) *News*

484. Friendship is a 50-50 deal but to be sure of keeping a dear friend, don't be afraid to go 51 per cent of the way once in a while.

—Kay Phelan, *Senior Scholastic*

485. You can make more friends in two months by becoming interested in other people than you can in two years by trying to get other people interested in you.

486. Six-year-old Mary was complaining of nothing to do. When her mother suggested that she ask some of her friends to come and play she said, "Well, I have two friends and one of them doesn't like me."

—H. J. Haskell, *Kansas City Star*

487. Teach the child to select his companions with care; the beginnings of vice or virtue are made within the circle of personal contacts.

—*N.E.A. Journal*

488. Friendship and wine are very similar; in the pure form they keep well indefinitely; and the more aged, the more satisfactory to heart and palate.

—Fernando Carbajal, *Rotarian*

489. If a dog can make friends, why can't you, without taking a course of lectures at $250?

490.
When you go walking down a street
No matter whom you chance to meet,
No matter if he's tall or slim,
No matter if he's Joe or Jim,
No matter if he's rich or poor,
No matter if he thinks the cure
To certain problems of the day
Is not the cure that you would say,
No matter what his race may be,
Remember only this, that he
Who is to you a stranger yet,
Is just a friend you've never met.

—Origin Unknown

Fundamentals

491. The nation's schools are now called upon to teach six R's instead of the traditional three. The new "R's" are, Responsibilities, Rights, and Relationships.

—Dr. Earl J. McGrath, former Commissioner,
U.S. Office of Education

492. Militarily speaking, today's three R's are rockets, radar and radioactive materials.

—*Cincinnati Enquirer*

493. I marvel at the lightning calculation by the salesgirls of the total cost of my "notions," plus $3\frac{1}{3}$ per cent sales tax; and the pretty bank tellers, without pencils, who compute my light bill, telephone

bill, water bill, and drop in the aluminum sluice-way the change I
get back from the check that I present.

—FREDERICK E. BOLTON, Dean Emeritus,
College of Education, U. of Washington

494. The term "fundamentals" is seemingly used interchangeably
with "essentials." The argument as to what constitutes fundamentals
has been raging since ancient times. Aristotle, Socrates and Plato
were also concerned about fundamentals; modern educators are
also concerned about the basic educational program.

—ROBERT D. FLEISCHER, Principal, Carnegie High School,
Carnegie, Pennsylvania

495. We can respond to the clamor of those who cry "go back to
the fundamentals—to the Three R's." Some who raise this clamor
have looked upon the world and do not find it cast in their own
image. They blame the school for this aberration. They would cut
education below the thinking level where the change called "progress" begins. They would restrict education to the simpler mental
skills of reading, spelling, writing, numbers. We can do that. We
can devote our time solely to these rudiments of learning. We can
create degrees of fascinating skill in reading, penmanship, spelling,
ciphering. And in two generations the American people would have
little to read, write, or spell about.

—Speech, WILLARD E. GIVENS, Former Executive Secretary, N.E.A., Third General
Session, A.A.S.A., 1952

Gifts—Giving

496. The old gent was telling his young girl friend of the difficulty he was having trying to find a gift for her.

"Oh," she said. "I think the nicest gift is always something you've
made yourself—like money."

497. God has given us two hands—one to receive with and the
other to give with. We are not cisterns made for hoarding; we are
channels made for sharing.

—BILLY GRAHAM, Evangelist

498. Is it fair to expect to get gold out of the sermon when you
put copper into the service?

—*Optimist*

Gossip

499.
Pigs gossip at the feeding trough
And chickens make a fuss;
Even kids at play sound off
At what is wrong with us!

But the chance to make a mole hill
Into a towering mountain,
Comes when the office personnel
Meets at the drinking fountain!

—*Quote*

500. A gossip is someone who will chin and bear it.

Carrolton (Kentucky) *News-Democrat*

501. Successful gossip columnist: Top man on the quote 'em pole.

—*Toronto Star*

502.
Gossip is the most deadly microbe;
It has neither legs nor wings,
It is composed entirely of tales
And most of them have stings.

—E. E. OPDYKE, *Mutual Moments*

Guidance

503. . . . This program of guidance should not stop at the college door; rather, in this relay called education, the guidance department of the high school should pass the baton to the guidance organization of the college. Of course, the program of guidance will limp or fail if the college does not have a guidance organization ready to take the baton; and, even if the college has a guidance organization, it will not achieve its potential effectiveness unless it gratefully accepts the baton from the guidance department of the high school.

—FRANK M. DURKEE, Assoc. Prof. of English,
Newark College of Engineering, *Bulletin,*
N.A.S.S.P.

504. The old maxim, "You can lead a horse to water but you can't make him drink," has been applied to the efforts of some teachers today in their attempts to fan the flames of learning. Proper guidance and some salt may make pupils thirsty.

505. To make any educational program function, there must be a full and well-prepared guidance organization. Such an organization can be justified many times over in cutting short that frustrating period of indecision in the lives of individuals who do not know what they want to do or of those who are in a training program for which they are unfitted.
—MARSDON A. SHERMAN, *Bulletin, N.A.S.S.P.*

506. Children are naturally creative just as they are naturally honest. If we can start early enough, our problem is not how to make them creative but how to keep them from being noncreative. . . . We can fan the flames of creativity instead of throwing water on them. And if we are really good, we can throw gasoline instead.
—D. KENNETH WINEBRENNER, *School Arts*

Habits

507. If you acquire enough good habits, the old ones will vanish, just as good grass crowds out the weeds.

508. Habits are either bobs or sinkers, cork or lead. They hold you up or hold you down.

509. A teacher, walking through a forest with a pupil, singled out four plants, ranging from a tender shoot to a small tree. "Pull them up!" she commanded.

The pupil managed the first three with increasing difficulty. The fourth was wholly beyond his strength.

"That," concluded the teacher, "is the way it is with our bad habits. When they are young, we can easily cast them out; as they grow older, they become more and more difficult to uproot."
—CARL HOLMES, *Speakers Magazine*

Happiness

510. If it's better to be happy than wise,
And he is happy who thinks he is,
Call him who is both sage and happy a prize,
While he who is wise, good and happy, consider a whiz.

511. The road to happiness lies in two simple principles; find what it is that interests you and that you can do well, and when you find it put your whole soul into it—every bit of energy and ambition and natural ability you have.

—JOHN D. ROCKEFELLER, 3rd

512. Oh, how I laugh when I think of my vague indefinite riches! No run on the bank can drain it, for my wealth is not possession but enjoyment.

—Author Unknown

513. Basis for happiness: something to do; something to love; something to look forward to.

—*Kanawha* (Iowa) *Reporter*

514. One thing I know; the only ones among you who will be really happy are those who will have sought and found how to serve.

—DR. ALBERT SCHWEITZER

515. Happy are the families where the government of parents is the reign of affection, and obedience of the children the submission of love.

516. Just think how happy you'd be if you lost everything you have right now—and then got it back again.

—*Journal of Living*

517. The school principal found the school custodian one day trying to keep the floors clean in spite of a steady inflow of mud on youngsters' feet. It was hard work but he was whistling merrily.

"Well, you must indeed be happy," observed the principal.

"No, I guess not," returned the custodian. "I'm just tryin' to *think* happy."

Help

518. *Dying man's request:* "Just bury me with my old Model T; it has pulled me out of many a hole."

519. Helping a blind man across a street is a fine thing to do. But it is far better to cure his blindness for he will have many more streets to cross.

Homework

520.   I am neither old nor stuffy,
I was tutored past McGuffey,
And I cut my second dentals
On the good old fundamentals,
But dear teacher, have a care,
You are giving me gray hair.

Please ease off this nightly domework,
I must do on Johnny's homework,
I tell you it must stop,
Or I'm bound to blow my top.
    —Person to Person, N.E.A.

521. *First Student:* "Have you heard about the new do-it-yourself idea?"
Second Student: "No. What is it?"
First Student: "It's called homework."

522. We may well ask ourselves how successful will the school be in teaching honesty when in the home father boasts gleefully at the dinner table about a sharp business deal or how lucky he was when the filling station attendant forgot to charge him for that extra quart of oil.
    —George E. Rotter, Social Education

Human Nature

523. He's been doing so well he's beginning to gripe.

524. An Indiana high school boy went with a tour group to Washington, visited the Lincoln Memorial, climbed the Washington Monument, and saw an array of other interesting sights. When he was asked by his parents what he enjoyed most, he answered, "Pillow-fights."
    —Griff Niblack, Indianapolis News

525. No matter what happens, there's always somebody coming along who knew it would.

526. All of us are potential members of a self-admiration club.

Man craves attention for his mental ability and athletic prowess, while woman places her hopes upon her physical attractions to bring herself into the limelight.

—Origin Unknown

527. "The human machine is a wonderful piece of mechanism."
"Yes. Pat a man on the back, and you make his head swell."

Human Relations

528. Five most important words—"I am proud of you." Four most important words—"What is your opinion?" Three most important words—"If you please." Two most important words—"Thank you." Smallest word—"I."

—*Indiana Telephone News*

529. Getting some group discussions started is much like the mating dance of the Great European Bustard, an old world game bird. First, there must be the approach, the drawing out, the acceptance, and finally, the summation.

—*Conference Sense,* Bureau of Naval Personnel, 1950

530. Little Brooksie, who is only five years old, came out the other day with a good lesson in human relations.

She was playing in the bathtub when she discovered a new trick.

"Mama, Mama," she called to her mother in the next room, "come see me do my new trick."

Her mother said that she was too busy. Brooksie screamed, moaned, wailed, cried and whined. But she had no luck. Mama didn't come.

Finally after a few minutes' silence Brooksie smiled and said, "Mother, you're so pretty and I love you so much, but I don't get to see enough of you. Won't you please come into the bathroom and let me look at you?"

Mama came.

—Napoleon Hill Associates, *Success Unlimited*

531. There are two things needed in these days; first, for rich men to find out how poor men live; and, second, for poor men to know how rich men work.

—*Rotary Key-Way*

532. Many human beings are like electric refrigerators—they slowly gather an ice formation which reduces their effectiveness considerably. These people need defrosting.

—J. George Frederick

Humility

533. As I moved near the sidelines of the floor while supervising the activities of a high school gym class, I suddenly found myself surrounded by half a dozen towheaded elementary youngsters.

"Coach, when's our first game?"

"Will I be on the team, Coach?"

"Can we stay after school and practice?"

"Coach, I think I'm doing better with my pivot shot; will you watch me?"

"Boys," I said, somewhat irritated, "you've interrupted my class. Don't bother me until the period is over."

As they shuffled away one by one, I turned back to my duties when a tug at my trouser leg halted me. "Listen," I said, and then paused when I saw the upturned, grinning face of a potential All-American. My intended rebuke melted to a feeble query, "What do you want, Jerry?"

"Coach," he said happily, "this is my birthday, I'm nine today."

Although I tried to say with sincerity the things one is supposed to say to a boy on his ninth birthday anniversary, I'm afraid my attempted recovery from a previous display of irritation was a miserable failure.

Then I noticed the cigar box in his arms. Now what? My spiritual stature shrank to a new low as I suddenly remembered that it was traditional in our elementary school for a pupil celebrating a birthday to treat his classmates and teachers. I felt as if I were looking up at Jerry. Opening the cigar box with a slightly soiled, chubby hand, he pressed the remaining contents, one popsicle, into my hand and beamed, "I've saved one for you, Coach!"

—M. Dale Baughman, *Indiana Teacher*

534. I had just won an oratorical contest in the Manila High School. Flushed with exultation over my victory, I ignored the congratulations of one of the other contestants. As we left the auditorium, my old father asked, "Why didn't you shake hands with Julio?"

I told him that I had no use for Julio, for he had been speaking ill of me before the contest.

I can still see my dignified, gray-haired father, as he put his arm around my shoulder and said, "Your grandfather used to tell me, 'The taller the bamboo grows, the lower it bends.' Remember that always, my boy."

"The taller the bamboo grows, the lower it bends." Throughout these many years that homespun advice on humility has helped to guide my life.

—CARLOS ROMULO, *Bulletin, N.A.S.S.P.*, March, 1957

535. True dignity comes only of humility. Pride is the ruin of dignity, for it is a worshipping of self, and that involves a continuous sinking.

—GEORGE MACDONALD

536. Humility is the virtue we prize most highly in other people —because it is the one virtue that makes them look up to us, whether we deserve it or not. Thus, our elevation of humility (in others) is evidence of our vanity.

537. One way to restore humility is to read the help-wanted ads. You'd be surprised how many positions there are which you are too ignorant, too unattractive or too old to fill.

—*Kiwanis Magazine*

538. The greater the intelligence, the more humble the individual because he realizes how meager is his knowledge, compared with the incomprehensive ocean of intelligence in this illimitable universe.

—BRICE DURBIN, *School Board Journal*

Humor

539. Humor is as highly serious and specialized a job as shoeing a mule, and darned near as dangerous if you flub it.

—OREN ARNOLD, *Kiwanis Magazine*

540. An epigram is a gag that's played Carnegie Hall.

—OSCAR LEVANT, *Good Housekeeping*

541. Humor is divided into three branches: Wit, humor, and yarn. The following are illustrations of each of these branches:

Wit: "Why does a Kentucky Colonel close his eyes when he takes a drink?" "Because he is afraid if he looks at the drink, his mouth will water and adulterate the drink."

Humor: The Kentucky Colonel had been drinking rather heavily, so the next morning his man John took some ice water up to him. When John knocked at the door, the Colonel said: "Who's there?" "John," said the man. "What do you have?" asked the Colonel. "Water," said the man. "Water!" said the Colonel. "What's the matter, is the house on fire?"

Yarn: The Colonel's old friend was a guest one afternoon and evening. The guest did not drink. Nevertheless, the Colonel sipped juleps all during the afternoon and evening. That night, the mosquitoes bothered the guest. The next morning the guest said to the Colonel's man: "John, how does the Colonel stand these mosquitoes?" John said: "Well, it's like this; during the fo' part ob de night, de Kunnel he so full of juleps he don't pay no 'tension to de skeeters, and during de second part ob de night de skeeters is so full ob juleps they don' pay no 'tension to the Kunnel.

—Source Unknown

542. A British poll was taken on who laughed at what and when. It showed that the British city dweller is more apt to laugh at jokes about current affairs while the countryman guffaws mainly at domestic humor. People over 40 laugh more at religion and drunkenness stories. Younger folks seem to go for "shaggy dog" stories.

543. Where does a joke originate? It's quite likely that some salesman thinks it up and tells his secretary, who spreads it widely enough to reach some house magazine editor. He prints the joke as a filler, after which eleven other house magazines print the joke. The newspaper finally prints it and then eleven other house magazines print the joke, crediting the newspaper. When the joke is about twelve years old, mass-media comedians discover it and use it successfully. Some fifty years later some sales manager tells the joke to his salesmen who nearly "die laughing."

Ideas

544. The despondent grasshopper was sure he could never survive the coming winter. He decided that the ant might hear his sad tale of aches and fears and offer some comfort and advice. To be sure, the ant was both optimistic and definite. "Easy now," said the ant. "All you have to do is to become a cockroach for the winter; crawl into that barn over there, be snug, comfortable, and warm until spring comes at which time you can return to the light and warmth of springtime—all your troubles over and your problems solved."

"But," said the grasshopper, "how am I going to change into a cockroach?" To which the ant readily answered, "Now I've provided the general idea; you'll have to outline the details for yourself."

545. We must treat ideas somewhat as though they were baby fish. Throw thousands out into the waters. Only a handful will survive, but that is plenty.

—ANNE HEYWOOD, *Forbes*

546. Remember that ideas are the valuable things in life. We need ideas more than we need money, because ideas will bring money and all other necessary things. Ideas are the life of riches. Ideas are the substance of our lives; without ideas we could not enjoy music, art, scenery, or riches. We must have some idea of what these things mean. A great painting is appreciated best by one who knows something of art. As we develop our ideas along the right lines, capacity to enjoy material things increases.

—LOWELL FILLMORE, *You Magazine*

547. "Well, then," his father went on, "if you have one dollar and I have one dollar, and we exchange, we each have one dollar. But if I have one idea and you have one idea and we exchange, we each have two ideas. Right?"

His son is still trying to figure it out . . . mathematically.

—ANN SCHOTT

548. The philosopher contemplates ideas; the teacher energizes ideas; the student generates ideas.

—LIONEL CROCKER, *Quarterly Journal of Speech*. Feb. 1953

549. There was a saucer on the desk while Henry Ford was speaking. He flipped it upside down. "You know atmospheric pressure is hitting there," he said, "at 14 pounds per square inch. You can't see it and you can't feel it. Yet you know it's happening. It's that way with ideas. The air is full of them. They are knocking you on the head. Just suspend in your mind the thought of what it is you want. Go about your business and suddenly the idea you want will come through. It was there all the time."

—GARET GARRETT

550. No field is ever completely worked out. A man with a bright idea can go over the old diggings and discover a gold mine which was overlooked in the first rush.

551. Ideas cross mountains, borders and seas. They go anywhere a man can go and endure long after he is gone. Ideas are indestructible because of their very nature. There is no defense on earth against them.

—WALTER GOLDSTEIN, *Houston Times*

552. Your most brilliant ideas come in a flash, but the flash comes only after a lot of hard work. Nobody gets a big idea when he is not relaxed and nobody gets a big idea when he is relaxed all the time.

553. Ideas are a dime a dozen . . . what is usually lacking is someone who can take an idea and give it concrete form.

—DR. JAMES B. CONANT

554. There's always a way to crack a hard nut, so long as you have the right kind of nutcracker!

555. Why don't you draw out some ideas from your idea bank and try on a few for size? Or do you have an idea bank? And if you do have, have you made any deposits lately?

556. Have you ever noticed that the smaller the idea, the bigger the words needed to express it?

—*Sunshine Magazine*

Ignorance

557. Ignorance has something to be said for it. It gives rise to about nine-tenths of the world's conversational output.

558. The most important thing a man can take to a new job is a little honest ignorance.

Imagination

559. Imagination was given to man to compensate him for what he is not, and a sense of humor was provided to console him for what he is.

560. The man who cannot wonder is but a pair of spectacles behind which there is no eye.

—THOMAS CARLYLE

561. Ask your small fry what happens to the wind when it isn't blowing. The variety of answers you'll get will surprise you.

—CEDRIC ADAMS, *Minneapolis Tribune*

562. Only he who can see the invisible can do the impossible!

563. To demonstrate the power of suggestion a chemistry professor held up a bottle labeled "Apple Blossom Perfume" and asked his students to raise their hands just as soon as they detected the odor. Within a few seconds after he had removed the stopper, nearly all hands were raised. The bottle contained only water.

564. The stinger of a bee is about one-thirty-second of an inch long. The other foot-and-a-half is imagination.

Importance

565. A business tycoon home from Washington glanced out the window and saw a huge log floating down river. Pointing it out to a friend, he exclaimed: "See that log? It reminds me of the Capitol. Close examination will reveal 10,000 ants on it—and each one thinks he's the pilot."

566. The wisest thing Woodrow Wilson ever said was one of the simplest when he remarked that, as President, he liked to put a man on an important job to see whether he grew or "just swelled."

—MALCOLM BINGWAY

567.   His key chain holds two dozen keys,
         He uses five in all.

The rest were made to fit the locks
Of doors he can't recall.

—WILLIAM W. PRATT

568. In the play of the same name, "Lightnin'," an old Civil War pensioner got his monthly check. He showed it to his friends and said:

"Look—see this signature! That's the President of the United States. Big man. And yu' see this? That's the signature of the Secretary of the Treasury. Another big man. Lots o' money."

Then turning the check over he pointed to the spot where he was to endorse it—and added proudly—"But you see there—here's where I sign it—and it's no good without my name."

Imitation—Imitator—Imitative

569. It is said that if you hold a stick in front of the foremost sheep in a flock that filed down a trail in the mountains, he will jump it, and every sheep following will jump when he reaches the spot, even if the stick is removed. So are many people mere unthinking imitators, blind to facts and opportunities about them.

—JOSEPH MORRIS and ST. CLAIR ADAMS, *It Can't Be Done*

570. Children are natural mimics. They act like their parents in spite of every effort to teach them good manners.

571. The village blacksmith finally found an apprentice willing to work hard at low pay for long hours. The smith immediately began his instructions to the lad; "When I take the shoe out of the fire, I'll lay it on the anvil; and when I nod my head, you hit it with this hammer." The apprentice did just as he was told. Now *he's* the village blacksmith.

Independence

572. Remember, kids, you must do your own growing no matter how tall your grandpappy was.

—RAY D. EVERSON, *Healthways*

573. *Moe:* "So you have a great deal of independence on your new job, eh?"

Joe: "You bet! I can come to work any time I want to before eight o'clock, and leave whenever I please after five."

Indispensability

574. History has recorded only one indispensable man: Adam.

575. A railroad shopman was called for jury duty. He begged to be excused on the grounds that he could not afford to be away from the shop. The judge was sarcastic. "I suppose you are one of those men who think the Pennsylvania Railroad could not operate without them," he said.

"No, your Honor," was the reply, "I know very well they could get along without me, but I can't afford to let them find it out."

He got excused.

Individuality

576. In the year 1939, just before the Second World War broke upon the world, a woman visited Dr. C. G. Jung of Switzerland and began to tell him of her personal difficulties and problems; then she paused and said, "Dr. Jung, I can't understand how a man like you has time to listen to our petty problems. An individual seems so insignificant with the whole world sliding toward an abyss." Dr. Jung paused a moment thoughtfully and then said, "But you see, the world problems begin with the individual."

—*N.A.S.S.P. Bulletin*

577. Nobody can make you feel inferior without your consent.

578. Who's the best audience you'll ever have? Probably yourself, say psychologists Anthony J. Smith, Harrison E. Madden and Ronald Sobol. They found that discussion group members recalled easiest the things they themselves had said, rather than statements made by their colleagues. And when they remembered what others said, it turned out that what was said fitted in with their own views. Apparently most of us go into discussions thinking we have an open mind. Actually, we're primed with our own beliefs—and are eager to have them supported by others. Understandably, we like what *we* say—and listen mostly to ourselves.

579. A college professor was trying to prepare his formal paper for delivery to the seminar. He was frequently and rudely interrupted by his five-year-old son's successful attempts at noisemaking in general. In desperation, he reached for a magazine with a world map on it, tore the map into little pieces, put them into a box and said, "Davey, I'll take you to the zoo if you can put this map together all by yourself."

With an enthusiastic "Okey-dokey," Davey went upstairs and left the professor thinking it would keep him busy at least for a couple of hours. What a surprised man he was when in about ten minutes Davey reappeared with the map all put together. The astounded father asked, "How in the world did you do that?" Davey just answered, "When are we going to the zoo?" The father again asked, "How did you do it? You don't know anything about world geography."

The lad said seriously, "Dad, you didn't see what was on the other side; there was a picture of a man, and I found out that if I got the man right, the world would be right."

Influence

580. To be successful, drop a pebble in a pool every day. That sounds cryptic until one reflects on the nature of a pebble dropped into a pool of water. Of course it goes to the bottom of the pool and is forgotten, but its influence lives long. When it penetrates the surface of the water, it creates ripples which spread and spread wherever there is surface.

The work which a teacher does in her day by day activities is like a pebble dropped in a pool. Every day the influence of the work goes farther, lasts longer, and carries far more influence than anyone imagines.

581. I sometimes wonder whether the average man knows his own strength, whether he is at all aware of the fortress he commands through influence and contact with fellow workers, with neighbors and friends, with younger people, in and out of his family.
—CHARLES E. WILSON

582. A tenant farmer's son, a 4-H enthusiast, became interested in soil conservation and adequate methods of the most effective use of fertilizer.

Although he was amused, his father grudgingly gave his permission for his son to "write" his initials in fertilizer in a new grain field.

As the grain grew, the whole family watched the initials grow greener and fuller than the rest of the field.

583. Some salesmen electrify their prospects; others merely gas them.

584. A nomad returned to the desert after a trip to America. As he unpacked his treasures, friends gathered around to ask what had most impressed him in the western world.

"Was it the tall buildings?" asked a friend.

"No," said the nomad, as he unpacked his shoes.

"Was it the wealth of Americans?" asked another.

"No," said the nomad, unpacking his robes.

"Well," they asked in chorus, "what *did* impress you most?"

"The American salesman," declared the nomad, as he released an outboard motor from it wrappings, and looked sadly over the bone-dry desert.

—WILLIAM C. KESSLER, *Quote*

585. Just as we can dig a channel to control the direction of a stream, we can control the direction of our children's activities through praise and recognition.

—NATALIE COLE

Initiative

586. Why not go out on a limb? Isn't that where the fruit is?

—FRANK SCULLY, *Forbes*

587. Some persons are like wheelbarrows. They stand still unless they are pushed.

Inspiration

588.   When things go wrong and you are tired,
Count your blessings and be inspired.

—M. DALE BAUGHMAN

589. To be an inspirational teacher, always use the A.I.D.A. formula: *A* is attention, *I* is interest, *D* is desire and *A* is action.

590. Any wife can help keep springtime in her husband's eyes by keeping a fresh flower in her hair. Any husband can help keep springtime in his wife's heart by supplying the flower.
—OREN ARNOLD, *Presbyterian Life*

591. Our colleges turn out young men by the thousands who have an abundance of carefully categorized information on many subjects, but who lack inspiration. Nothing of permanent value has ever been accomplished without inspiration. The successful person is the one to whom come the right thoughts at the right time.

Intelligence

592. Common sense is genius in homespun.
—A. N. WHITEHEAD

593.   All through night the keen-eyed owl
            Hunts the forest on the prowl.
            Daylight finds him still and winking,
            Just as if he's thinking.

            People say he's sage and deep;
            Actually, it's just lack of sleep.
—Author Unknown

594. Real intelligence is a creative use of knowledge, not merely an accumulation of facts. The slow thinker who can finally come up with an idea of his own is more important to the world than a walking encyclopedia, who hasn't learned how to use the information productively.
—D. KENNETH WINEBRENNER, *Argonaut*

595. A man's intellect is judged by his ability to disagree without being disagreeable.

596. Someone has figured out that the peak years of mental activity must be between the ages of four and twenty. At four we know all the questions; at twenty we know all the answers.

597. Intelligence is like a river . . . the deeper it is, the less noise it makes.

598. There are two kinds of cleverness and both are priceless. One consists of thinking of a bright remark in time to say it. The other consists of thinking of it in time not to say it.

—GALEN DRAKE

599. Today we are told that the bright student is bright enough to keep his mouth shut, an act that in some mysterious way is supposed to keep his nose clean.

—HAROLD LASSWELL, *The Education Digest*

600. The trouble with the world is that the stupid are cocksure and the intelligent full of doubt.

601. The man of intelligence understands the value of sound knowledge and provides himself with it. The ignorant despise knowledge and are punished with "poor luck."

—W. D. HOARD

Interest

602. Interest is the opposite of water; it travels naturally upward, but it is difficult to pump down.

603. You can learn a lot about a person by asking his companions where they would look for him if he were lost. Where would they expect to find him on Sunday morning? Where would they look first on Saturday night? After a small lad was reported lost by his parents, police and helpful citizens searched and searched to no avail. After what seemed an eternity, his parents found him in the theater watching a science-fiction show over and over. Perhaps they would have found him sooner, had they remembered his interests.

Jokes

604.   If he can remember so many jokes,
       With all the details that mold them,
       Why can't he recall, with equal skill,
       How many times he's told them.

—*Atlas News*

605.

I see no reason why some folks
Never chuckle at my jokes,
Unless, perhaps, it somehow bears
Upon the fact I don't at theirs.

—SYDNEY R. BARON

606. Some of the jokes in this book, but not many, resemble Santa Claus the year around—they have whiskers, too.

Judgment

607. Be careful what you tie yourself onto. A farmer who tied his cow's tail to his leg while he was milking said before they had gone around the barn seven times he knew he had made a mistake.

608. In a biography of the life of Cecil Rhodes, there's a story about a judge who was called upon to settle a dispute between two brothers over an inheritance of land. Said the wise old judge: "Let one brother divide the land, and let the other brother have first choice."

609. A literary critic's five-year-old son struggled through *The Three Little Pigs*, his first work of fiction. Finishing the story, the lad said judiciously, "Dad, I think this is the greatest book ever written."

—*This Week*

610. If the school is to be judged by its poor products, why can't a factory be judged by its scrap pile?

—MARIE FRASER, *Indiana Teacher*

611.

When you're forming your opinions, do it carefully, go slow;
Hasty judgments oft are followed by regretting—that I know.
And in arguments be careful, not too quickly to decide—
Try to look upon the subject from the other fellow's side.

—Author Unknown

612. When a neighbor asked Mohammed how he might make amends for falsely accusing a friend, he was told to place a goose feather on each doorstep in the village. The next day Mohammed said, "Now go and collect the feathers."

The man protested, "That's impossible—a wind blew all night and the feathers are scattered beyond recall."

"Exactly," said Mohammed, "and so it is with the reckless words you spoke against your neighbor."

Juvenile Delinquency

613. Samuel S. Leibowitz, Brooklyn judge, on juvenile delinquency: "It would be well to get back to the days when the mere look of a teacher was enough to freeze a kid in his tracks."

614. If the hot breath of the draft and the icy threat of war were eliminated from the national scene, I'm convinced that 50 per cent of so-called juvenile delinquency would disappear overnight.

—Source Unknown

615. A boy who had stolen six automobiles was hauled into juvenile court and a woman probation worker said to the judge, "We feel that this defendant is a sick young man."

After the hearing the probation worker was asked why she considered the boy sick. She replied, "Why, he's sick because he stole six automobiles."

Knowledge

616. In *The New Republic,* English instructors Arthur Norman of the University of Chicago and Lewis Sawin of the University of Colorado, told the amazing results of a test given 359 freshmen and sophomores at a Southern state university. Of 20 famous names presented the students, only four—Adlai Stevenson, John Dillinger, Peter Townsend and Karl Marx were known by more than half.

617. Knowledge comes by taking things apart—analysis. But wisdom comes by putting things together.

—John A. Morrison, President, Anderson College

618. It takes a smart man to conceal from others what he does not know.

—*Phi Delta Kappan*

619. If a little knowledge is a dangerous thing, the remedy is to advance further into the unknown . . . not to retreat into enforced ignorance.

—Dean Rusk, President, Rockefeller Foundation

620. What we need is not the will to believe, but the wish to find out, which is the exact opposite.
—BERTRAND RUSSELL, *Scientific Monthly*

621. You can always spot a well-informed man. His views coincide with yours.

622. Inclination is the first step to knowledge.

623. There can be no knowledge and no truth without accurate facts. But all the facts in the world do not add up to knowledge.

624. Knowledge is the beginning of tolerance and tolerance the beginning of understanding.
—JOHN WESLEY COULTER, *Education*

625. To know is a great thing, all by itself. It gives you a living, yes; it also gives you fun, interest, value as a human being.

To know one specific field expertly may give you your fame, your reputation, and niche in life. But to know life itself, in all its variety, its goodness and pain, its glory and squalor, you need to know something about many fields.

And if you care enough, you will know.
—Author Unknown

626. It wasn't until late in life that I discovered how easy it is to say, "I don't know."
—SOMERSET MAUGHAM

627. A man borrowed a book about penguins from the public library. Three days later he returned it with the plaintive protest, "This book tells more about penguins than I want to know."

628. Man has made some machines that can answer questions, provided the facts are previously stored in them, but he will never be able to make a machine that will ask questions . . . The ability to ask the right questions is more than half the battle of finding the right answer.
—TOM WATSON, JR., *Parent's Magazine*

Language

629. The most unfortunate letter in the alphabet, some say, is the letter "e" because it is always out of "cash," forever in "debt," and never out of "danger."

That's all true. Still, it's never in "war," always in "peace," and always in something to "eat." It is the beginning of "existence," the commencement of "ease," and the end of "trouble."

—Builders

630. "Simplify-ed English," a world language designed to be learned in a single day, was scoffed at by Omaha *World-Herald* writer Evelyn Simpson. Some of its rules are: (1) three suffixes— "ing," "ed," and "s" are hyphenated, (2) all verbs take endings "-ing" and "-ed" and there are no irregular verbs, and (3) only personal pronouns permitted are: "I," "you," "he," "she," "it," "we," "you-s" and "they." Comments Miss Simpson: "Thus I am writeing this column; you am, he am, she am reading it; we am real gone and they am looking for we am with strait jackets."

631. Say what you will about the American language. It is, next to kissing, the most exciting form of communication that man has evolved.

—OREN ARNOLD, *The Kiwanis Magazine*

Laughter

632. The smile is an inaudible, subdued, and gentle form of laughter. Movements about the eyes as well as the mouth are visible. Upward and backward go the mouth corners, the zygomatic muscles contract, and the orbicular muscles narrow the upper and lower eyelids.

In the laugh greater muscle movement prevails—the sound of laughter is created by deep inspirational and jerky contractions of the chest, especially of the diaphragm. The head nods to and fro; sometimes the entire body is in visible movement. The lower jaw may even quiver up and down. According to Darwin, a movement such as this is also characteristic of some species of baboons when they are extremely well pleased.

Frequently, the mouth is opened during laughter, sometimes to an appreciable extent. The nose seems to contract during hearty laughter and the skin on the bridge of the nose has a tendency to wrinkle. There may also be slight wrinkling of the forehead. This is one reason some women avoid laughing.

633. Laughter is the sensation of feeling good all over and showing it principally in one or two spots.

634. Some laugh "Ha-Ha"; others laugh "Ho-Ho" especially if there's plenty of room. Old maids laugh "He-He-He."

Laws

635. There are two million laws in force in the United States. If a man could familiarize himself with them at the rate of ten each day, he could be qualified to act as a law-abiding citizen in the short space of six thousand years.

636. Everybody who says this country has too many laws knows of another law that ought to be passed.

637. What we need is a child-labor law to keep children from working their Moms and Dads to death.

Laziness—Lazy

638. Many individuals are so opposed to work that they are willing to prosecute opportunity for trespassing.
—Douglas Meador, *Matador*

639. Even if you are on the right track, you will get run over if you just sit there.
—*Friendly Thoughts*

640. Even if money did grow on trees, some people wouldn't shake a limb to get it.
—Al Spong, *Quote*

641. British scientists, pausing to watch three construction workers wheeling loads of bricks, were impressed by the fact that two were pushing their wheelbarrows, while the third pulled his.

Convinced that they had stumbled on something that possibly could revolutionize the British construction industry, the scientists called their staffs together. But though they held lengthy discussions, no one could come up with a logical reason why one man

109

was pulling his wheelbarrow. Consultants were brought in and the conferences continued until at length someone suggested calling the eccentric bricklayer and asking him.

This was done and the man was ushered in with great formality, told to sit down and take his time in answering the question because it was of the greatest scientific importance.

After taking his time as instructed, the puzzled bricklayer said: "Gov'nor, sure I can tell you why I pull my wheelbarrow. I can't stand the sight of the bloomin' thing."

Leader–Leadership

642. A man who wants to lead the orchestra must turn his back on the crowd.

—JAMES CROOK

643. Effective leadership means effective speaking. Men, like bullets, go furthest when they are smoothest. Tact and leadership demand effective speaking. Leadership is yours—if you speak for it.
—EDMUND MOTTERSHEAD, *Trained Men*

644. One man in a thousand is a leader of men. The other 999 are followers of women.

645. A wise superintendent I knew, who lived when horses were an important factor in our daily life, once said, "A leader should never get so far ahead of his followers that his tugs get loose from the singletree."

—EDWIN A. LEE, Dean, School of Education, Univ. of California, *Quote*

646. If you're not afraid to face the music, you may some day lead the band.

647. The man who knows "how" is always sure of employment, but the man who knows "why" is his boss.

648. The question "Who ought to be boss?" is like asking "Who ought to be the tenor in the quartet?" Obviously, the man who can sing tenor.

—HENRY FORD

649. A leader is best when people barely know that he exists; not so good when people acclaim him; worst when they despise him. But of a good leader, who talks little, when his work is done and his aim fulfilled, they will all say, "We did this ourselves."

—LAO-TSE, Chinese sage

650. In both leadership and steamship the cry is "full steam ahead."

—M. DALE BAUGHMAN

651. Good leadership makes for mental health and its absence makes for mental ill-health. And synonymous with "mental health" and "mental ill health" are the terms "efficiency" and "inefficiency."

—DR. WILLIAM MENNINGER, Speech to American Association of Advertising Agencies

652. One of the basic qualities which a leader in a democratic setting must acquire is the habit of renouncing power or authority over others. The democratic leader is a person who knows how to discover the will of the group, and who knows the secret of releasing the energies of the group. He is a catalytic agent who influences group action but never dominates.

—E. C. LINDEMAN, *Phi Delta Kappan*

653. "Look, I'm just like the fellow who had a bull by the tail!" A friend shouted, "When are you goin' t' let go?" The man replied, "I don't know, the bull's got charge now!"

654. We will greatly increase our understanding of leadership phenomena if we abandon the notion of "leadership" as a trait, and concentrate instead upon an analysis of the behavior of leaders.

—ANDREW W. HALPIN, Professor of Education, Montana State University, *Educational Leadership*

Learning

655. Some students don't apply what they know. There was the student who failed in everything but the course "How to Study." Another student failed in all but religion, only to be expelled for getting drunk.

656. Learning is any change that takes place in a pupil's method of thinking, feeling, or doing.

—PARKER

657. The real, uncoerced zest for learning goes out of education when it is reduced to a routine transmittal of pre-digested information.

—HAROLD C. CASE, Boston University, *Education Digest*

658. Back in the old days it was a boy himself, rather than his teacher, who had to explain why he could not read.

—CY N. PEACE

659. Little boys would learn to write much sooner if blackboards had the appeal of fresh cement.

—*Florida School Bulletin*

660. Bright people of 20 do not become dull by 60, nor do dull young people become moronic by 60. An individual at 60 *can* learn the same kinds of knowledge, skill and appreciation at 60 that he could at 20 years of age.

—WILMA T. DONAHUE, *Education for Later Maturity*

661. Learning is recognized as a life-long process. Even if a genius could learn in school all there is to know about everything, he could be out of school only a short time before the accumulation of new knowledge would make him a back number.

—PHILIP H. FALK, *American Library Association Bulletin*

662. There is nothing mysterious about true learning. It takes place all the time, but, like all creative processes, it is more likely to be in the form of spontaneous combustion than to be the response to methodical coercion.

—MARY H. B. WOLLNER, *Education*

663. To some pupils learning is a lot like pouring sorghum molasses out of a pitcher. It comes slowly.

—M. DALE BAUGHMAN

664. Thus a child learns, more through trial than error, more through pleasure than pain, more through experience than suggestion, more through suggestion than direction.

Thus a child learns, through affection, through love, through patience, through understanding, through belonging, through doing, through being.

Day by day the child comes to know a little bit of what you know;

to think a little bit of what you think; to understand your understanding. That which you dream and believe and are, in truth, becomes the child.

As you perceive dully or clearly; as you think fuzzily or sharply; as you believe foolishly or wisely; as you dream drably or goldenly; as you bear false witness or tell the truth—thus a child learns.

—Chalkdust, *National Schools*

665. I don't think much of a man who is not wiser today than he was yesterday.

—ABRAHAM LINCOLN

666. It's a great pity that things weren't so arranged that an empty head, like an empty stomach, wouldn't let its owner rest until he put something in it.

—OLIN MILLER

667.   We learn of vice and virtue
             From very different points,
             The good we learn at mother's knee,
             The bad at other joints.

668. On the one hand, learning is the sum total of what is known, as that which is handed down by books and learned men . . . On the other hand, learning means something which the individual *does* when he studies.

—JOHN DEWEY

Lecture—Lecturing

669. As the professor prepared to give his lecture on pragmatism, he found that his audience consisted of only three persons. His comments at the beginning of his remarks were as follows:

"Plato sometimes had Aristotle as his only listener to lectures which he delivered in Athens. When such was the case, he merely proceeded with his lecture as usual, remarking that when he had Aristotle for a hearer, he had the better half of Athens. On the same principle, I congratulate myself on this evening's audience."

670. "I shall now attempt to explain what I have in mind," said the professor as he read carefully his prepared notes.

Leisure

671. A study of 1,000 adults conducted at New York University revealed that 87 per cent started developing skills that they use in leisure time before they were 12, and 67 per cent before they were 10.

—Parents Magazine

672. It is respectfully submitted that the paramount question in American life today is "What'll we do now?"

673. Leisure time may be as deadly as the most virulent disease unless the time is profitably employed. Anyone who is content to sit around hour after hour and twiddle his thumbs is not only losing life but is losing every chance for becoming successful and happy.

674. In pursuing any hobby we need to be extremely careful lest it become so fascinating to us that it becomes our master, taking up too much of our time and thought, and preventing us from attaining success in the main show. It should always be remembered that a hobby is only a side line—not the big thing to be done in life.

Life

675.
Life itself can't give you joy,
Unless you really will it;
Life just gives you time and space—
It's up to you to fill it.

—Optimist

676. My philosophy is to make the most of all that comes, and the least of all that goes.

—Luke Pease, Television program, *Life Begins at 80*

677. A man spends the first 30 years of his life throwing rocks at the target; the next 30 years examining the target to see where the rocks hit; and from then on, he sits around and cusses rock-throwing in general.

—P. K. Sideliner

678. In 1923, a group of the world's most successful financiers met at the Edgewater Beach Hotel in Chicago. Present were:

The president of the largest independent steel company.
The president of the largest utility company.
The greatest wheat speculator.
The president of the New York Stock Exchange.
A member of the President's Cabinet.
The greatest "bear" in Wall Street.
The president of the Bank of International Settlements.
The head of the world's greatest monopoly.

Collectively, these tycoons controlled more wealth than there was in the United States Treasury, and for years newspapers and magazines had been printing their success stories and urging the youth of the nation to follow their examples. Twenty-five years later, let's see what happened to these men.

The president of the largest independent steel company—Charles Schwab—lived on borrowed money the last five years of his life, and died broke.

The greatest wheat speculator—Arthur Cutten—died abroad, insolvent.

The president of the New York Stock Exchange—Richard Whitney—was recently released from Sing Sing.

The member of the President's Cabinet—Albert Fall—was pardoned from prison so he could die at home.

The greatest "bear" in Wall Street—Jesse Livermore—committed suicide.

The president of the Bank of International Settlements—Leon Fraser—committed suicide.

The head of the world's greatest monopoly—Ivar Kreuger—committed suicide.

All of these men had learned how to make money, but not one of them had learned how to live.
—Johnson County News, Greenwood, Indiana

679. One man gets nothing but discord out of a piano; another gets harmony. No one claims the piano is at fault. Life is about the same. The discord is there, and the harmony is there. Study to play it correctly, and it will give forth the beauty; play it falsely, and it will give forth the ugliness. Life is not at fault.
—Indiana Teacher

680. Many young poeple starting out in life believe that freedom means the right to do the things that they want to do, regardless of whether or not that right interferes with the rights and comforts of others. They mistake license for freedom; they are spiritually near-sighted. They want to be free to see life. This is a noble desire, but it is too often misunderstood and turned in the wrong direction. They should know that living does not consist in the dissipation of life but in the conservation of life.

—LOWELL FILLMORE, *You Magazine*

681. From the time an infant tries to get his toes in his mouth, life's a continual struggle to make both ends meet.

682. In our lives today, yours and mine, we shall find that when we refuse to be alarmed by appearances or bound by conditions, when we declare we are more than appears on the surface, we link ourselves to a wisdom and a power we can use to advantage in all the ways of our life.

—IRENE M. CLEMONS, *Weekly Unity*

683. A cynical grandfather has observed that life is a period of time in which the first half is spoiled by one's parents and the last half by one's children.

684. One of the largest organizations in the world is the "Ancient Order of Intenders." There are no dues, but it costs you plenty to belong. It's easy to join. You simply start each day with the intention of accomplishing big things. Something comes along to throw you off the track. Then you decide your red-letter day will be to-morrow—that day never comes. The alibi-folks try to substitute intentions for initiative, apologies for action, and promises for performance.

685. The clock of life is wound but once,
And no man has the power
To tell just where the hands will stop
At late or early hour.

686. Three rules of life were given me some years ago. I pass them on, for I have found them practical. The first is "Go," the second is "Keep Going," and the third is "Help Someone Else to Go."

—THEODORE ADAMS

687. You get a thorn with every rose; but ain't the roses sweet? This world that we're a-living in, is mighty hard to beat.

688. Things could be worse. Suppose your errors were tabulated and published every day, like those of a ball-player?

689. Men spend their lives in anticipation, in determining to be vastly happy at some period or other, when they have time. But the present time has one advantage over every other; it is our own.

—COLTON

690. When we moved into apartment 33-8, Veterans' Housing at Indiana University, we found this note taped to a wall:

To the next occupant: Please tolerate the tame mouse which runs around this apartment. He is affectionately known as Nibblemaster. He thoroughly enjoys any and all delicacies! He is not vicious, so let him survive and he will provide many hours of enjoyment.

—M. DALE BAUGHMAN

691. We live a life luxurious beyond the dreams of millions upon millions of the earth's inhabitants. We are lucky. We were born into it. The least we can do with this magnificent heritage is to preserve it and pass it along as rich and as pure as it came to us.

—*Eagle*

692. To remain master of the soul's household is to be like the sandalwood tree, which remains truly itself even in violence and death, and imparts its fragrance even to the blade of the ax that cuts it down.

—FULTON OURSLER

693. To make happiness a goal is never to know it. To make happiness a tool is never to lose it.

—*Nuggets*

694. Keep skid chains on your tongue. Always say less than you think. Preserve an open mind on all debatable questions. Discuss but don't argue. It is the mark of superior minds to disagree and yet be friendly.

—DR. WILLARD GIVENS

695. Talking with John Dewey, several months before his 90th birthday, a young doctor blurted out his low opinion of philosophy.

"What's the good of such clap-trap?" he asked. "Where does it get you?"

The great philosopher answered quietly, "The good of it is that you climb mountains."

"Climb mountains!" retorted the youth, unimpressed. "And what's the use of doing that?"

"You see other mountains to climb," was the reply. "You come down, climb the next mountain and see still others to climb." Then putting his hand gently on the young man's knee, Dewey said, "When you no longer are interested in climbing mountains to see other mountains to climb, life is over."

—MAX OTTO, *John Dewey*

696. Do not dream your experiences—experience your dreams. One reality is worth a thousand dreams.

—FRANK C. ROSS, *Hobbies*

697. The measure of a life is not its duration, but its donation.

698. He who postpones the hour of living rightly is like the rustic who waits for the river to run out before he crosses.

699. Days are like little stations placed along life's railroad track,
Each twenty-four hours finds us passing through one and, to none can we come back,
May this station be the grandest of the stations we have passed;
And may many more await you, each one grander than the last.

700. Some people are getting just like their car; the older they get the more knocking they do.

701. Most folks make more enemies by what they say than friends by what they do.

702. The belle must not sit so long primping before the glass as to miss the party, and the man must not work so hard and burden himself with so many cares as to have no breadth of interest left for things free and intellectual.

703. "There's lure in leftovers," said one good cook.
One wonders if this idea could not be applied to life.

704. Psychologists believe that no person should keep too much to himself. And so does the Internal Revenue Service.

—FLOYD R. MILLER

705. Accept the impossible, do without the indispensable, and bear the intolerable.

706. The distance on life's journey is marked not by the number of leaves torn from the calendar, but by the number of good deeds done.

—*Sunshine Magazine*

707.   Life is like a journey taken on a train.
With a pair of travelers at each windowpane.
I may sit beside you all the journey through,
Or I may sit elsewhere, never know you.
But if fate should make me sit at your side,
Let's be pleasant travelers,—it's so short a ride!

—Author Unknown

708. We have done much to raise our standards *of* living; now, we need to turn our efforts to the much more important task of raising our standards *for* living.

—KENT RUTH, in *Coronet*

709.   Never mind about tomorrow—
It always is today;
Yesterday has vanished,
Wherever none can say.

—Author Unknown

710. The sooner a man is convinced that there are no shortcuts in life, the better. Some men never learn it. To the end of their lives they have a notion that there is a shortcut to wealth, a shortcut to reputation, a shortcut to health, a shortcut to happiness—if they could only find it. They walk along the high road with a continual sense of grievance. Every now and then they deviate to the right or left to reach in a step the fields of desire, but it always ends in their coming back to the main road again, a little behind where they left it.

—Quoted in *NEA Journal*

711. *This I believe.* I believe that we are brought into life for a purpose, and that this purpose is improvement. That is the law of nature. Improvement means mental and physical fitness. Without these, we are discarded. . . .

—EDWARD R. MURROW

712. The difficulties, hardships, and trials of life, the obstacles one encounters on the road to fortune are positive blessings. They knit the muscles more firmly and teach self-reliance. Peril is the element in which power is developed.

—W. MATHEWS

713. Live every day of your life as though you expected to live forever.

—DOUGLAS MACARTHUR

714. We never find the future. It's always a dream. Someday when we are old we may realize that all these years we've been living the future every day of our lives!

—*Luther Life*

715. Beware the feather-brained man who also has lead in his bottom—he has to be unbalanced.

—HAL BOYLE

716. There are few things in life more pitiful than a man who can only brag about the things he doesn't do.

—HAL BOYLE

717. The supreme duty of every man is to make a life . . . anyone can make a living.

—*Lion Magazine*

718. I sat at the bedside of a dying man not long ago. He said, "Don't feel sorry for me now; I died 20 years ago," and I knew what he meant. Twenty years before he had lost the bite out of him. Twenty years before he had lost his attack toward life. It seems that there are some people who were just born in the objective case. They don't like anything.

—WILLIAM H. ALEXANDER

719. Many of us need the prayer of the old Scot, who mostly feared decay from the chin up: "Lord, keep me alive while I'm still living."

—*Nuggets*

720. No life is so hard but you can't make it easier by the way you take it.

—ELLEN GLASGOW

721. Life is no brief candle to me. It is a sort of splendid torch which I have got hold of for the moment, and I want to make it burn as brightly as possible before handing it on to future generations.

—GEORGE BERNARD SHAW

722. Find your pace; then work without haste or rest.

723. How many "wrong turns" can be made? In the United States of America alone, there are more than 23,000 ways to make a living. The odds are clearly not in favor of the hit-or-miss chooser.

—DAN PROCTOR, President, Oklahoma College for Women, *Rotarian*

724. Too many men conduct their lives on the cafeteria plan—self-service only.

—*Office Executive*

725. Every life is unsatisfactory until its owner has made up his mind what he means to do with it.

—*Information*

726. It was recently reported that all the monkeys in Forest Park Zoo in St. Louis were to be sent to a rest home. It seems that they were about to crack up, watching the anxious faces of all the visitors walking by.

727. The great use of a life is to spend it for something that outlasts it.

—WILLIAM JAMES

728. To live content with small means; to seek elegance rather than luxury, and refinement rather than fashion; to be worthy, not respectable, and wealthy, not rich; to study hard, think quietly, talk gently, act frankly; to listen to stars and birds, to babes and sages, with open heart; to bear all cheerfully, do all bravely, await occasions, hurry never. In a word, to let the spiritual, unbidden and unconscious, grow up through the common. This is to be my symphony.

—WILLIAM H. CHANNING, *The Lion Magazine*

729. Millions long for immortality who can't even amuse themselves on a rainy Sunday afternoon.

730. Reflection of a disillusioned and forlorn old man in his twilight years: "Life's heaviest burden is to have nothing to carry."

731. The trouble with people these days is that they want to get to the promised land without going through the wilderness.

—Reading Railroad Magazine

732. Ah, life is suddenly brighter, sweeter, fortune no
longer fickle,
Here's time left on a parking meter from somebody
else's nickel!

—STANLEY DEARSTYNE

733. Be careful how you live; you may be the only Bible some people ever read.

—LAWRENCE C. DERTHICK, U.S. Commissioner of Education

734. Nothing left loose ever does anything creative. No horse gets anywhere until he is harnessed. No steam or gas ever drives anything until it is confined. No Niagara is ever turned into light and power until it is tunneled. No life ever grows until it is focused, dedicated, disciplined.

—BISHOP CLIFFORD NORTHCOTT, *Christian Advocate*

735. Most of us can make ends meet—what we're trying to do is get them to overlap a little bit.

—CEDRIC ADAMS, *Minneapolis Tribune*

736. Two men were discussing their status in life. "I started out on the theory that the world had an opening for me," said one.
"And you found it?" asked the other.
"Well, rather," replied the first. "I'm in the hole now."

—*Arkansas Baptist*

737. No one has any right to find life uninteresting or unrewarding who sees within the sphere of his own activity a wrong he can help to remedy, or within himself an evil he can hope to overcome, or within another a life he can assist to greater heights.

—*Odd Moments,* Sunshine Private Press

Listening

738. One of the subjects which should be taught in every grade through college is the art of listening.

739. A good listener is not only popular everywhere, but after a while he knows something.

—Wilson Mizner

740. Concentration, listening and memory are interrelated. Listen and concentrate for less trouble in remembering. The Lord gave us twice as many ears as mouths, didn't He? Reckon He knew what He was doing.

741. The best recipe for the art of conversation comes from the Arabic. The pupil asked the sage how he could learn to be a good conversationalist.

"Listen, my son," replied the sage, holding up an admonishing finger.

"I am listening, father," said the pupil after the silence. "Continue your instruction."

"There is no more to tell," replied the sage.

—*Topicks*

742. Not long ago I was hostess to my bridge club. It's customary for the husbands of the members to make themselves scarce when the wives entertain. This particular night, however, our game was long and my husband returned before the girls left. He greeted everyone, then went into the bedroom and read, apparently paying no attention to our rapid-fire conversations. But after the last guest had left he said, "I have just one question. Who listens?"

—Avis Thunman

Man—Mankind

743. Mankind falls into three classes; immovable, movable, and those that move.

—*Phi Delta Kappan*

744. Funny thing about a man: He has to have a certain brand of cigar, but any licker will do. He criticizes the government, and doesn't turn out to vote. He condemns women for using rouge, and falls for it every time. He talks about the folly of over-work, and plays poker till 3 A.M. He talks about the rotten service, and tips the waiter a half. He is glad if the train is late enough for him to catch, and sore that it is late as soon as he gets on. He goes to church on Sunday, and to the devil the rest of the week, making the odds 6 to 1. He hasn't the nerve to refuse money to a grafter, but will stand off the man he really owes. He will spend a hundred dollars on a good time, and be sore all day if he breaks the crystal of his watch. He laughs at his wife's judgment, and always asks her for advice. He thinks one way and acts another, and if there were a third way to do it, he would do that. Yes, sir, funny creature, a man.

—Healthways

Marriage

745. The book salesman was proposing to his girl. "I realize," he said, "I'm not really much to look at."

"Yes, I know," she answered, "but that'll be all right. You'll be on the road most of the time."

746. Did you hear about the young teacher who said to his girl friend, "Bet you wouldn't marry me, would you?" She not only called his bet but raised him five.

Memory

747. The biology professor peered at his class and said, "The time has come for us to dissect a frog. I have one in my pocket for the experiment." He took a crumpled paper bag out of his pocket and extracted from it a very tired-looking cheese sandwich. The professor trembled visibly, and ejaculated, "Goodness me, I distinctly remember eating my lunch."

748. Selection is the very keel on which our mental ship is built. And in the case of memory, its utility is obvious. If we remembered everything, we should on most occasions be as badly off as if we remembered nothing.

—William James

749. Mayor Frank J. Moyer, losing his bid for renomination in the Republican primaries at Lackport, New Jersey, expressed his feelings in verse:

> "And now among the fading embers,
> These in the main are my regrets;
> When I am right no one remembers—
> When I am wrong no one forgets."

750. "What's that piece of string tied around your finger for, Mike?"

"That's a knot. Forget-me-not is a flower. With flour you make bread, and with bread you have cheese. This is to remind me to buy some pickled onions."

751. Even though your brain will forget more than 90 per cent of what you learn during your lifetime, it may still store up as much as 10 times more information than there is in the Library of Congress, with its 9 million volumes.

—Lawrence Galton, *Pageant*

752. An executive found this message on his desk: "Your wife called. Wanted to remind you of something which she couldn't remember but thought you would."

—Herb Caen, *San Francisco Examiner*

753. I had one most regrettable weakness as a headmaster. It was difficult for me to remember faces and to associate names with them. I was not quite so bad as the headmaster of a neighboring school, who, on one occasion after a baseball game, shook hands with all the members of his own team as if they were visitors and invited them to spend the night.

—Claude M. Fuess, *Independent Schoolmaster*

Merit Rating

754. In New Zealand where inspectors evaluate teachers, rating them in six categories, there is a common joke.

A teacher anticipating a visit instructs his class, "Raise your right hand if you know the answer; raise your left hand if you don't."

755. One of the arguments against paying an outstanding teacher another 20 or 30 per cent above the norm is that it is too hard to judge what makes a really good teacher. But that's a pretty strange line from a profession that prides itself on its measurement devices for the pupil, in every field from social adjustment to mechanical aptitude.

—Wisconsin State Journal

756. Merit rating reduces professionalism in teaching and tends to reduce teachers to the role of laborers, rather than encourage them to be competent professional employees. It forces supervisors to become inspectors, rather than professional leaders in the improvement of instruction. . . .

—Study Conference on Merit Rating,
Dept. of Classroom Teachers

Mind

757. We are all aware of the dangers of being narrow-minded; but few of us are aware of the opposite danger of becoming so broad-minded that we end up flat-headed.

—SYDNEY J. HARRIS, *Chicago News*

758. There is discipline ahead—walking with the army and wearing a uniform doesn't make a man a soldier.

759. The United States is developing an acute shortage of precious natural resources—high voltage brainpower.

Government officials report that the national deficiency in "creative" talent, which first showed up in science and engineering, now extends through the whole spectrum of business and professional skill.

—LOUIS CASSELS, Champaign-Urbana *News Gazette*

760. Stagnant minds are the greatest obstacles to progress.

—WILLIAM D. DANFORTH

761. The mind of a leader makes one a leader.

762. A woodpecker pecks out a great many specks of sawdust
While building a hut,
He works like a digger to make the hole bigger,
He's sore if his cutter won't cut.
He doesn't bother with plans of cheap artisans,
But there's one thing can rightly be said:

The whole excavation has this explanation,
He builds it by using his head.

—Author Unknown

763. The human mind is not a deep freeze for storage, but a forge for production.

—W. A. DONAGHY

764. The great American desert is not located in Idaho, New Mexico, or Arizona. It is located under the hat of the average man. The great American desert is a mental desert rather than a physical one.

—J. S. KNOX

765. The pleasures of the senses pass quickly; those of the heart become sorrows, but those of the mind are ever with us, even to the end of our journey.

—Spanish Proverb

766. A disorganized mind is unprepared for reality and easily frustrated.

—*Marten Ten Hoor*

767. I met Mr. Average Man on the street and we exchanged ideas; now my mind is a blank.

768. Whatever the mind can conceive and believe, the mind can achieve.

—NAPOLEON HILL

769. Some minds are like concrete; all mixed up and permanently set.

770. Take your typewriter apart. Separate each screw, bolt, and spring. Dump all the parts into a wash machine, turn on the switch, and wait. After a week of churning, look. There is your typewriter, neatly re-assembled, each part in its proper place, all letters and numerals in their standard position—

"Nonsense!" you say. "You could charge the parts with all the energy you can think of; you could let the parts churn for a million years and they would never churn themselves into a typewriter. It takes a mind to assemble a machine."

—Origin Unknown

771. You can't be a mental loafer and have a good memory.

—JAMES W. WEINLAND, New York University

772. An informed and disciplined mind is the greatest asset a man can have.

773. One of the advantages of having an open mind is that once in a while something good drops into it.

—DAN BENNETT, *Quote*

774. Human minds are like wagons. When they have a light load, they are much noisier than when the load is heavy.

775. Minds, like streams, may be so broad that they are shallow.

—*Sunshine Magazine*

776. It's all right, sir, to let your mind wander, provided you don't try to follow it.

777. The less a narrow-necked bottle and a narrow-minded man have inside them, the more noise they make pouring it out.

—*Weekly Progress*

778. The human mind is like a parachute; useless unless open.

779. You know that two objects cannot fill the same space at the same time. Your mind can be compared to that space; you can't keep your mind filled with negative thoughts or doubts if you have it filled with positive, powerful, and creative thoughts. Consider your mind a room with but a single door, and you have the key. It rests with you to decide who is to come through the door. . . .

—By CLAUDE BRISTOL © 1957 by Prentice-Hall, Inc., from
The Magic of Believing for Young People, Published by
Prentice-Hall, Inc., Englewood Cliffs, New Jersey

780. My mind is made up; don't confuse the issue by presenting the facts.

Mistakes

781. The only way to avoid mistakes is to gain experience and the easiest way to gain experience is to make some mistakes.

782. Last week I saw a man who had not made a mistake in 4,000 years. He was a mummy in the British Museum.

—H. L. WAYLAND

783. A father, counseling his son, instructed him to drive a nail into a post every time he did an evil thing and to remove one nail each time he performed a good deed. The son did as instructed but observed with regret that he could not pull out the nail holes. In life we may turn over a new leaf, mend our ways, and improve our behavior, but the nail holes remain as proof of our mistakes.

784. The irresponsible, lazy husband of a rural lady died. As the last rites were being said and the minister was saying all the good things about the dead man, the widow nudged her sixteen-year-old son and said, "Son, go up and look—I think we might be at the wrong funeral."

785. A beautiful blond had been prepared for the operation and left on a stretcher outside the operating room; while awaiting the nurse's return, a young man in a white smock appeared, lifted the sheet, peeked under and left without saying a word; another did likewise. As a third approached, the patient asked, "What am I here for, an operation or observation?" "I don't know," said the third young man, "you'll have to ask the doctor—I'm one of the painters down the hall."

786. It was almost time for school to be out in the spring and a seventh grade boy was asking his Dad for an advance on his allowance. Dad asked the reason and the son replied, "Well, my teacher is leaving our school and the class wants to give him a little momentum."

787. A student spent part of his summer vacation working as stage hand in a summer theater until he made one disastrous mistake. The chorus was making a quick change on a dark stage when somebody hollered for "tights." He thought they said "lights."
—Seng Fellowship News

788. I have made mistakes, but I have never made the mistake of claiming that I never made one.
—James Gordon Bennett

789. Learn from the mistakes of others—you can't live long enough to make them all yourself.

790. The biggest mistake is the fear that you will make one.

129

Misunderstanding

791. An Irishman named O'Shea came to America and wanted to attend a big league ball game. To his dismay, he found all seats were sold out. However, the management gave him a high flagpole seat. When he returned to his own country, his people asked him, "What kind of people are the Americans?"

He said, "Fine people. They gave me a special seat at the ball game, and just before the game started, they all stood up and sang, 'O'Shea can you see . . . ?"

—Quote

792. A woman had 8 children in 11 years. The night the oldest one, 12-year-old Sally, tried on her Confirmation dress, her mother said, "Sally, honey, I think you're beautiful." The youngster's face lit up. Then her mother added teasingly, "Of course, I'm prejudiced."

Sally's face fell. "Oh, Mother," she wailed, "not again!"

—Cappers Weekly

793. Cincinnati has installed some king-sized "Walk" and "Don't Walk" signs at intersections where pedestrian traffic is heavy. Traffic screeched to a halt at one intersection the other day as a little old lady blithely crossed against the light. A grim-faced policeman was waiting on the opposite curb. "Lady," he said, "do you realize you walked against the sign?"

"What sign?" she asked.

"That big orange 'Don't Walk' sign."

"Oh, that," she said. "I thought that was put up by the bus company."

—Ollie M. James, Cincinnati Enquirer

794. A young minister was preparing to take the pulpit of an older, experienced pastor. On the latter's last Sunday in the pulpit, the young man sat in the pews and marveled at the fiery sermon. When it was finished, he asked the retiring minister how he managed to be so inspirational.

Explained the experienced pastor, "There are two secrets: (1) That glass on the rostrum does not contain water but gin—sip it slowly, and (2) Know the Bible."

The outgoing preacher stayed to hear his successor's first effort.

130

After the sermon was completed, the young man asked, "Well, how did I do?" The experienced one answered, "Fair—but I said 'sip' not 'gulp' that gin, and I think you'll find that David slew Goliath; he didn't get him down and beat hell out of him."

795. He was a bit shy, and when she threw her arms around him and kissed him for bringing her a bouquet of roses, he started to leave.

"I'm sorry I offended you," she said.

"Oh, I'm not offended," he said, "I'm going for more roses."

796. A lady tourist in sunny California was keeping her guide busy answering questions. As they drove along in the country she turned to her guide and asked, "What kind of a tree is that?"

"That's a fig tree," he replied.

"But it can't be," she insisted in perplexity.

"But it is," stated the driver. "That's a fig tree."

"Goodness," exclaimed the old lady with a blush, "I always thought that fig leaves were bigger than that."

797. A New York plumber of foreign origin, with a limited command of English, wrote the National Bureau of Standards and said he had discovered that hydrochloric acid quickly opened drainage pipes when they got clogged and asked if it was a good thing to use. A Bureau scientist replied: "The efficacy of hydrochloric acid is indisputable, but the corrosive residue is incompatible with metallic permanence." The plumber wrote back thanking the scientist for telling him the method was all right. The scientist was a little disturbed and showed the correspondence to his boss, another scientist. The latter wrote the plumber: "We cannot assume responsibility for the production of toxic and noxious residue with hydrochloric acid and suggest you use an alternative procedure." The plumber wrote back that he agreed with the Bureau—hydrochloric acid works fine.

A top scientist, boss of the first two, broke the impasse by tearing himself loose from technical terminology and writing this letter. "Don't use hydrochloric acid—it eats hell out of the pipes."

798. A father and his son went for a ride on a trolleycar. The boy seemed to be completely absorbed in the passing landscape and his father, feeling a bit mischievous, lifted the boy's cap from his head and pretended to throw it out the window. The boy began to cry, so his father whistled and placed the cap back on his head. He made believe that he was able to bring back the cap by a mere whistle. The lad's tears disappeared and he grinned impishly. "That's fun," he said, "let's do it again"—and he grabbed his cap and threw it out the window.

Modern Age

799. An older lady was trying to teach a kindergarten class an old favorite song, "This is the way we wash our clothes," accompanied by washboard motions. The children didn't understand since none of them was acquainted with a washboard. On second thought, the teacher led them in the tumble action of our automatic washers.

800. There's a new wonder-pill so powerful that you can't take it unless you're in perfect health.

801. Americans who once expressed their love of our rocks and rills, our woods and templed hills, can now sing: "We love our expressways and parking lots, big cloverleaves and traffic knots."

—Lewis H. Mumford, *Quote*

802. The American Way—using instant coffee to dawdle away a half-hour coffee break.

803. The Ben Franklins and Thomas Jeffersons have been replaced by men in gray flannel suits, most of whom prefer Univac to Plato.

—Senator Stuart Symington

804. It takes a lot of jack to lift a modern car and to raise a modern kid.

—*Empire Magazine*

805. We find ourselves, at mid-century, in a world that is like a drum: strike it anywhere and it resounds everywhere.

806. Miss Sylvia Porter quotes Gilbert, of the Gilbert Youth Research Co., who polled 5,000 children: "We asked children of six and seven to identify currency and coins. The one item they could all identify was the dollar bill. Some of them had never seen a penny. It's a trend of the times."

—*Education Summary*

807. The Russians may be a step ahead in science, but certainly not in some phases of the cultural arts, particularly music.

One record album includes "Harry Sputnik and his satellites singing 'Out of This World!'"

808. A well-adjusted teacher is one whose intake of energy pills overbalances his use of tranquilizers just enough to leave him sufficient energy for the weekly faculty meetings.

—M. DALE BAUGHMAN

809. Now planes are so fast you don't have time to get acquainted with the hostess.

810. As if a woman's life were not hard enough, now she has to decide which super-market checkout line to get on the end of.

—*Cappers' Weekly*

811. Modern man is one who drives a mortgaged car over a bond-financed highway on credit-card gas.

—CY N. PEACE

812. The three R's used to stand for reading, 'riting, and 'rithmetic. Today there are four R's, and they stand for rockets, radiation and rock'n roll.

—ROBERT D. GIDEL, *National Safety News*

813. The minute men of today are the ones who can make it to the refrigerator and back with a sandwich while the commercial is on.

814. Ashes to ashes and dust to dust—if cigarettes don't get you the fallout must.

—DAN KIDNEY

Modesty

815. Modesty: The art of encouraging people to find out for themselves how important you are.

—*Public Safety*

816. A modest man often seems conceited because he is delighted with what he has done, thinking it better than anything of which he believed himself capable, whereas the conceited man is inclined to express dissatisfaction with his performances, thinking them unworthy of his genius.

—HESKETH PEARSON

Morale

817. Morale: The spunk that keeps your hands and feet working when your brain says it can't be done.

—Typing Tips

818. Morale doesn't appear as from a well-spring at the bottom, but rather as from a fountain from the top.

Motivation

819. I believe there are no poor students, only unmotivated students.

—FREDERICK MAYER, Professor of Philosophy,
University of Redlands, *Phi Delta Kappan*

820. It was desire that brought progress to the world. Without it, we all would still be living in a primitive age. Everything we have in our modern world is the result of desire. Indeed, desire is the motivating force of life itself. . . .

—By CLAUDE BRISTOL © 1957 by Prentice-Hall, Inc., from
The Magic of Believing for Young People. Published by
Prentice-Hall, Inc., Englewood Cliffs, New Jersey

821. Dr. Edward Rosenow, who become world famous as a member of the staff at Mayo Brothers Clinic, likes to tell of the incident that caused him to become a doctor. It happened when he was an eleven-year-old boy living with his family, on a farm in the backwoods of Minnesota. One day his brother became rather violently ill, and, while the family sweated it out there on the farm, the father rushed to town for a doctor. When the doctor arrived, he examined the sick boy. He looked in his throat, his eyes, and his ears. He took his temperature, and his pulse. He felt his abdomen. All this time young Edward was standing behind a chair studying the anxious expressions of his parents. Presently, the doctor turned to the parents, smiled, and said, "You can relax now—your boy is going to be all right." And Edward Rosenow was so impressed with the effect that announcement had on his parents that he says, "I decided that very day that I would become a doctor so I could put light in peoples' faces."

—KENNETH McFARLAND, *Bulletin, National Association
of Secondary School Principals*

822. In general, the teacher makes only indirect use of the physical and physiological motives, although those latter are always in the background and cannot be disregarded by the teacher.

It is the social and intellectual motives to which the teacher appeals in most direct fashion and which he applies most freely.

—J. M. STEPHENS, in *Educational Psychology*

823. I myself have always gloried in democracy as a free, competitive society—a society that encourages each person to make the best of his abilities, whether of brain or brawn. I think of democracy as using all manner of incentives—marks, ribbons, salaries, degrees, positions, money, honors, diplomas, buttons, badges, and what not. Have we not made increasing use of the "carrot" of rewards and less of the "stick" of poverty, denial of educational opportunity, and so on? Children, too, live in our competitive society. Shall we deny them the rewards for achievement that we provide so generously for adults?

—WILLIAM D. BOUTWELL, *National Parent-Teacher*

824. About three weeks before an annual alumni dinner, a member received a letter from the club president, asking him to serve on the reception committee and be there at 7 sharp. A scarlet ribbon marked RECEPTION COMMITTEE was enclosed. He hadn't meant to go. The dinners were usually a bore. But since he had been asked to be on the committee . . . By the time he arrived, almost all 400 members of the club were there, each wearing a scarlet ribbon marked RECEPTION COMMITTEE.

Objective

825. A traveler in Switzerland tells us that, uncertain of his way, he asked a small lad by the roadside where Kandersteg was, and received the most significant answer that was ever given him. "I do not know, sir," said the boy, "where Kandersteg is, but there is a road to it."

—HARRY EMERSON FOSDICK

826. The unanswered question is, who decides what the objectives of education should be, and on what basis? Should this question be left to the educators? The wiser among them are reluctant to accept the responsibility. Should this question be left then to the community? This is not always acceptable, for reasons known to most educators. Should it be left, then, to the power groups? This is precisely where it will be left if allowed to go by default, as many administrators know.

—GEORGE D. SPINDLER, Associate Professor of Education, Stanford University, *Educational Leadership*

827. A pretzel has small sense of direction. It cares not where it begins, and even less where it ends. It twines in and out, under and over, going nowhere. Some men are like that. Constantly crossing and recrossing their steps, ending up where they began.

—*Phoenix Flame*

828. You probably know about the lemmings. The lemmings are interesting folks. They're small rodents. One group lives in Siberia. They do mighty well in Siberia. They adjust well to the climate, to the living conditions, and to each other. Parent lemmings teach their offspring all of the skills of living in Siberia. They do so well that they multiply rapidly. In a few generations there are thousands and thousands of well educated young lemmings.

Then something happens to friend lemming. He decides he wants to "get somewhere"—and off he starts. Travelling hundreds of miles, he climbs mountains, inundates plains, swims rivers, crosses marshes. Lemmings who are in poor physical condition and the ones who have received only D's and C's in lemminology—the science of amphibious operations—drop by the wayside.

Parents and schools are proud to see that the most apt lemmings continue to adjust nicely to their life problems. The horde dwindles as the coastal foothills are reached and a remnant of the original starters make it to the ocean. Here the weary, but well-trained lemmings who have survived, pause not for a moment. They walk into the ocean and start to swim again as they were taught. The class valedictorian swims out to sea, bravely breasting the tide as head after head disappears. Finally, he is by himself, tired but swimming flawlessly. (His swimming teacher would have been proud but he had died on one of the early mountain passes, because his training had been too specialized—not enough general education.) Then the class valedictorian, too, sinks from sight.

You see, friend lemming's education provided all the necessary skills, but not a direction. Are we whelping well-educated lemmings?

—Robert L. Lamborn, Headmaster, McDonough School, McDonough, Maryland. *Phi Delta Kappan*

829. When Henry Ford wanted safety-glass for one of his new models, he went to his tried and tested engineers for help. All 130 of them knew too many reasons why safety-glass could not be produced.

Finally, a young engineer, who knew no reason why it couldn't be done, set to work and developed safety-glass.

830. If you go duck hunting, you aim at the point where the winging bird is going to be rather than where he is when you fire. Is there a lesson here for education?

Too often, says Dr. Harold Rugg, former professor of education, Columbia University Teachers College, we aim our education plans at the point where the children are now or even where they were a generation ago.

We need to aim at the point where children will be when the education plans mature, says Dr. Rugg.

831. The first Ford shook and rattled all over, but it got there; Wanted: more Ford people today.

832. The person who makes a success of living is the one who sees his goal steadily and aims for it unswervingly.

—Cecil B. De Mille

833. With an armload of papers, the newsie, too young to read, sat weeping along the street curb. When an observing passer-by asked the trouble, the little boy held up the front page and said, "Read me the headlines, please; I've lost my holler." Some people are a bit like the unfortunate boy; they have lost their objective and have forgotten their "holler."

834. The world steps aside to let any man pass who knows whither he is going.

—David Starr Jordan

Obstacles

835. Napoleon saw Italy, but not the Alps. He had an objective and knew where he was going. Washington saw the Hessians at Trenton. A man of smaller stature would have seen the Delaware choked with ice.

The majority sees the obstacles; the few see the objectives; history records the successes of the former while oblivion is the reward of the latter.

836. Most of us carry our own stumbling block around with us. We camouflage it with a hat.

—Healthways

837. In the park, a little girl was learning to skate by a sort of trial and error method, and experiencing falls in the process. She was resting from her labors when a boastful little boy rolled up to her side and taunted, "I can skate better than you can." "Yes, I suppose you can," the little girl agreed. "But," she added proudly, "I'll bet you mind falling down more than I do."

—Christian Science Monitor

838. An elderly woman watching a tennis game saw how often the ball hit the net. Exasperated, she declared, "Why don't they take down the net?"

Some folks cannot comprehend the value of obstacles or opposition. They never realize the satisfaction and exhilaration experienced by those winning against odds.

—Capitol Life Contact

Opinion

839. Folks would think more of the judgment of experts if the experts were more expert at agreeing.

—Sam the Sexton, Together

840. Most of us like a person who comes right out and says what he thinks—especially when he thinks as we think.

Toastmaster

841. Opinion: A definite conclusion reached after examining one's preconceived ideas.

842. Always listen to the opinions of others. It probably won't do you any good, but it will them.

843. To some people almost any question is like the moon; they see only one side.

—*Good Impressions*

Opportunity

844. I'm going back to college if I don't get any better job opportunities! Not a single company has offered me more than Dad's already making!

845. Opportunities do not come to those who wait; they are captured by those who attack.

—William H. Danforth, *I Dare You*

846. The trouble with opportunity is that it always looks bigger going than coming.

—Sylvia Strum Bremer, Davenport, Iowa, *Daily Times*

847. When opportunity knocks, don't be hesitant. Open the door and welcome it. More than that, seize it and hang on. If it has called at the wrong address, however, it may escape.

—M. Dale Baughman

848. If there be righteousness in the heart,
There will be beauty in the character,
If there be beauty in the character,
There will be harmony in the home.

If there be harmony in the home,
There will be order in the nation.
If there be order in the nation,
There will be peace in the world.

—Chinese Proverb

849. The reason many people never get anywhere in life is because when opportunity knocks they are out in the back yard looking for 4-leaf clovers.

—*American Salesman*

850. Blessings brighten as they take flight.

—Jacob Dolson Cox, Jr., *Material Human Progress*

851. To every man there openeth a way, and ways.
The high soul climbs the high way, the low soul gropes the low;

139

And in between on the misty flats, the rest drift to and fro;
But to every man there openeth a high way and a low,
And every man decideth the way he will go.

—Author Unknown

852. Can you imagine anyone looking at the rushing, tumbling waters of Niagara Falls—power beyond imagination—and saying, "I'll take a cupful," or even the weaker soul who, in a small voice, entreats, "Just a thimbleful for me."

853. We often receive letters from young people or their parents asking where the best opportunities for the future lie. Our answer is that special opportunities do not exist in the particular industry or profession—they exist *within* men themselves.

—CHARLES KETTERING, *Short Stories of Science and Invention*

854. The American with his eye always out for business got his first view of the Sahara Desert. "Man!" he said. "What a place for a parking lot!"

—BONNIE BRAY

855. Moses G. Farmer, reading of Bell's telephone discovery, claimed that he spent many sleepless nights, condemning himself for his own failure to make the invention. He admitted that he had been blind to this wonderful opportunity and that the idea had been clear in his mind on several instances.

856. Opportunity is
. . . . What the strong man makes for himself.
. . . . What the industrious man asks for.
. . . . What the lazy man dreams about.
. . . . What the weak man waits for.
. . . . What the wise man sees and makes the most of.

—*Optimist*

857. Opportunity is like an egg. Once it is dropped, its composure disintegrates.

—DOUGLAS MEADOR, *Matador* (Texas) *Tribune*

858. An opportunist is one who meets the wolf at the door and appears the next day in a fur coat.

859. Another reason many people do not hear opportunity knocking is that it usually knocks early in the morning and they sleep late.

—*Cincinnati Enquirer*

860. Ain't it a fact! Opportunity merely knocks—temptation kicks the door in!

Optimist—Optimism

861. An optimist and a pessimist were defined by a speaker at a meeting as follows: "An optimist is a man who sees a light that is not there, and a pessimist is the fool who tries to blow it out."

862. An optimist notes the green lights. A pessimist sees the red. A philosopher is color-blind.

863. How can you concentrate on a rosy future, when you permit thoughts about a blue past?

—M. DALE BAUGHMAN

864. The prophets of gloom always remind me of the early Boston merchant who said, "When whale oil is gone, the world will be plunged into darkness!"

He didn't know about Texas—or about Tom Edison. I don't even remember his name. Pessimists are never important people, and vice versa.

—PAUL HARVEY, *News*

865. The difference between a pessimist and an optimist is that if you fall into a deep hole, an optimist will pull you out, but a pessimist will get in with you.

—*National Safety News*

866. An optimist is a guy who tells you to cheer up when things are going his way.

867. The optimist says, please pass the cream. The pessimist says, please pass the milk. The realist says, please pass the pitcher.

—*Columbia*

868. There is no danger of developing eyestrain from looking on the bright side of things.

—*Cheer*

869.   If you can smile when things go wrong
                And say it doesn't matter.
             If you can laugh off cares and woe
                And trouble makes you fatter,
             If you can keep a cheerful face,
                When all around are blue,
             Then have your head examined, Bud,
                There's something wrong with you.
             For one thing I've arrived at,
                There are no ands and buts,
             A guy that's grinning all the time,
                Must be completely nuts.
                                            —Author Unknown

870. An optimist is a fisherman who takes along a camera.
                                            —*Saturday Evening Post*

871. "Who are those people who are cheering?" asked the recruit as the soldiers marched to the train.

"Those," replied the veteran, "are the people who are not going."
                                            —*News and Views*

872. An optimist is a guy who falls from a 20-story building and at every story shouts, "I'm all right so far."

873. Finish each day and be done with it. You have done what you could. Some blunders and absurdities no doubt crept in—forget them as soon as you can. Tomorrow is a new day; begin it well and serenely, and with too high a spirit to be cumbered with your old nonsense.
                                            —RALPH WALDO EMERSON

Orator—Oratory

874. Trying to settle a problem with oratory is like attempting to unsnarl a traffic jam by blowing horns.

875. Two friends met on the street. One was dressed in a new outfit from head to foot. The other wore tattered garments. Said the tattered one, "You must have a good job. You are certainly all dressed up."

"I am an orator," was the reply.

"What is an orator?"

"Well," said the other, "if you meet a man and ask him how much is two and two and he says it is four, he is not an orator. But if you ask *me* how much is two and two, I will respond to you in the following language, viz, namely, to wit: 'When, in the course of human events, it becomes necessary to take the second numerical and superimpose it upon the figure two, then I say unto you, and I say it without fear of successful contradiction, that the consequential result amounts to four.' *That* is an orator, which I am."

—ALBEN W. BARKLEY

876. Joseph Parker gives some good, sound advice to students of oratory. "Remember that the eloquence of mere words has no power in this generation. The eloquence that dimples in the sunlight and wimples in the moonlight and splashes in silver waves into golden foam upon the amber sand—and otherwise makes a fool of itself has gone onto the everlasting nothingness out of which it came." We might say, get up and say something that is something, or excuse yourself on the grounds that you have laryngitis, lumbago or lockjaw. Anything is better than to stand up and make others suffer.

877. An orator? A man who says vague things with extreme violence.

878. An orator is one who makes loud noises from the throat sound like deep messages from the brain.

Organized—Organization

879. Joining a club is like the home run hitter taking his stance; after that, there has to be a swing and a follow-through.

880. Kas George, a farmer in my home county, always plowed with a team of mules. He continually hollered "Gee" and "Haw" but the mules didn't seem to comprehend; at least they didn't "Gee" and "Haw" when they should. "Then go wherever you durn please," said Kas, "the whole field has got to be plowed anyway."

Life has to be lived and field has to be plowed; but you'll not get far if you let mental mules lead you around the field.

881. A team is a number of people who work together, but you know which one is playing left field and which one is pitching. A "group" often tends to be a team with 9 voluntary short stops all agilely covering that spot on the diamond; with great voids around the rest of the place.

—HAROLD F. SMIDDY, Vice-President, General Electric Company

882. An old hill farmer was showing his grandson the precision of his aim with his bullwhip as they drove along in the buckboard. A bullwhip is some 25 to 35 feet long with a solid handle, tapered down, with a fine end slightly frayed. When a butterfly suddenly fluttered in front of the buckboard, the rustic lashed out and neatly divided the butterfly. Mouth agape, the youngster complimented, "Boy, that's something!"

As they drove along they soon observed a herd of cows some 20 feet away. Buzzing flies made one cow switch and writhe. Thinking this would make a worthy target, the grandson challenged, "I bet you can't hit a fly on that cow's horn." At that the bullwhacker leaned back, cut loose and clipped a fly off the cow's horn. "Gosh, that beats all," exclaimed the astonished lad.

Later on the youth saw a hornets' nest hanging from a tree limb; the hornets were buzzing around and around quite noticeably. Still an unbeliever, the lad dared, "I bet you can't knock the bottom out of that hornets' nest." The old-timer looked straight at his challenger and declared, "Sonny, are you daff? I can cut a butterfly in two at 30 feet. I can knock a fly off a cow's horn at 25 feet, but you're asking for trouble. You're a little young to understand, but that I'll not do." Dumbfounded, the lad asked "Why?" "Sonny," he said, "them's organized, and you have no business monkeying with anything that's organized."

Parking

883. Parking place: An unfillable opening in an unending line of automobiles near an unapproachable fireplug.

—Future

884.　　　　When Noah sailed the waters blue,
　　　　　　He had his troubles same as you.
　　　　　　For forty days he drove his ark
　　　　　　Before he found a place to park!

Patience

885. You can do anything if you have patience. So says a noted MD and he adds: "Sometimes it takes time."

To offer proof of his statement, he said: "You can carry water in a sieve—if you wait until it freezes."

886. Patience is not an isolated thing. It is an intelligent desire with a willingness to work and an understanding of how much effort and time will be required.

—CHARLES KETTERING, *Short Stories of Science and Invention*

887. There's only one endeavor in which you can start at the top and that's digging a hole.

888. The reason people confuse *patience* and *interest* is simple enough. The same thing that inspires the keenest interest in one person might completely bore another.

This is illustrated in a homely way. Of two neighbors, one found little boys and girls a definite annoyance at all times. He asked the other, who seemed to attract them, how he could be so patient with children.

"Me, patient!" the man replied in complete surprise. "Why, I'm not patient, I just like kids."

889. Life is composed of waiting periods. The child must wait until he is old enough to have a bicycle, the young man until he is old enough to drive a car, the medical student must wait for his diploma, the husband for his promotion, the young couple for savings to buy a new home. The art of waiting is not learned at once.

—HOWARD WHITMAN, Condensed from *Better Homes and Gardens*

Perseverance—Persistence

890.
One step won't take you very far;
  You've got to keep on walking;
One word won't tell folks who you are;
  You've got to keep on talking;
One inch won't make you very tall;
  You've got to keep on growing;
One deed won't do it all;
  You've got to keep on going.

—*Arkansas Baptist*

891. With ordinary talent and extraordinary perseverance, all things are attainable.

—T. F. Buxton

892. Nothing in the world can take the place of persistence. Talent will not: nothing is more common than unsuccessful men with talent. Genius will not: unrewarded genius is almost a proverb. Education will not: the world is full of educated derelicts. Persistence and determination alone are omnipotent. The slogan "Press on," has solved and always will solve the problems of the human race.

—Calvin Coolidge

893. STAYbility is as important as ability.

—NEA Journal

894. The people who keep sawing wood in all kinds of weather are the ones who have the biggest woodpile at the end of the season.

—G. E. News

895. To rise over the disappointment of a moment is one of the signs of progress toward maturity. An assistant found Thomas Edison one morning at 2 o'clock, wreathed in smiles. Expecting that Edison had solved the problem in research he had been carrying on for years, the assistant said: "You've solved it! you've found the answer?" And Edison said: "Not a blamed thing works; now I can start over again."

—Voice Writing

896.   It's the steady, constant driving
To the goal for which you're striving,
Not the speed with which you travel,
That will make your victory sure.
It's the everlasting gaining,
Without whimper or complaining
At the burdens you are bearing,
Or the woes you must endure.
It's the holding to a purpose
And never giving in;
It's the cutting down the distance

By the little that you win;
It's the iron will to do it
And the steady sticking to it;
So whate'er your task, go to it!
Keep your grit and plug along!
—Author Unknown

Personality

897. History books have slipped up on this story. Thomas Jefferson and some friends were out horseback riding. A stranded traveler asked Jefferson for a lift across a swollen creek.

"Why did you ask me, instead of my companions?" queried Jefferson.

"There are some personalities which seem to say, 'No' and there are others which seem to say, 'Yes,' answered the stranger.

"Theirs said 'No!' and yours said, 'Yes.'"

—Bob Hansen, *Eagle*

898. Before you crack an eggshell, you don't know in what condition the egg will be. People are much the same, and we should all "crack the outer shell" before we decide what kind of person someone is.

—Jeanne Sillay, *Power*

899. By the time a child is eight years old his personality has developed into a somewhat permanent pattern. After that there is little to do but try to make the most of what is there. In general, there is little possibility of future synthesis. The pattern remains, even though some darning, patching and repairing may be done.

900. Some arresting advice: "If you want to be popular, live so that a blind person would like you." *Lasting* popularity depends not on a pretty face or being handsome, but upon inner qualities that communicate themselves to others through media other than sight.

901. Everyone can give pleasure in some way. One individual may do it by entering a room, and another by going out.

Persuasion

902. The north wind and the sun disputed which was the most

147

powerful, and agreed that he should be declared the victor who could first strip a way-faring man of his clothes.

The north wind first tried his power, and blew with all his might, but the keener his blasts, the closer the traveler wrapped his cloak around him, till at last, resigning all hope of victory, he called upon the Sun to see what he could do.

The Sun suddenly shone out with all his warmth; the traveler no sooner felt his genial rays than he took off one garment after another, and at last, fairly overcome with heat, undressed and bathed in a stream that lay in his path.

Persuasion is better than force.

903. Blessed are they who have nothing to say, and who cannot be persuaded to say it.

Philosophy

904. If education is to become a profession with its distinctive discipline, then efforts to formulate an "integrated" program must come to grips with three significant philosophic-methodological questions:

What is integrated?

What does the integrating?

With what standards or criteria do we determine whether or not integration has been achieved?

—NATHANIEL L. CHAMPLIN, Ass't. Prof. of Education, Wayne University, *Educational Leadership*

905. What's yours is mine and I'll take it.
What's mine is mine and I'll keep it.
What's mine is yours and I'll share it.
Wanted: More people with the last named philosophy!

906. *Dr. Sara Jordan, leading ulcer specialist:* "Quit being a 'heller' and be a 'what-the-heller'! The philosophical attitude will be good for your ulcer, your heart, and the rest of you."

907.   I watched them tearing a building down,
A gang of men in a busy town;
With a ho-heave-ho and a lusty yell,
They swung a beam and a side wall fell.

I asked the foreman, "Are these men skilled?"
He gave a laugh and said, "No, indeed!"
Just unskilled labor is all I need.
I can easily wreck in a day or two,
What builders have taken a year to do!"
And I thought of myself as I went my way,
Which of these roles have I tried to play?
Am I a builder who works with care,
Measuring life by a rule and square?
Am I shaping my deeds to a well made plan,
Patiently doing the best I can?
Or am I a wrecker who walks the town
Content with the labor of tearing down?
                                    —Author Unknown

Physical Attributes

908. Blessed are they who have big feet, for they shall be well balanced.

—Dr. T. T. Mason

909.   Although I'm a very short fellow,
I know of a thing that's divine.
For no matter how high a man's head is,
His feet are always level with mine.

—Paul Huls

910. An old-timer hitched up old Dobbin and took his daughter for a ride in the country. When highwaymen approached the buggy, he quickly admonished his daughter, "Quick now, hide your pearl necklace in your mouth."

The hold-up was completed and the masked men rode off with their loot, all except the concealed necklace.

The old-timer philosophized, "It's a shame your mother wasn't along. We could have saved both the horse and buggy."

Plan

911. He who only plans is a dreamer; he who only works is a drudge; but he who plans and works his plans is a conqueror.

912. The man who fails to plan, plans to fail.

149

Poise

913. Poise is the art of raising the eyebrows instead of the roof.
—*The Lion*

914. Poise is that quality which enables you to buy a pair of shoes without seeming conscious of the hole in your sock.

Popularity

915. A man doesn't sacrifice self-respect to win popularity. If he respects himself, he doesn't feel any need for popularity.

916. Remember Grandpa's remark about the cantankerous mule who was more troublesome than useful: "The more he kicks the more unpopular he becomes."

Potentiality

917. There is in every man something greater than he had begun to dream of. Men are nobler than they think themselves.
—PHILLIPS BROOKS

918. Many men possess a hundred acres of possibilities but keep about one-half acre under cultivation.
—*Indiana Issue,* Indiana Temperance League

919. One of the saddest experiences which can ever come to a human being is to awaken, grey-haired and wrinkled, near the close of an unproductive career, to the fact that all through the years he has been using only a *small part* of himself!
V. M. BURROWS, *Indiana Freemason*

920. We are not such pygmies as we sometimes think. I believe we are actually giants, with potentialities far greater than we perceive. We use less than 10 per cent of our powers, we are told; why not try to release another small percentage at least? Even 1 per cent of what we have would be 10 per cent added to what we use, and 10 per cent is a large margin of profit in any enterprise.
—GARDNER HUNTING, *You*

Power

921. Contemplate your powers, not your problems.

922. A certain youth was fond of swimming but he had never swum farther than one-half mile in his life. One day he was challenged to attempt a five-mile swim. When he passed the first half-mile, he naturally began to lose his wind. Very soon his heart began to pound, he gasped for breath, and his face assumed an agonized look. Just as he was about to give up, he suddenly drew a deep breath, then another and another, and his troubles were gone. Since he had never before experienced "second wind," it seemed a miracle to him. His new-found strength propelled him on and on and he finished the five miles tired of muscle, but breathing easily and confidently.

To him this was a new discovery, for he had never known that power was within him. It's true that every distance runner knows the power of second wind. In every long race the runners are tempted to give up, just before second wind comes. Always they go through the breathless stage, and always follows the miracle to carry them onward. Yes, here is a power, unknown to many, that can take men *ten times as far* as most people can go.

In every man not only is there a vast lung power in reserve, but there is also an amazing reserve supply of mind power and general physical power.

Practice

923. "If Heaven's a place of rest," grumbled Uncle Dodd Buckner, "my hired man's going to be all practiced up for it."
—Burton Hillis, *Better Homes & Gardens*

924. A visitor once came upon Pablo Casals practicing very slow scales upon the 'cello. "But, master," the visitor said, "surely you do not need to practice scales!" The musician replied, "Ah, my boy, the whole problem in playing the 'cello is how to get from one note to the next."

925. No one is born with skill to do anything. A man may have a special aptitude; that is, some things come to him relatively easily, yet he must practice them if he is to excel. This is true of all callings, from heading a large company to playing a piano. The most skillful are those who practice the very most.
—*Efficiency Magazine*

Praise

926. Giving praise is like making love to an old maid; you can't overdo it.

927. There is something sweeter than receiving praise; the feeling of having deserved it.

928. Praise is like a shadow. It follows him who flees from it, but flees from him who follows it.

—Quote

929. One of his marshals sought an audience with Napoleon. His purpose: to boast about a great victory which had just crowned his arms.

At length he talked to his chief, giving in detail the brilliant strategy by which he had routed the enemy. Of course, what he wanted, what he expected, perhaps what he deserved, was praise.

Napoleon, deep, quiet, incisive, inscrutable, listened attentively, patiently to the entire recitation, long as it was, dull as it was. But then in place of praising the soldier, Napoleon asked him one question. The question was: "What did you do the next day?"

Here was a man who realized, as all of us must, that there never is a time when anyone can be content to rest on his laurels—and that the time to prepare for new victories is the moment when victory is ours.

—Origin Unknown

930.   Wouldn't this old world be better,
If the folks we met would say:
I know something good about you"
And then treat us just that way? . . .

Wouldn't it be nice to practice
This fine way of thinking too:
You know something good about me,
I know something good about you?

—Author Unknown, The Lion

Prayer

931. Two boys were being chased by a goat; it seemed that the distance would be completely reduced before the boys reached the fence. One said to the other, "Why don't you try praying; say that prayer that your Dad says before you eat."

And so the other prayed, "Lord, make us grateful for that which we are about to receive."

932. The Midwest farmer has come a long way since the frontier grace at meals:

> Mush is rough,
> Mush is tough,
> Thank Thee, Lord,
> We've had enough.

Prejudice

933. A prejudiced person is anyone who is too stubborn to admit that I am right.

934. A man with a prejudice is somewhat like the shoemaker who thinks there is nothing like leather.

935. It is amazing that a narrow-minded person can stack so many prejudices in a thin vertical column.

—Grit

936. Studies show that 80 per cent of the American people show some degree of prejudice, and that children in an all-white school in New York City show the same basic prejudice as children in Georgia.

Preparation—Preparedness

937. Chance favors only the prepared mind.

—Louis Pasteur

938.
> For all your days prepare,
> And meet them ever alike,
> When you are the anvil, bear,
> When you are the hammer, strike.
> *—Edwin Markham, Pennsylvania School Journal*

939. I shall never forget a ride I had in the early days of 1955. A lumber merchant friend of mine drove me in a jeep up Mt. Cushman in Vermont. Near the top of the mountain I noted some six-inch deciduous seedlings. I asked him when they would be good as lumber and he replied, "In the year 2015 A.D." Since that was far beyond his span of years, I asked him why he had planted these trees and he replied, "Because my grandfather planted some on the other side of the mountain for me."

—PHILIP LOVEJOY, Speech before the Biennial Council, *Phi Delta Kappa*, 1955

940. Sign over the ice cream counter in a drug store: Take home a brick; you might have company.

941. Nobody wants to buy an awning; they just want the shade. Nobody wants to buy an umbrella; they just want protection from the rain.

942. Life insurance is something you have to buy when you don't want it to have it when you do want it.

—WILL ROGERS

Pride

943. A visitor once watched a group of slaves slouching and shuffling off to their work. One tall, broad-shouldered fellow strode on, his head held proudly erect.

"Who is that?" the visitor asked.

"Oh," was the reply, "he's the son of an African King. He never forgets that."

944. Pride is to the character, like the attic to the house—the highest part, and generally the most empty.

—*Sunshine Magazine*

945. A farmer with one cow was sold a milking machine after the salesman promised it would lighten his chores considerably.

He looked Bossy to the machine, went about his chores and ate supper, completely forgetting Bossy.

He realized his mistake by 9 P.M., jumped out of bed and rushed to the barn. The pail was full and fifteen gallons of milk were on the floor. Bossy was a tired cow, standing spraddle-legged with sweat pouring off her whiskers.

"How do you feel?" gasped the farmer.
Answered the cow: "Pooed but proud!"

—Illinois Education

Principal

946. The school principal is a mighty force—
    1. To the child
        He is a friend and protector.
    2. To the teacher
        He is a guide and advisor.
    3. To the parent
        He is a counselor and neighbor.
    4. To the school superintendent
        He is a trusted officer.
    5. To the community
        He is a leader and interpreter.
    6. To the teaching profession
        He is a pioneer and builder.
    7. To democracy
        He is a loyal and active citizen.

—Author Unknown

947. If he gets things done, he's a dictator;
If he asks others for advice, he lacks competence.
If he has fun, he's doing it for show;
If he does not, he's not easy to work with.

If he sticks to fundamentals, he's antique.
If he engages in experimentation, he's too progressive.

If he insists on order and discipline, he's too firm.
If the pupils run wild, he's much too easy.

If he sells popcorn and candy, he's on the toboggan;
If he doesn't, he's a poor business man.

If he has a sense of humor, he's not intellectual.
If he doesn't have, he's a prig.

If he's efficient in community relations, he's a politician;
If he isn't, he's a square from Delaware.

155

If he always agrees or keeps still, he's a rubber stamp;
If he has strong convictions, he's too blunt.
If he strives to improve the school, he's too idealistic;
If he chooses to coast instead, he has lead in his pants.

—Origin Unknown

948. The school principal was trying to make the fundamental doctrines of the Declaration of Independence clear to his class.

"Now, boys," he said, "I will give you each three ordinary buttons. You must think of the first as representing Life; the second as Liberty; and the third as representing the Pursuit of Happiness. Next Monday I will ask you to produce the three buttons and tell what they stand for."

On Monday the teacher said to the youngest member: "Now, Johnny, produce your three buttons and tell what they stand for."

"I ain't got 'em all," the boy replied, holding out two of the buttons. "Here's Life and here's Liberty, but Mamma sewed the Pursuit of Happiness on my pants."

949. A high school principal is a television composite—he has the omnipresent energy of a Superman; the detective skill of a Joe Friday; the up-to-the-minute mind of an Edward R. Murrow; the easygoing manner of a Dave Garroway; the directorial ability of a Robert Montgomery; the talent-finding ease of an Ed Sullivan; the question-asking talent of a Hal March (without the $64,000 incentive); and the sense of humor of a Jerry Lewis.

—Marjorie Scott, *Clearing House*

950. *Some good advice to beginning principals:* You are not required to finish the job; neither are you permitted to lay it down.

951. The outgoing principal was instructing his successor about human relations. "And remember, now, we have nothing but kind and cooperative patrons—until you try to change their reserved seat at basketball games."

—M. Dale Baughman

952. Sign on a principal's desk: "If you can keep your head while all those about you are losing theirs, you simply don't understand the situation."

953. Did you hear about the pessimistic principal who had just endured another hectic morning at school? As usual, he had an idea in the back of his mind to take his vengeance out on his wife at the earliest opportunity.

When the bell sounded for lunch, he caustically remarked to his secretary, "Well, here it is time to go home to lunch. If lunch isn't ready, I'm going to raise hell, and if it is ready, I won't eat a damn bite!"

—M. Dale Baughman

954. An advertisement announcing the existence of a vacancy in a principalship and listing the qualities desired in the new principal:

"There is a vacancy for a principal in a challenging school and we are open for applications. We would like to consider a man for this good post who has the wisdom of Solomon, the patience of Job, the strength of Samson, and the piety of St. Luke; we desire that he have the personal appearance of Clark Gable, the eloquence of Franklin D. Roosevelt and the sagacious judgmental ability of Winston Churchill seeking a U.S. loan; we require that he have the interest of the race as closely at heart as Brigham Young but coupled thereto the restraint of St. Paul; we stipulate that the applicant have the dominance of the Roman, the understanding of the Greek, and the self-denial of the Hebrew; he must pay for his religion like a Presbyterian, work on it like a Methodist, and enjoy it like a Baptist . . . In short, we want a plum good principal who is not leaving his previous post by invitation of the brethren."

955. A hunter, unsuccessful in his quest for game, was returning to his car when he chanced to meet a small boy. "Where can I find something to shoot?" The truant lad blinked for a moment and then hopefully exclaimed, "Here comes my principal."

Principles

956. Some people confuse principles with rules. A principle is something inside one; a rule is an outward restrictor: to obey a principle you have to use your mental and moral powers; to obey a rule you have only to do what the rule says.

Problems

957. The measure of success is not whether you have a tough problem to deal with, but whether it's the same problem you had last year.

958. In problem solving, get more hose or get closer to the fire.

959. It is wise not to solve any problems that you do not have to solve. Save your time, your nerves, and your brains until you are certain that a problem exists and that you are the person who has to do the solving. Many problems, like storms, never arrive in spite of threatening skies.

—EDWARD HODNETT

960. It is truly amazing that from so humble an origin as the oyster comes the pearl—on occasion. People, when irritated, fuss, fume and blow their tops; the oyster acts quite differently. When an irritation is set up inside the oyster by foreign particles, he quietly exudes a substance which allays the friction, covers the sore spot, and miracle of miracles, the substance hardens, forming a pearl.

Oysters that have never been irritated, never had a problem. No problem, no pearl.

Profession

961. There are at least three dimensions to a profession. The width, the height, and the depth, of that which may be called a profession, can be described. The three D's of a profession may be said to be Dedication, Development, and Discipline.

—TED WILSON BOOKER, *Georgia Educational Journal*

962. Things are seldom what they seem. Skim milk masquerades as cream; high-lows pass as patent leathers and jack-daws strut in peacocks' feathers.

—WILLARD HURST, *Public Relations Journal*

Progress

963. All progress is born of inquiry. Doubt is often better than over-confidence, for it leads to inquiry, and inquiry leads to invention.

—HUDSON MAXIM

964. Very much of what we call the progress of today consists in getting rid of false ideas, false conceptions of things, and in taking a point of view that enables us to see the principles, ideas, and things in right relation to each other.

—W. D. HOARD

965. In the early 1870's a U.S. Congress became greatly alarmed over the size of the federal budget, and determined to cut it. Finally a senator arose to announce a solution. It seems that he had been investigating the Patent Office. After noting the staggering total of entries in the records, he had concluded that it would be impossible to invent anything else. Therefore, they might well discontinue the Patent Office, and appropriate no more money for it. The savings here would provide the desired decrease in the federal budget.

966. To some school administrators, progress is simply creating bigger and better circles to run around in.

—M. DALE BAUGHMAN

967. If he were living today, I am sure Thomas Edison would look around and say, "Let us not become egotists just because we have made some progress. There are many problems yet to be solved and it seems, too, there are just about as many things to be done now as there were when I was a boy, but the opportunities are so much greater. So let's get to work."

—CHARLES KETTERING, *Short Stories of Science and Invention*

968. You can't do today's job with yesterday's tools and be in business tomorrow.

—HELEN MACKINTOSH, *NEA Journal*

969. Progress, you must admit, always involves a certain amount of risk. After all, you can't steal second base and still keep one foot on first.

—*Bremerton* (Washington) *Sun*

970. Some people are like what the farmer said about the mule: awfully backward about going forward.

971. Among the many new powdered and condensed foods, a new one has been invented to keep you from dying of thirst on the desert. It consists mainly of evaporated and powdered H_2O. It is called Neverthirst. All you do is add water.

—*The Paseo Press,* Paseo High School, Kansas City, Missouri

972. If you don't think that we've made progress, just remember that the only packaged product in Abraham Lincoln's grocery store at New Salem, Illinois, was breakfast cocoa.

973.   Beneath the spreading chestnut tree,
The smith has customers from far and near,
For now he's selling gasoline,
Hot dogs and root beer.

974. You will never falter standing still. The faster you go, the more chance there is of stumbling but the more chance you have of getting somewhere.

975. Every year it takes less time to fly across the ocean and longer to drive to the office.

—RAYMOND DUNCAN

976. The world's moving so fast, the man who says it can't be done, is interrupted by someone doing it.

—ELBERT HUBBARD

Progressive Education

977. A little girl with a cold was urged by her mother to stay home from a progressive school. "But I can't, Mother," the girl insisted. "This is the day when we start to make a clay model of a cow, and I'm chairman of the udder committee."

978. A little English girl was taken from the city to the country where she saw her first sow. It was an enormous animal squatting in the pigpen and the farmer's wife said, "Big, isn't she, Doris?"
"Why shouldn't she be big," replied Doris. "I saw her a while ago and she had ten little ones blowing her up.

—PERCY WAXMAN

979. It is curious that at the present time, when freedom is threatened with destruction, the very education that could save it is in popular disrepute. Progressive education is the only education ever devised that is harmonious with the demands of a free society.

—ERNEST O. MELBY

980. Extreme progressive education is a dead-duck. Those who have written recently about the perils of progressivism have had to go out of their way to find the beast.

—GEORGE LEONARD JR., *Look Magazine*

981. Teachers and college professors should take to the rostrum to dispel the charge that there is a current "traditional-versus-progressive" controversy. Modern education is very much with us; the science of education is young and there is room for improvement. The job of educating the public in this professional area rests with the school personnel themselves.

—PHILIP OLGIN, Associate Professor of Education,
Long Island University, *Phi Delta Kappan*

982. Upon finding fresh footprints in his new concrete sidewalk, a college professor decided that they must have been made by his neighbor's young sons. Seeking to avoid a possible quarrel, he merely suggested to the boys' father that he might caution his sons against destruction of the property of others.

The father grew indignant at the professor's suggestion and neither agreed that mischief had been done nor apologized. He declared that reprimanding his sons was out of the question, since it might stifle their natural impulses. He went so far as to suggest that the professor was both stuffy and unremembering of his own youth. He finally ended his speech in obvious irritation with the query, "Don't you like boys at all?"

"Oh, yes, I like them well enough," said the professor, "but in the abstract, not the concrete."

Psychology

983. One parent described his 10-year-old boy as having a handful of "gimme" and a mouthful of "oblige."

984. My two-year-old son floored me with this one day: "The cow says 'moo, moo'; the dog says 'bow-wow'; the duck says 'quack, quack'; Mommie says 'no, no!'"

MRS. T. S. DOBSON, *Parents Magazine*

985. Shoe salesmen are taught always to say, "Madam, your right foot is smaller than the left," not "Your left foot is larger than the right." Some restaurants sell the "sizzle," not the steak. Mattress manufacturers sell "sleep." The baker sells "taste."

One youthful salesman was fired because he was caught by his boss standing outside a birth-control clinic selling vanishing cream.

986. Spanking had one advantage over modern child psychology. It made the child smart.

—HAL CHADWICK

987. A child specialist gave this advice to a mother: "You'll have to handle this child carefully; remember you're dealing with a sensitive, highstrung little stinker."

—*Scholastic Teacher*

988. If you tire of the noise from your son's drum and he can't be separated from it, just give him a knife and ask him if he knows what's inside.

989. Stopping for gas in an Iowa town, I found a line of cars at a filling station which displayed a sign: "Your tank full free if you guess how much it takes." After I had guessed—and lost—I asked the busy proprietor how his plan had worked out. "Fellow guessed right about 2 years ago," he said, "but it only cost me $1.30. And we don't get any 'Gimme a dollar's worth' customers any more. Everybody makes a guess and fills up."

—M. F. McGRATH, *Rotarian*

990. *Farmer, plowing with one mule:* "Giddap, Pete! Giddap, Barney! Giddap, Johnny! Giddap, Tom!"
Stranger: "How many names does that mule have?"
Farmer: "Only one. His name is Pete, but he don't know his own strength, so I put blinders on 'im, yell a lot of names at 'im, and he thinks three other mules are helping 'im."

991. Psychologists say that parents should never ask a child a question which can be answered negatively. One father registered strong complaints after using such tactics for a time on his five-year-old son. All went well for a time as he would say, "Which do you want to eat, son, your tomatoes or your lettuce?" "Do you want to wash your hands or brush your teeth?"
When they were downtown shopping and reached the toyshop, the youngster asked, "Hey, Dad, which do you want to buy me, roller skates or a wagon?"

992. Repairs were being carried out on the roof of an asylum by a local builder who had asked for an inmate to assist him. All went well until lunchtime, when the builder's assistant clutched him around the neck and said: "Come on, let's jump down."

The builder was frightened almost out of his wits, but suddenly had an inspiration that saved his life.

"Oh, nuts," he replied, "anybody could do that. Come on down and let's jump *up*."

—*Lion*

993. The PTA mothers were much alarmed at the report that one of their number had allowed her 8th grade son to have his own latch-key. Afraid their own children would demand the same privilege, they tackled her on the subject. When she understood what they were talking about, she laughed.

"Oh," she said. "Sure, I let him have it to show off to his friends —but it doesn't fit the door!"

—Lois Carney, *Magazine Digest*

994. Child psychology is what parents use in letting their boys and girls have their own way.

—Franklin P. Jones, *Saturday Evening Post*

PTA

995.
If you're nominated chairman of a
   specially good committee,
And it's just the job you wanted and
   You're sitting very pretty,
Please don't pretend you're horrified and
   Hide behind an attitude
Of pseudo-self-effacement, and an utter
   Lack of gratitude!
Nod your head to show acceptance, with
   A smile to show your pleasure,
And resolve that if elected you will give
   Your finest measure.
But—if you think you hate the job, and
   Do not want to take it,

Get up at once and in a voice as firm as
    You can make it,
Say thank you for the honor, show your
    Real appreciation
Then briefly state your reasons and
    Decline the nomination.

        —Illinois Parent-Teacher

996. The PTA is a 12-year course with homework, but no classes; study programs, but no examinations. It's elective, not required. It's work—but it's fun.

One of the smartest things you, as a parent, can do is to sign up for the course when Tommy or Susie is ready for kindergarten—and stay with it from dolls to dates, from marbles to auto-driving.

High school PAT-ers know its satisfactions: they are what bring on that reminiscent wistful tone when they say: "Yes, I'll be graduating in June."

997. A middle-aged lady with two children in high school was emotionally shocked when she discovered she was pregnant again.

"Doctor," she moaned, "I just don't see how I can go through with it again."

The sympathetic doctor asked, "Did you have much trouble with your other pregnancies?"

"Goodness no!" replied the lady, "my other babies never hurt me at all physically; it's the PTA that gets me down."

998. Every law-enforcement officer would agree with the parent-teacher organizations that in planning for the future of America's children, parents, teachers and religious advisers must give consideration to adequate religious training, the instillation of discipline, and the inculcation of responsibility. But the majority, I think, would go further. They would urge that parent-teacher associations strive to bring the local law enforcement officer into the circle of the young child's acquaintance.

        —J. Edgar Hoover, *National Parent-Teacher*

999. The growing child benefited from the improved mutual understanding on the part of teachers and parents. He created a third bond of responsibility between them. This resulted in a 3-way relationship—a parent-teacher-child relationship, which demonstrated the inter-dependence of home, school and community.

—ARNOLD GESELL, Research Consultant, Gesell Institute
of Child Development. *National Parent-Teacher*

Public Opinion

1000. The pressure of public opinion has been compared with the pressure of atmosphere; you can't see it, but it's there just the same; 14.7 pounds to the square inch.

—Speech by WILLIAM G. WERNER

1001. Schoolmasters, like people in business, I suggest, should always be ready to sit in the classroom and take notes when the public speaks its mind.

—Speech by WILLIAM G. WERNER

1002. Public sentiment is everything. With public sentiment nothing can fail; without it, nothing can succeed. Consequently, he who molds public opinion goes deeper than he who enacts statutes or pronounces decisions. He makes statutes or decisions possible or impossible to execute.

—*Freeways to Friendship*, W. HAROLD KINGSLEY,
California Teachers Association

1003. There is more wisdom in public opinion than is to be found in Napoleon, Voltaire, or all the ministers of state, present or to come.

—Talleyrand, speech in the French Chamber of Peers

1004. "Have you brought many people to your way of thinking?"

"No," answered the great politician. "Public opinion is something like a mule I owned when I was a boy. In order to keep up the appearance of being the driver, I had to watch the way he was going and follow on behind."

Public Relations—Publicity

1005. There's no need for continuous publicity so:

Preachers should preach only one sermon or so a year. People are against sin anyway, so why harp on it.

Teachers do not need to review lessons. Tell the pupils once and they won't forget.

165

But if you want to be foolish like the bell ringer at Notre Dame Cathedral, where the bell has been rung every day for six centuries to let people know it's there, you might consider continuous publicity.

—Author Unknown

1006. Management is at last growing to understand that every policy decision, every operating move, has a public relations aspect that must be considered. Industry today regards public relations as a management function along with research, engineering, distribution, manufacturing and personnel.

—PAUL GARRETT, *Public Relations Journal*

1007. An evangelist in Texas recently published a lengthy list of 679 sins. He was swamped with requests for the list by a surprisingly large number of folks. It seemed that they were afraid they had been missing something.

1008. You know about the Sphinx. It never told anything to anybody. It just sort of stood around and looked wise and didn't give out any information. Finally it was forgotten, and got covered up with sand and people had to dig to find it. Not many did.

A school district can be like a sphinx, silent and uninformative. Then people forget it, or, if they do think about it, aren't very interested. We don't want that to happen to us. We want to tell people all about our school district—and we want the staff of our school district to have the answers to questions that they might ask.

—La Mesa-Spring Valley (California) District Handbook

1009.
    The codfish lays a million eggs
    While the faithful hen lays one,
    But the codfish does not cackle
    To inform us what she's done;
    So we disregard the codfish,
    While the faithful hen we prize,
    Which only goes to prove
    It pays to advertise!

—Author Unknown

1010.
    I keep six honest serving men,
    They taught me all I knew.

Their names are What and Why
And When and How and Where and Who.
—Kipling

1011. Teachers . . . develop a nose for news as sharp as your eye
for monkey-business in the classroom and as alert as your second-
sight for discipline.

—Speech by William G. Werner

1012.   Don't cry, little story, please don't cry,
Can I help it if there you lie,
With precious hours gone to naught
In preparation and careful thought.

Not every story suffers your fate,
So tell your successor not to be late,
Maybe next week he'll hit page one
To show you that it can be done.

—*Pipeline to Editors,* Michigan Community Study,
Michigan State College

1013. Whatever or whoever is in the sun will either ripen or
wither.

—German proverb

1014.   If in life you would succeed
And your accomplishments you wish to enhance,
You must stir it and stump it
And blow your own trumpet,
Or believe me, you haven't a chance.

—Author Unknown

1015. The proprietor of an old-fashioned general store, was once
approached by an advertising specialist. The salesman received an
abrupt "Nothing doing" to his sales pitch. Explained the store-
keeper, "Been in business twenty years and never have advertised."

Looking down the main village thoroughfare as he turned to
leave, the city traveler remarked, "What is that large white building with the steeple?"

"Why, that is our church," answered the merchant.

"Been serving the people very long?" asked the stranger.

"Yes," was the answer, "about 75 years, I guess."

"Well," the traveler made his point, "they still ring the bell every Sunday, don't they?"

1016.   He who whispers down the well
              The things he has to sell
              Will never make as many dollars
              As he who climbs a tree and hollers.

                                        —Author Unknown

1017. Several years ago a man appeared in a small Pennsylvania town and hired the opera house for one night; he engaged no ushers or other helpers. Nearly a month preceding the day for which the hall was rented, he posted a huge sign, conspicuous and appealing, which read, "He is coming!"

One week before the night of the performance the sign was re-placed by one which read: "He will appear at the Opera House on October 31!" On the day just before the event the sign said simply, "He is here!" The morning of the fateful night: "He will be at the Opera House tonight at 8:30!"

That night the promoter sat in the box office and sold tickets at $1 per person to a full house. When the curtain went up inside, however, all the audience could see was a final sign reading: "He is gone!"

1018. The wise school administrator learns all he can about his community's organizations, including the order of town and gown, the spit and whittle clubs, the league of powder-room specialists, and the legion of boiler-room gripers.

1019. February's heroes, Washington and Lincoln, probably would be puzzled by the term *public relations.* Yet both men faith-fully adhered to an ideal that should underlie all good public rela-tions—the ideal of *service*—to people, community, nation.

1020. According to Dun and Bradstreet, 95 per cent of all busi-ness failures are from the ranks of non-advertisers.

It's like the feller says, "When business is good, you ought to advertise; when it's bad, you've got to.

1021.   "Are parents permitted
                    To visit the classes?

Do we need an appointment
Or legalized passes?"

"Not only permitted
But urged!" we replied,
"For months upon months
We have earnestly tried
To make our school parents
Feel welcome and free
Any day, any time
Unannounced, to come see.

"You're entitled to visit.
We want you to know
What we're doing to help
John and Mary M. grow!"
—*Education in our Town,* parents' newsletter of the
Grosse Point (Michigan) Public Schools

1022. A school without a public relations program is like winking at a girl in the dark. You know what you're doing, but no one else does.

1023. Many good school administrators still plant four seeds to the hill as did the Indians:

One for the blackbird,
One for the crow,
One for the cutworm,
And one to grow.

1024. International public relations might be improved if the ratio of praise to censure were at least 2 to 1.

1025. Some newspapermen hold that the best news stories are about beauties, babies and beasts. School administrators need to learn to identify the beauties, babies and beasts in school news reporting.

—M. DALE BAUGHMAN

1026. Gigg-Nu, the first public relations expert, stood on the hilltop and told fellow dwellers in the Pleistocene Apartment Project how he slew an ichthyosaurus with a club. Thus he publicized his prowess, promoted his prestige, won the favor of his people, and was elected chief.

But this wasn't enough for Gigg-Nu; for he was public relations-wise. He knew that if he wanted to hold office he would have to keep his talents ever fresh in the minds of the people. So he selected a large rock with a flat surface situated beside the trail over which everyone had daily to pass. There he chiseled in picture words the story of his hunting feat. Day by day and every day the greatness of Gigg-Nu was held before the public eye and in the public mind.

He succeeded because he used all available means of communication: there were only two—oral and graphic—yet his technique was as modern as a present day soap opera, which proves that in the field of public relations there is really nothing basically new.

Now, as in Gigg-Nu's day, there are only two human facilities for the reception of words, ideas and impressions—the eyes and ears, two ways to reach them; the spoken word and written word.
—*Freeways to Friendship,* W. HAROLD KINGSLEY,
California Teachers Association

1027. The second important factor in building school-community relations is the use of printed materials. The local newspaper can influence many important school decisions. Publicity on any part of a school activity is news, particularly if it is unfavorable

There is a "closed season" protecting ducks, quails, rabbits and groundhogs, but school principals are evidently expendable, and therefore, enjoy no protection from the "pot shots" of any ambitious newspaper reporter. If the local newspaper editor can be induced to visit the school and spend some time in classes, he may become a supporter of our modern school.
—CHARLES STEEL, *Bulletin, N.A.S.S.P.*

1028. Public school relations are of two kinds, public and private. According to research, school administrators have both kinds, but the latter are more numerous than the former. Public relations are best "carried on" in every professional act. In fact, it is as difficult to avoid public relations as private ones. Some authorities claim that every school administrator is a public relations counselor in the rough. Others say, "Phooey." At times the preponderance of evidence would seem to rest with the phooeyites.

The best authorities have soured on the term "public relations" and prefer to use something more pedagogical and obtuse like "school interpretation." Both terms are sliced from the same piece, probably.

—FREDERICK MOFFITT, Chalkdust, *Nations Schools*

Pupil

1029. *Teacher:* "Tommy, where are elephants found?"
Tommy: "Elephants are so big that they hardly ever get lost."

1030. Senior boy's plea to his date just before the prom. . . .
Roses are red,
Violets are blue
Orchids are much too high!
Won't dandelions do?

1031. We present without comment the response of a 4-year-old of our acquaintance, who was asked how he occupies his time in nursery school. "Oh," said the kid airily, "I fight and take tests."

1032. *Teacher:* "Is your father well enough to go back to work?"
Pupil: "No, and he won't be for some time."
Teacher: "Why?"
Pupil: "Compensation has set in."

1033. Rom Tyers, one of my high school classmates, occasionally took a day off from school to go rabbit hunting. He always signed his absence blank with the excuse, "Taking shots."

—M. DALE BAUGHMAN

1034. On the first day of school there were not enough seats for all the pupils. The teacher asked one little tyke, "Will you sit on a stool for the present?" The little fellow went home at the end of the day, disillusioned, and told his parents, "I sat on that stool all morning and never did get a present."

1035. This happened a few days before the moon eclipse last fall, writes Nadine Caldwell, sixth grade teacher at Talco. She overheard the following while her pupils were having a five minute break.

"Linda, are you going to watch the moon eclipse tonight?"
The reply was; "I guess so. What channel is it on?"
—Texas Outlook

1036. Children who are proficient readers have a great advantage over their friends. They can finish a comic book before the druggist tells them to put it down.
—Maurice Seitter

1037. "Did you enjoy your first day at school?" a father asked his young son upon his return from his first day at kindergarten.

"I've never been to such a place," he answered. "There was a lady there who didn't do anything but try to restore order."

1038. A substitute teacher in a large city school prepared the 10:30 lunch for kindergarten. Then she pulled up a chair to join them. "Now, let's eat," she said. No one touched his food. Again she said, "Come on, children, let's start to eat." There was silence. Finally, a little tousle-haired lad said, "Hell, we ain't prayed yet."
—John Harold in *Midland Schools*

1039. Little Lindy's version of the nursery rhyme, "Little Miss Muffet," goes like this: "Little Miss Muffet sat on a tuffet eating her curls at play."

1040. After end-of-term prizes were distributed in the fourth grade, Rusty's mother asked him if he got an award. "No," he replied, "but I got a horrible mention."
—*Mississippi Educational Advance*

1041. Boys and girls like math. If they had a choice, they'd keep it and throw out sports. The problem is getting teachers to like it.
—Dr. Richard Madden

1042. *Teacher:* Construct a sentence using the word exchange.

Student: The frequency of absorbable radiation depends upon the elastic constant of the molecule and the process of energy exchange is therefore in accord with the equipartition theory.

1043. The school my daughter's enrolled in
Provokes me to laud it,
My little blondie, sharp as a pin
Is sure to earn a plaudit.

Her teacher is outstanding
And makes her work a joy,
Oh, how her mind's expanding!
(Wonder what she can do with our boy?)

—M. DALE BAUGHMAN

1044. The child who is always two jumps ahead of his class usually sits nearest the door.

—RAYMOND DUNCAN

1045. Braddy came to school with pockets full of bubble gum, which he shared with his classmates and a surprised teacher. He quickly explained, "I just became a brother this morning."

1046. There are only two ways to handle Junior high school youth; does anyone know what they are?

1047. Telephone conversation between two 7th grade boys: "All right, page 11, problem 8—what answer does your Dad get for that one?"

"He can't solve it so he's checking with a C.P.A."

1048. Normal children love school . . . [When they don't] it's because the school or teacher they went to was impossible or they had been so conditioned by improper home training that only a special school could overcome it.

—DR. KARL MENNINGER

1049. After Willie gave "Nile" as the answer for the principal river of Egypt, his teacher said, "That's right. Now can you tell me the names of some of the smaller tributaries?"

Willie hesitated a moment, then said, "I guess it would be the juvenile."

—*North Carolina Education*

1050. Some students drink at the fountain of knowledge—others just gargle.

1051. The teacher asked Perry to tell her what a hypocrite is. Replied Perry, "It's a boy who comes to school with a smile on his face."

1052. Seeking to bolster his son's flagging interest in attending school, a father displayed a picture of Pilgrim lads on their way to school. "Now, Billy," he said, "see how happy these boys are on their way to school. Why can't you have that attitude?"

"Shucks," moaned Billy, "I wouldn't mind going to school either, if I could shoot Indians on the way."

1053. A safety sign read: "School—Don't Kill a Child." Beneath was a childish scrawl: "Wait For a Teacher."

—Great Lakes Bulletin

1054.   When we have the classes sifted
             And thus isolate the gifted,
         Shall we integrate, accelerate, or segregate?
         Just how are the gifted lifted?
         —H. M. GRANT, *Forum of New Brunswick Education*

1055. Comment of a junior high school boy, enrolled in general science: "One thing about the speed of light—it gets here too early in the morning."

1056. For a brighter future tomorrow, identify the gifted child today.

1057. The little girl was telling her teacher about her baby teeth coming out. One tooth was loose and she had already lost three. She said: "Pretty soon I'll be running on the rims."

1058. The teacher had asked her class the difference between a primitive man and a modern man.

One of the brighter pupils answered, "When his wife talks too much, modern man goes to his club, while the primitive man reached for it."

1059. There was the lazy pupil who took up playing the trombone because it is the only instrument on which you can get anywhere by letting things slide.

1060. A sophomore in the English class of Katherine E. Andrews of Trenton, Missouri, gave an example of a collective noun:
    "Garbage can."

1061. In commenting upon the conduct of young people 2,000 years ago, Socrates is said to have remarked: "The children now love luxury; they have bad manners, contempt for authority; they show disrespect for their elders and love chatter in place of exercise. They no longer rise when elders enter the room. They contradict their parents, chatter before company, gobble up dainties at the table, cross their legs, and tyrannize their teachers."

1062. An inexperienced young driving pupil, tackling downtown traffic for the first time, stalled the engine of her car at a busy intersection.

"Don't get excited now," soothed the driving instructor, "Just use the old noodle."

"Oh, dear," the flustered girl muttered, "Now where is that thing?"

1063. During a recent election when the people of Texas were voting on Amendment 4 (the amendment designed to improve the Teacher Retirement System in Texas) a fifth-grade boy was noted marching up and down in a schoolhouse where the people were voting, and shouting, "Vote for Amendment 4. Let's retire all of these teachers."

—Waco *News Tribune*

1604. A five-year-old girl came to kindergarten one day dressed in faded blue jeans, over which she wore a frilly petticoat and a party dress. Pinned to the dress was this note from her mother: "I hope you don't think this was *my* idea!"

1065. The teacher had her class write a short composition on the subject "water." One pupil seemed to be having difficulty, but finally he turned in his paper and this is what he wrote:

"Water is a light colored liquid which turns dark when you wash in it."

—*Wisconsin Journal of Education*

1066. *Teacher:* "John, how was iron discovered?"
John: "I heard Dad say they smelt it!"

—Burt Cohen

1067. Spring: An Essay

Spring is my favorite season of the year because we have spring vacation and right after spring vacation we have summer vacation.

When spring comes the weather is much more pleasant and the teachers give us less homework.

In spring lots of tornadoes come and everyone is hoping that one will come and destroy the school. And with the tornadoes comes rain and hail which might flood the city. Then not one person will have to go to school.

Spring is my best season of the year.

—BRYAN HAMRIC, sixth grader, Dallas, Texas, carried in the *Dallas Morning News*

1068. The bumptious student in the adult evening class in wood-working was a master at one thing—telling other people he could do it better. It soon became apparent that his talk was a cover up for his bungling. He matched the wrong woods, made mistakes in measurements and used the wrong tools in wrong ways. Throughout, he chattered along, ignoring both the helpful comments and frank criticisms of his classmates.

When he had almost completed his pride, a small chest of drawers, he asked for advice, however. "I can't decide how to finish it—shellac or varnish," he said. "What do you guys think?"

One of the men who had tried in vain to help him earlier studied the botched chest from every angle, and then said, "Why don't you just stucco it?"

—DONALD SYNGG, *Saturday Evening Post*

1069. Miss Teechum was genuinely startled when she discovered a full-size puddle on the floor of the kindergarten coat hall. She told the class of her discovery, but, being a true disciple of progressive methods, announced that no one would be punished. In a quite serene manner she announced, "We'll all bow our heads, close our eyes and at the end of five minutes I'll go to the coat hall. I imagine the puddle will be mopped up."

The all-believing youngsters, along with Miss Teechum, closed their eyes as planned. At the end of the five-minute period, the teacher arose and marched confidently to the scene of the crime. To be sure, the evidence, the little puddle, had disappeared. But down at the other end of the hall was another puddle similar in dimensions; above it was a scribbled sign which read, "The phantom strikes again!"

1070. A high school teacher has just given us a note from one of his pupils that indicates how far we've come since the days when getting to and from school was a simple pedestrian matter. "Dear sir," the note reads, "I could not submit this homework yesterday because I could not find a parking space, so I went right back home."

—New Yorker

1071. *Grouping—Old Style:* As far back as 400 A.D. teachers categorized their students into four groups:
1. Sponges, who soak up everything, good and poor, significant and trivial.
2. Sifters, who check the undesirable, and save the desirable.
3. Funnels, who retain not a particle.
4. Strainers, who collect the bad, and permit the best to pass.

1072. "Jimmy," scolded his mother, "your teacher reported that you have been fighting with two boys and you gave one a black eye. Is that correct?"

"Yes, Mom," answered Jimmy. "You see it's like this—those boys are twins and that's one way I can tell them apart."

1073. Haven't we all wondered about deaf people?

My daddy is deaf—just deafer than ding! I asked him last night 'bout an important thing; he kept right on reading, though loud I had shouted. He paid no attention, and I almost pouted!

Then I *whispered* to mother if I might please go to a small Freshman party—she never says "No."

Daddy turned square around, and the law down he laid! "These parties in midweek play hob with your grade!"

—Ruth Smeltzer

1074. A nun asked her second-graders if anyone could tell her the 4 seasons of the year. A little boy said, "Yes, Sister; marbles, baseball, football, and basketball."

1075. Some pupils are like blotters. They soak it all in, but get it all backwards.

—Future

1076. *Teacher to little boy who had played hooky the previous afternoon:* "What did you do all afternoon?"

Boy: "I was shooting craps, teacher."

Teacher: "That must stop. Those little things have as much right to live as you have."

1077. Too many pupils today major in alibiology.

1078. High school senior's contribution to the poetry magazine:
> By her glorious hair I was bitten,
> She's really the charmingest girl, sir:
> In her arms any man would find bliss, sir.
> But what struck me most about her
> Was her hand when I started to kiss her.

—Yale Record

1079. *Teacher:* For goodness sake, Peter, what happened to the seat of your trousers?"
Peter: "I was trying to drown our cat and I sat on the pail to keep her from jumping out."

1080. A gambler's seven-year-old son, asked to count in school, responded promptly: "1, 2, 3, 4, 5, 6, 7, 8, 9, 10, Jack, Queen, King."

1081. The first-grade pupils were taken to the county fair. One little boy watched the proceedings with much interest; finally he turned to his teacher and asked, "Why does that man go around patting and pinching the cows?"

"He's doing that," answered the teacher, "because he wants to buy a cow and he's trying to make sure that he will get good meat."

A few days later, the boy excitedly told his teacher, "I saw the bread man trying to buy our cook."

1082. Schoolboy, complaining to chum: "I used to stay home all week with a cold. Along came these miracle drugs and it's back to school the next day."

*—*GEORGE CLARK, *Chicago Tribune,*
New York News Syndicate

1083. At the conclusion of a nature lesson, the teacher said, "Now don't you think it's wonderful how the little chicks get out of their egg shells?" Whereupon a little girl piped up with, "What beats me, teacher, is how they get in."

1084. *Teacher:* "What's your cat's name, Joey?"

Joey: "Ben Hur."

Teacher: "That's a funny name for a cat. How did you happen to pick such a funny name for a cat?"

Joey: "Well, we just called him Ben until he had kittens."

1085. In Ontario, a teacher asked in an examination, "In the fall, why do wild geese fly south?"

In seven words, a schoolboy solved one of nature's mysteries that has baffled waterfowl experts since they were recognized as experts. His answer was, "Because it is too far to walk."

—KEITH C. SCHUYLER, *V.F.W. Magazine*

1086. A first-grader thus described to his father how his school day began; "Well, first you have to be in your chair when the bell rings. Next, we say our morning prayer, and the pledge to our flag, and sing *America*. Then Mr. York, our principal, does the commercial."

—MAXINE PETTIBONE, *Instructor*

1087. The rural school teacher, on the first real cold spell of winter, cautioned her pupils about the dangers of playing on ice-covered ponds and streams. She admonished, "Now, pupils, you must be sure the ice is safe. I had a little brother, only eight years old. One day he went skating on the lake with his new skates. He broke through thin ice and drowned."

After a period of silence, a freckle-faced lad in the back of the room raised his hand and asked eagerly, "Where's his skates?"

1088. A third-grade boy overheard his second grade teacher talking to some other teachers about him. He interpreted the remarks as complimentary, went home beaming and told his mother how much his last year's teacher liked him. "What makes you think that, Paul?" asked his mother. His reply was, "Because I heard her say that one of the happiest days in her life was the day that Paul was promoted into grade three."

1089. Approaching the school building one morning, one first-grader said to another, "Do you think that man will ever reach the moon by rocket or other projectiles?"

"Certainly not," said the other. "There are too many unknown forces in the substratosphere . . ."

179

The ringing bell ended the conversation. One lad remarked, "Silence that dreadful bell—it means we gotta go in and squeeze clay."

1090. "I don't know what to do, Pop," sighed the young son. "Teacher says I have to write more legibly but if I do, she'll find out that I can't spell."

—Texas Outlook

1091. The child is the real ambassador between home and school. He transmits fact and fiction, messages and communicable diseases. He carries home, without cost to the taxpayer, invitations, classroom reports and announcements—also pencil stubs, chalk ends and seemingly endless quantities of used paper.

In exchange the teacher receives from the home written excuses, uncensored communications, and through the "lost and found," some interesting cultural by-products, including comics, playing cards and 45 R.P.M. records.

—Winston Roesch, University of Michigan Extension Serv.

1092. Our first-grade daughter came home one day extremely disillusioned because, as she said, "Teacher has never seen a goat." When asked why, she came back with, "Because I drew one for her and she didn't even know what it was."

1093. *Teacher:* "If your mother gave you a large apple and a small apple and told you to divide with your brother, which apple would you give him?"

Johnny: "Do you mean my big brother or my little brother?"

1094. A pupil was asked to paraphrase the sentence: "He was bent on seeing her." He wrote: "The sight of her doubled him up."

—Hoyer Grams, *Sunshine Magazine*

1095. According to the creative thinking of one pupil, " 'Nothing' is a balloon with its skin peeled off."

1096. A small boy announced to his parents that his reading class was to be divided into divisions. "I'm in the top one," he said, "and the other is for backward readers. But we don't know who is going to be in the other one, because there's not a kid in the room who can read backward!"

1097. Did you know that school children are getting stronger? To be sure a new-type school desk would stand up under juvenile squirming it was tested by being hit 30,000 times with a 40-pound sandbag.

—HAL BOYLE

1098. After all, the little red schoolhouse has something over the little-read pupil.

1099. The six-year-old went off to school looking very grown up in a new blouse and skirt. When she came home, her mother asked if anyone had commented on her new outfit.

"Yes, the teacher did," said Jackie. "She said as long as I was dressed like a lady, why didn't I act like one."

—*Cappers Weekly*

1100. In an essay on "Things I am Thankful For," a little boy listed "My glasses," explaining "they keep the boys from fighting me and the girls from kissing me."

1101. *Teacher:* "How did you like Venice?"
Pupil: "Oh, we stayed only a few days—the place was flooded."

1102. The teacher wound up her talk on animals by asking, "And from the skunk we get fur; isn't that right, Johnny?"

"I'll say it is," said Johnny, "As fur as possible."

1103. "Willie," said the teacher, "if fuel oil is selling at 20 cents a gallon and you pay your distributor $40 how many gallons will he bring you?"

"About 190 gallons," answered Willie, after some thought.

"Why Willie, that isn't right," said the teacher.

"No, Ma'am, I know it ain't," said Willie, "but they all do it."

1104. The best cure for an ailing schoolboy has always been a holiday.

1105. Little Claude's mother had reluctantly allowed her precious child to attend public school. She gave the teacher a long list of instructions. "My Claude is so sensitive," she explained. "Don't ever punish him. Just slap the boy next to him. That will frighten Claude."

—*Philadelphia Bulletin*

1106. One morning as the children came in I noticed one little boy was crying. When I asked why, he held out two one-dollar bills and said, between sobs, "I can't remember which dollar is for my pictures and which one is for my lunch ticket."

—MARJORIE M. ARTHUR, *Texas Outlook*

Quality

1107. Hats off to the man who is a little better than his word, a little more liberal than his promise, a little larger in deed than he is in speech.

1108. Men know what they want, and they know when they have found a power higher than their own. That power may be called the best thing to strive for. Everything else is subordinate to it. But when we find the best to be found in life, everything else fits into place.

The significant thing is that the best is not far from us. We do not have to search to the end of the world. Fine living and life's big treasures are not matters of geography. These are near at hand.

—NATHAN HOWARD, *Gist*

1109.
If a task is once begun,
Never leave it till it's done.
Be the labor great or small
Do it well or not at all.

—Author unknown

1110. It is good work well done that holds the fabric of civilization together and gives a sense of significance to the individual life.

—*N.E.A. Journal*

Raise

1111. "You can't come in here and ask for a raise just like that," said the superintendent. "You must work yourself up."

"But I did," replied the young teacher, "look, I'm trembling all over."

1112. "I'll have to have a raise, sir," said the teacher to the superintendent, "or I'll have to leave the profession. There are three companies after me."

"What three?" demanded the superintendent.
"Light, telephone, and gas," was the reply.

1113. Address to a superintendent upon requesting a raise:
As planned:

I think you will admit, sir, that the quality of my teaching during the last three years has been such that it would be difficult to duplicate my services. More in pain than in anger I say that it has been a matter of profound surprise to me that you have not seen fit to recognize and reward my value to the school in some substantial way. I honestly believe I have been extremely patient. I have continued to improve my effectiveness with unremitting zeal, and I think I may flatter myself that my efforts have not been without result. I have here, carefully recorded, a report of the increased knowledge of my pupils during the past nine months, due in great part, undoubtedly, to my skillful teaching. Reluctantly, I must force you into a decision, but I am surely obligated to say candidly that unless you see the matter in the same way that I do, I shall feel it necessary to deprive the school of my services.

As delivered:

Well, there is one other thing, sir, that is, if you're not too busy—in fact, the truth of the matter is exactly—well, sir, I was just wondering whether—of course I know this is a bad time—really, I have been pleased to see the school improving some of late and I am quite sure that my own pupils are—but to tell you the truth, sir, I have been thinking—of course, it's just as you think best and I want to avoid insisting, but after all, perhaps I have erred in mentioning it, but I was thinking that possibly you might consider the idea of a possible future raise in salary at some future time.

Reading

1114. The comic book has become the principal cultural manifestation of our epoch, plus such additional inspiration as may be obtained from the second-hand car and the local tavern.
—Robert Hutchins

1115. No furniture is so charming as books, even though you never open them or read a single word.

—SYDNEY SMITH

1116. No other human being is necessary to the reader at the moment of reading. He can take his book with him to the jungle or the desert, on the ocean, or the mountain top. He can select his company at will, and rid himself of it by a turn of the hand. It is potentially an inexhaustible resource; all ages of history; all countries; all varieties of human beings, and even of animals and feelings, hopes and fears, conquests and failures, victories and defeats; the real and the ideal—all are available at the turn of a page for the reader's contemplation and understanding.

—Author unknown

Reason

1117. There's a mighty big difference between good, sound reasons and reasons that sound good.

—BURTON HILLIS, *Better Homes and Gardens*

1118.

Gentlemen:

Why is it that your switch engine has to ding and dong and fizz and split and bang and biss and pant and grate and grind and puff and bump and chug and hoot and whistle and toot and wheeze and jar and jerk and perk and howl and snarl and growl and thump and boom and crash and jolt and screech and snort and slam and throb and roar and rattle and yell all night long?

After due deliberation the local railroad management replied with the following letter:

Dear Sir:

Sorry, but if you are to get meats and sweets and breads and spreads and beans and jeans and shorts and skirts and cakes and rakes and socks and dippers and slippers and lotions and notions and hooks and eyes and cherry pies and candy bars and nuts in jars and sugar and spice and everything nice to make you happy all your life—you'll have to put up with the noise of the railroad.

Recreation

1119. *Fishing:* a disease for which there is no cure; catching but not contagious. It formerly infected only savages, small boys and the ne'er-do-well; but now it attacks presidents, governors, judges, doctors, lawyers, congressmen, senators, ministers, priests, rabbis— 20 million people. In extreme cases the fever can be reduced by placing the patient in the hot sun for several hours.

—Fishing Almanac

1120. A baseball park, as everyone knows, is a hot-dog stand that has floor shows.

—HAROLD COFFIN

1121. Possibly the greatest waste in public works in some communities is the failure to use school facilities for recreation when they are not being used for education.

—GEORGE HJELTE

Relativity

1122. The difference between a groove and a grave is only a matter of depth.

1123. Professor Albert Einstein, giving his explanation of his theory of relativity: When you sit with a nice girl for two hours, you think it's only a minute. But when you sit on a hot stove for a minute, you think it's two hours. That's relativity."

Another explanation of the Einstein theory of relativity goes like this: "The Einstein theory is concerned with time. Suppose you're on your honeymoon for two weeks. Sometime later your mother-in-law comes to visit for two weeks. The lengths of time are precisely the same, yet they seem different relatively."

1124. If man had the relative jumping power of a flea, he could hurdle the Empire State Building. If man had the beetle's pulling power, he could tow a locomotive engine.

1125.   In every way in which we live,
           Our values are comparative.
           Observe the snail who with a sigh,
           Says: "See those turtles whizzing by."

—Author Unknown

Report Card

1126. When the teacher comments on the report card that James is an individualist it perhaps means in a nice way that James is a trouble-maker. Robert is a well-adjusted, wholesomely integrated individual,—Jackpot, brother, you're in. Bobby is teacher's pet! Michael does not socialize well, may mean that Mike is always beating some other kid's brains out. Frank's personality evidences a lack of social integration—this is a nice way of saying that Frank is a stinker!

1127. *Dad:* "What's this low mark on your report card?"
Junior: "Maybe it's the temperature of the schoolroom."

1128. Father found on his daughter's report card a note, "Good worker, but talks too much."

After signing the card, he wrote, "Come up and meet her mother sometime."

1129. The birth announcement of our friend's son was in the form of a report card. It read:

Subject	Grade
Crying	A
Sleeping	B
Kicking	A
Eating	A

1130. *Student to teacher:* "I can't get that report card back for you—you gave me an A in something and they're still mailing it to relatives."

1131. Timmy came home from school with his January report card which was anything but good. When his mother saw it, she cried out, "What happened this month?"

"Why, nothing unusual," answered Timmy, "you oughta know—things are always marked down right after Christmas."

1132. *Pupil on report card signing day:* "There comes Dad! Mom, what will we show him first: my report card, your new hat, or the broken window?"

1133. "Your little boy is really very bright," the note accompanying the report card read. "But he spends entirely too much time playing with the girls. However, I am working on a plan to break him of the habit."

So Mama signed the card and sent it back with this penned note: "Let me know if it works, by all means, and I'll try it out on his father."

1134. The small fry, trying to explain the significance of his poor grades on the report card to his disgruntled dad, said, "Don't forget —we're studying all new stuff this year."

1135. A junior high school English teacher jokingly told her pupils on report day that if their parents wouldn't let them come home because of bad grades, they could all come to her home to live. That evening when she came home from dinner, she found 41 pupils sitting on her porch.

—LINDA FEICH, *Pennsylvania School Journal*

1136. A fifth grade youngster, undergoing serious chastisement for his poor report card, asked:

"Well, Dad, what do *you* think is wrong with me—heredity or environment?"

1137. A college freshman home for the Christmas holidays was asked by his Dad, "Well, son, how are your marks at school?" To which the youth answered cryptically, "Under water." "Now just what do you mean by that expression?" demanded the impatient parent. "It's like this," said the son reluctantly, "they're all below 'C' level."

1138. Parents of a three-year-old received a nursery school report card on their daughter. "Emotionally immature," the report read.

"If you can't be immature at the age of three," the mother commented, "when can you be?"

—*Scholastic Teacher*

Research

1139. Basic research is what I am doing when I don't know what I'm doing.

—WERNHER VON BRAUN

1140. If you copy anything out of one book, it is plagiarism. If you copy it out of two books, it is research. If you copy it out of six books, you are a professor.

—From an address by Bishop FULTON J. SHEEN

1141. Research is of great importance to a profession . . . while certain kinds of problems can be solved only by highly trained research specialists, other problems of equal importance can be solved only as teachers, supervisors, and principals become researchers.

—*Teachers Newsletter*

1142. Intelligent ignorance is the first requirement in research.

—CHARLES F. KETTERING

1143. A man will turn over half a library to make one book.

—SAMUEL JOHNSON

1144. To start out on a new project is something like taking a trip from New York to the West Coast. We must know our destination and understand about how long the trip will last. We must realize that we will have to be on the train for several days. No intelligent person would become impatient and get off the train at Kansas City and then complain that the train was not in Los Angeles.

—CHARLES F. KETTERING, *Short Stories of Science and Invention*

1145. Research, to some so-called investigators, is like fashion. They follow the popular fields, and shift as the fashion changes. A leader starts a new line of study; all the so-called researchers quickly follow. Fortunately, their number is small. We do not need many researchers; what we need today are searchers.

—LOUIS N. KATZ, *Journal of American Medical Association*

1146. Research is like saving. If postponed until needed, it is too late.

1147. Maybe one of the reasons people are so easily discouraged is because of their education. During all of our years at school, we were examined two or three times a year. If we failed once, we were out. In contrast, all research work is 99.9 per cent failure and if you succeed once, you are in. If we are going to progress in any line we must learn to fail intelligently so we won't become discouraged at the 99.9 per cent failure.

1148. One measure of the maturity of a science is the extent to which problems for investigation have been identified. The greater the volume of research in a field the more extensive are the new areas identified for investigation.

—CARTER V. GOOD, Dean, Teachers College, *Phi Delta Kappan*

Respect

1149. To many teachers today, contract ties are given about as much respect as Christmas ties.

1150. Too often respect for others is like the button in the parlor game—now you have it, now you don't.

Responsibility

1151. If the boss hands you a tough job, he isn't picking on you. He's complimenting you. Batting practice pitchers aren't selected to hurl the first game of the world series.

1152. The average American home has two children. The average American classroom has 21 children. Plain arithmetic, if nothing else, makes it evident that the parents' responsibility is greater.

—RICHARD L. NEUBERGER, *Eagle*

Resourcefulness

1153. Little Mary insisted that she be allowed to serve the tea when her mother was entertaining one afternoon. Mother, with crossed fingers, consented. However, she became annoyed by the long delay and asked, "Why did you take so long, child?"

"I couldn't find the tea-strainer," answered Mary.

"Then how did you strain it so well?"

"I used the fly-swatter."

—*Iowa State Green Gander*

1154. The dean of a girls' school was troubled because the girls insisted on crossing the street in front of the school without going to the corner. Warnings, penalties, and lectures did no good. Finally, the dean had a sign painted and set it up in the middle of the block. From that time on, the girls always walked to the corner before crossing the street. What did the sign read? "Cattle Crossing."

1155. A traveling salesman in a Western state enroute to the next town in his car, came upon a man running desperately along the road. The salesman stopped and invited the runner to get in.

"Emergency?" the driver asked.

"No," puffed the stranger. "I always run like that when I want a ride. Never fails."

—Frank L. Remington

1156. In a small church in southern Illinois, a bus driver came in at the beginning of the service and sat in the very first row. After the sermon the preacher, talking to the man, asked why he had occupied that position all alone. The bus driver explained, "I sat up there to see what you did to make everyone move to the back."

—Harry C. Vaughn

1157. A motorist came upon a young man carrying a gasoline can along the side of the road. He stopped and asked him to get in. When they were on their way again, the motorist asked, "Do you want out at the first gas station?" "Absolutely not," replied the stranger, "this gasoline can is my suitcase—it always gets me a ride."

Rest—Relaxation

1158. It may be wise to "make hay while the sun shines," but it is equally important to "saw logs while the moon shines."

—M. Dale Baughman

1159. A vacation provides a long-awaited rest, except for the checkbook.

1160. The office is a retreat where one can relax from his strenuous home life.

Rules

1161. A high school principal, trying to convince some students who felt "fenced in" by the many school rules, told the story of a kite. It seemed that the kite wanted its tail cut in half so it could be free to roam the skies. Its tail was cut in half and it swooped to the ground. "Now, boys," admonished the principal, "the tail wasn't holding the kite down—it was keeping it up." That's the way with school rules—actually they *give* you freedom rather than *take* it away.

1162. The Boston School Committee recently directed that the following commandments be read biweekly to pupils in Grades 7 through 12:

1. Don't let your parents down; they've brought you up.
2. Stop and think before you drink.
3. Be smart, obey! you'll give orders yourself someday.
4. Show-off driving is juvenile; don't act your age.
5. Ditch dirty thoughts fast or they will ditch you.
6. Pick the right friends to be picked for a friend.
7. Choose a date fit for a mate.
8. Don't go steady unless you're ready.
9. Love God and neighbor.
10. Live carefully. The soul you save may be your own.

1163. These simple poems, driving home a lesson, appeared in the daily bulletin of the Queen Anne Junior-Senior High School, Seattle, Washington.

When quarter tests come and your bluff is called,
Knowledge is revealed by what you scrawled.
You will realize then that your failure to study
Made your score low 'cause your ideas were muddy.
Start studying now while yet there is time,
Ere ten weeks test bells the simple truth chime.

1164. All 7th and 8th graders, we remind you once more,
In case there are some who didn't hear it before,
When satisfying thirst or pangs of hunger at noon,
Please stay in the lunchroom, don't fly over the moon
Some lately have landed at a local beanery,
Who say they're just out to enjoy the scenery.

1165. If I could get to bed on time every night,
And set my old alarm clock reasonably right,
The chances are I wouldn't be so late
And every morning have to face my fate.
As it is now, I generally miss my bus;
Parents and school make an awful fuss;

Haven't had time for my breakfast food;
And arrive at school in an awful mood;
Beginning tomorrow I'll make it my rule
To be right on time and just play it cool.

Rural Education—Rural Life

1166. Every rural child has the right to teachers, supervisors, and administrators who know rural life and who are educated to deal effectively with the problems peculiar to rural schools.

1167. In some of our early rural schools education was often secured in a practical manner. Pupils studied astronomy through the roof and geology through the floor. There was even natural ventilation.

1168. A hick town is a place where you wait for a dog to cross in front of your car because he's a friend of yours.

—PAUL LARMER

1169. I'm for hot chocolate on cold winter nights and porch swings on warm summer evenings.

—PAUL LARMER

1170. In the rural village you can put a quarter in the milk box and be reasonably sure the milkman will get it.

1171. A man was driving through sparsely settled mountain country one day when he passed a teenager standing beside a beat-up truck. He pulled out, offered him a lift and then asked, "Motor conk out?" "Nope," the youth replied as he clambered in. "Cars most often whizz right by here, so I got Decoy for a little o' nothin'. She has no wheels on the ditch side, her tires are filled with sand, and she's not blessed with an engine. She's no trouble at all and always gets me to school."

1172. A deeply religious backwoods woman was called into court as a witness. She had never been in court before and knew nothing of legal proceedings and terminology. When she was put on the witness stand and asked to swear in, she explained she was a very religious person and didn't believe at all in swearing.

"But the law requires it," explained the judge.

192

The old lady meditated a moment and then expostulated, "Well, if I have to, I have to! Hell! Be damned. Hell! Be damned!"
—Link

Safety

1173. America has more than 50 million motor vehicle missiles, some of them not very well guided.
—Rushville (Indiana) Republican

1174. Mathematics equation: the number of blasts that come from auto horns in a traffic jam is equal to the sum of the squares at the wheels.
—Indiana Telephone News

1175.   A nut at the wheel
              A curve in the road
              A peach on his right
              Fruit salad tonight.
—Great Lakes Bulletin

1176. *Sign near Colorado Springs:*
"The average time it takes a train to pass this crossing is 14 seconds—whether your car is on it or not."
—Pageant

1177.   The curfew tolls the knell of parting day
              A line of cars winds slowly o'er the lea;
              The pedestrian plods his absent-minded way,
              And leaves the world quite unexpectedly.
—Michigan Educational Journal

1178. Some automobile trips are just about as safe as playing patty-cake with a mule's hind legs.

1179. A man pays 50¢ for a shave. It cost $5 to shave a dead man. A wool overcoat costs $50. A wooden one $500. A taxi to the theater costs $1 for a round trip. But one to the cemetery costs $10 for one way.
Stay alive and save money.
—Powerfax

1180. A speaker was talking to a bunch of teen-agers about things that happened in the West in an early day. He said Billy the Kid had killed 21 men when he was 21 years old.

A girl that had been listening open-mouthed said, "And what make of a car did *he* drive?"

—Cappers Weekly

1181. Some second-graders were identifying geometric forms held up by their teacher. When she showed them a square, they shouted "Square." A triangle was just as easy. And almost all knew what a rectangle was. Then she held up an 8-sided shape.

"What is this one?"

To a child they told her, "A stop sign!"

1182. The "safety in numbers" theory may be responsible for many committees.

Salesmanship—Selling

1183. Peddlers quote prices first. Salesmen give them last.

1184. Some salesmen need the wind taken out of their sales!

1185. We were listening to the encyclopedia salesman who finally climaxed his pitch with a hearty "Yes ma'am! You merely put a tiny bit down, and don't make another payment for three months." My wife appeared surprised and then asked, "Who told you about us?"

1186. Anyone can kiss a girl once. The art is in being invited again! It's the same in salesmanship. It's the first impression that your prospect gets of you, your product, and your company that counts up to long-run profits.

—250 Successful Sales and Promotion Letters

1187. An American and a British shoe salesman traveled on the same boat to West Africa, each representing different shoe companies. After landing, they looked around, and what struck them first was that all the natives were barefoot. The Britisher cabled his head office: "Nobody here wearing shoes. Coming home by next ship."

The American salesman cabled his chief: "Nobody here wearing shoes. Send one million consignment. Market wide open."

194

Scheduling

1188. Scheduling in the school of the future will be a very intricate thing. Courses will be indefinite in length; they will not necessarily meet one period a day, five days a week, but may meet all day long, once a week or once a month. A course (course—the use of this term indicates that we haven't yet been able to remove at least one inhibiting mental set!) will be completed when the instructor and the students feel that the need for it has been met.

—ROBERT C. McKEAN, San Francisco State College,
Phi Delta Kappan

1189. To most high school principals making the daily schedule is like getting olives or pickles out of a narrow-necked jar. After the first one, the rest come easier.

Scholarship—Scholarships

1190. *Unusual scholarships:* Men named Murphy—Harvard. Girls who won't drink—Simmons College, Boston. Boys who won't smoke or drink—M.I.T.

1191. What America's colleges and universities need to do next: Provide with each scholarship the guarantee of a free-parking space.

School

1192. Now I would say more explicitly that in the junior high school we ought to have what I would call "seeding" going on in all the major areas of knowledge.

—HAROLD HAND, University of Illinois

1193. We need great souls to make great schools,
Or all our walls were laid in vain,
Youth to ask more questions, not more rules,
More than Latin, to make plain.
The road of life lies just ahead,
And there is youth just as the dawn,
And the road of life is here to tread,
We need great souls to lead us on.

—DR LEWIS EVANS, Speech at First General Session of the
American Association of School Administrators, 1952

1194. Did you hear about the upper-class mother who told the headmaster in a private school, "I don't see why the masters can't get along with Johnny; all the other servants do."

1195. The school faces destiny. It must create in the young a more dynamic intelligence, a surer initiative, a self-disciplined character, a broad and liberal social outlook.

—Joy Elmer Morgan

1196. The junior high school movement is just like a steam shovel —it's picking up.

—M. Dale Baughman

1197. Irate supporters of small schools converged on the Iowa legislature and offered some positive views of the school situation:
1. Morals problems in small schools are much less serious.
2. Colleges would just as soon enroll in their chemistry courses students who had not taken high school chemistry.
3. High school pupils usually take the easiest courses if they are offered a wide variety.
4. A large school isn't always superior to a small one.
5. Elimination of the small school would hurt the Iowa State Basketball Tournament for Girls.

1198. A proud mother wished to enter her five-year-old daughter in an exclusive school where the minimum age was six.

"She can easily pass the six-year-old test," the mother told the principal. But the teacher was openly skeptical as he said to the little girl, "All right, say some words."

The precocious child looked at the man with great dignity for a moment, then asked her mother, "Purely irrelevant words?"

1199. 1. "At the opening of the fall term, children come pouring in until the seats and all other available places are overflowing. . . ."
2. "In general, reading has not been successfully taught in our primary schools. Good readers are the exceptions."
3. "It [the Federal Government] has not felt that education was one of the interests which it must foster and promote, and its policy has therefore been both inconstant and inadequate."

The first statement was made in the National Education Association proceedings of 1879; the second and third statements were made in the National Education Association proceedings of 1873.

1200. Since each learner is unique and learns in relation to his uniqueness, we will need to change our schools in the next decade so that they will be human-centered instead of "lesson"-centered.

—EARL C. KELLY, *Educational Leadership*

1201.
Will it be:
In school today,
Or in and out of jobs tomorrow?

Cash in the pocket today,
Or dollars in the bank tomorrow?

Hot rods today,
Or a good car tomorrow?

A big guy today
And the little guy tomorrow?

Out of school today,
And out of luck tomorrow?

1202. A Freshman class, working on the improvement of sentence construction, were considering the sentence, "Hurrying to school, his shoes came off at the corner."

"What's wrong with it?" the teacher asked.

The students suggested several things, all of them wide of the mark. They seemed completely baffled. A minute of silence was suddenly ended by a loud chuckle and a voice that said, "I know what's wrong with it. 'Hurrying to school!' "

—ETHEL H. GERSTEIN, *High Points*

1203. Our schools' greatest enemies today are ignorance and lack of understanding. Their best ally is well-informed citizens—and their numbers are increasing daily.

—ROY E. LARSEN

1204. A school fight is always easy to start, because practically everybody thinks he's an authority on education.

—*Boston Globe*

1205. I believe it is possible for our schools to do far more for children with special gifts and talents than at present, without jeopardizing our best educational policy.
—DR. JAMES BRYANT CONANT

1206. We are told that there are 31 million children in the public schools of America. How many is that? If all of the children of America were to march from the Atlantic Ocean to the Pacific Ocean and back again in columns of four, each column of four an arm's length from the one preceding it, the first children would have made the entire trip and returned to the Atlantic before the last of the children would have started the nation-wide trek.
—*Sunshine Magazine*

1207. "Will you join me in wishing for every child in the world a school—

Where knowledge of self and of all humankind
Contrives to build in his heart and his mind
Full measure of faith and the grace that bestows
Strength and compassion wherever he goes;
Where the talents that lie in his soul inbound,
Awaken to live; where confidence found
In his own deft skill, releases the key
For freedom to grow and growth to be free?"
—MRS. JOHN E. HAYES, President, National Congress
of Parent-Teachers, 1952

1208. After several practice drills, the pupils in a new school plant invited the superintendent and president of the school board to watch them in their fire drill. When the alarm rang, the 300 pupils evacuated the building in one and one-half minutes.

Pupils went back to classes, proud and pleased. A while later when the noon whistle blew, the principal, still in possession of his stop watch, made a test from idle curiosity. This time the building was cleared in less than one minute!

1209.   The school bell rings and sidewalks fill
With cleaned-up Jack and curled-up Jill;
And Mother hums a jaunty tune—
They're Teacher's problems 'til next June!
—*Quote*

1210. The public schools in 1957 are in the same position that banks were in 1931. In a year or two, or three, more and more of them will become educationally insolvent. Unfortunately, or perhaps fortunately, there can be no run on the schools that will force them to close.

—BEARDSLEY RUML

1211. For me, purpose and meaning are given to university service because I believe:

That the public school system, including the colleges and universities, provides cohesiveness in American life. Schools are the neutral ground where partisans on all other issues—religious, economic, political, social—may join in a common effort for furthering the public welfare.

—DAVID DODDS HENRY, President, University of Illinois, Installation Speech

1212. School leaders are represented as ringmasters of the *Circus Maximus* and their standards of integrity have been permitted to disintegrate alarmingly. Schools have become entertainment bureaus for parents, clubs and communities. "Big money" has bored into high school athletics and fictional purity of athletes and subsidization of coaches and staff salaries out of earnings have resulted.

—Committee of Pennsylvania Supervising Principals' Association

1213. Our public system of education at present is geared to mesh with the early years of life. We eat of the plate of education for 20 years and then, like the bear, we hibernate. The bear hibernates for the winter only and then comes out to eat again. Most of us, however, after the early feast of education are likely to hibernate educationally for the next 50 years.

—HUGH W. NORMAN, *Community Teamwork*

1214. Schoolhouse doors should open both ways—outwards so that teachers can go out and see what the world is like, and inward so that other people can come in and help with the school.

—BESS GOODYKOONTZ, *Phi Delta Kappan*

1215. Spotted by a summer-school student on the door of the office of the university president: "This office closed for the summer. For anything important, see the janitor."

—MARGUERITE M. McCONNELL

199

1216. We see tomorrow's schools as no box which packages learning in time containers (8:30 to 3:30) or bundles of age groups (6 through 11, 12 through 14 or 15 plus) or some specific or temporary educational structure (departmentalization or subject matter integration).

—School Executive

1217. There are two obvious methods in getting a full-grown girl into a bathing suit. Of course one can make the essential measurements and then select the garment which matches the measurements. One could, of course, select at random such a garment and then expect the figure to adjust to it. The latter method is well-known, since it is how many school courses are fitted to pupils.

1218. Fifty years ago the National Education Association "indicted" American pupils for (1) a disregard for authority, (2) lack of respect for age and wisdom, (3) a weak appreciation of the demands of duty and (4) a disposition to follow pleasure rather than obligation. It could be verse:

1219.
They disregard authority,
Respect for age they lack,
They follow pleasure most often
And duties they do slack.
You think I mean the kids and so
I do, those of fifty years ago.
—IRVING LEIBOWITZ, *Indianapolis Times*

1220. It is said that the teacher fears the principal and superintendent; the principal fears the superintendent and is suspicious of the supervisor; the supervisor is suspicious of the principal and fears the superintendent; the superintendent fears the school board; the school board fears the parents, and the parents fear the children. The children do not fear anyone.
—O. C. MILLER, The Democratic Way to Better Schools, Exposition Press, Inc.

1221. This is a school. It is where human beings go to learn things they don't know. Besides human beings, there are some girls and a teacher. The teacher is there to see that nobody does anything and the little girls are there for stool pigeons. Once in a while you get a chance to stick a pin in one but another one always sees you, so you are outnumbered. When the girls grow up, they get to be teachers and have their own mob of stool pigeons.

At school you have reading, writing, arithmetic, spelling, history, and recess. Recess is so you can forget what you learned in the morning before you start something new. Reading is looking at words instead of pictures. Arithmetic is stuff like you have three and you give John two. Baloney! I wouldn't! History is what happened before you got to school, which is plenty. It keeps happening all the time, so the later you start to school, the worse off you are.

You don't have to go to school in the summer, but you have to start in September unless somebody burns it down. (But nobody ever does.) They make up for not making you go to school in summer by giving you homework when they get you again. Homework is what your father does until it gets too hard, and then he buys you an encyclopedia so you can do it yourself. You go to school in the morning, and you have to stay until afternoon, so it spoils the best part of the day unless you play hooky. Then you have to write a note from your mother saying you were sick.

Grown-up people think you give the teacher an apple every morning, but that is propaganda put out by the teachers who like apples. If your mother gives you an apple for the teacher, you eat it on the way to school unless you are a girl. Every month they give you a report card which you bring home. You get your father to sign it if it is good and your mother if it's no good, which it usually is. When you start school again in September, they give you a brand new teacher as the last one is worn out and got married. She is like the old teacher except she knows more. . . .

—Written by a 9-year-old Quiz Kid
From the South Dakota Smoke Signals

School Administration—Administrators

1222. There are still classroom teachers, perhaps, who think it was no typographical error that caused a statement in a much-read newspaper to appear:

"What this country needs is a more vigorous program for the braining of administrators."

—Lois Edinger, Speech at A.A.S.A. Convention, Atlantic City

1223. Sometimes, it appears that "democracy" and "efficiency" are like the gingham dog and the calico cat—natural enemies.

1224. George Washington could broad jump 23 feet, a record in those days. Today we have school administrators who can side-step farther than that.

1225. The experience of many administrators is not unlike that of the robin who returned to home base somewhat ruffled and worn out, with tail feathers in disarray.

"Have you been fighting over me?" asked its mate; to which Papa Robin replied, "Nope, I simply got caught in a badminton game!"

1226. When you get to the end of your rope, tie a knot in it and hold on!

1227. Beatitude for school administrators: "Blessed are they who go around in big circles for they shall be called big wheels."

1228. The beamish superintendent spoke and kindness filled his eyes. "Dear Teachers," said he happily, "I have a neat surprise! The Board of Education at its meeting yesterday unanimously voted you a large increase in pay. For months the local Tax League has gone to bat for you and the entire district is convinced you have not had your due. They know your work is harder and have seen your classes grow. So if you'll pass in single file, I'll now give out the dough." APRIL FOOL!

—FREDERICK MOFFITT, Chalk Dust, in *Nations Schools*

1229. Sign outside superintendent's office door:

Friendly calls ....10 minutes
Friendly calls when busy .... 9 minutes
Life insurance agents ....15 seconds
School supply salesmen with the
    "latest" .... 3 seconds
Book salesmen with samples .... 2 hours
Friends inviting us to lunch .... 2 hours
Friends wishing to talk hunting and
    fishing ....All Day
Wives ....No time

Girl Friends ....All night
Irate Parents .... 6 minutes
Teachers wanting raises .... 2 seconds
Bill and tax collectors ....All day (Tomorrow)

1230. To no other school activity do teachers give so willingly of their extra-class time as to the lamentable but absorbing practice of complaining about the appointed head of their school organization, the school principal.
                              —MINIVER CHEEVY, *New York Supervisor*

1231. One of the most important tasks of the school administrator is to know people, and especially children, intimately; be accepted by them; be a real friend.
                              —WALTER COCKING, Editor, *School Executive*

1232. A superintendent's observations on New Year's resolutions:
All honor to these heroes, may they meet no cold rebuff!
But, as for me, I must admit I'm made of softer stuff.
My New Year's resolution is simple and clear-cut:
I'll try to keep my conscience clear and keep my big mouth
    shut.
When speakers speak and panels pan,
When bricks hurl through the air,
When snipers snipe and battlers bat,
When words fly everywhere,
Serene and calm I'll go my way
And neither cringe nor strut,
And, heaven helping me, I'll try to keep my big mouth
    shut.
                              —FREDERICK MOFFITT, Chalk Dust, in *Nations Schools*

1233. Definition of an acrobatic administrator: One who, when he opens his mouth, puts his foot in it and stands on the fence all at the same time.

1234. The superintendent visited the ailing vice-principal in the hospital. "Now, Bill," he said, "don't worry. Everybody at the school will pitch in and do your work—as soon as we can figure out just what you have been doing."

1235. You don't need to go to a gypsy tea-cup juggler when you

203

pick a superintendent or principal—just listen for one preposition. That word is as significant as shibboleth to the ancient Gileadites; or the consonant by which American soldiers identified their Pacific enemies in World War II. Of course, that doesn't imply that an administrator is a teacher's enemy or that it is a question of pronunciation, but just that those three are all key sounds. The word to listen for, in those interviews in schools, agencies, colleges, and hotel lobbies in which you decide upon your place for work for the year, is the preposition "under" when applied to members of the teaching staff.

—JENNIE L. PINGREY, *Bulletin, National Association of Secondary School Principals*

1236. A high school principal was told by his physician to get out from behind his desk and get more exercise. He even persuaded the portly administrator to give up driving his car to and from his school office.

The principal did not agree, however, that he should run, since it might prove too conspicuous on Meridian Street. Finally, the adamant doctor succeeded in convincing him that he might roll a tire on his daily excursions. This would be less conspicuous since onlookers would think he was taking it to a garage for repairs.

He subsequently made arrangements to park his tire at a nearby gasoline station for 25¢ a day. Everything worked well for about two weeks and he was learning to like his exercise. Then, one day an unknowing assistant sold the tire. The manager apologized and said, "I'm getting in some new tires tomorrow and you can have one of them."

"Well," agreed the principal, "I suppose that's fair enough but what worries me is how am I going to get home tonight?"

1237. *School administrator's observations on the month of October:*
Weather prophets make their autumn predictions on the supposition that October always has at least 20 "fair-weather" days. School administrators know better, for October is the month of broken femurs on the gridiron, broken heads at the first meeting of the Parent-Teacher Association, and broken promises from the harried textbook companies. There are few days of unbroken weather in October.

—FREDERICK MOFFITT, Chalk Dust, in *Nations Schools*

1238. A superintendent received this letter of recommendation for a prospective teacher. "I write you in support of the application of Miss Jones, who is looking for a position which offers more money and less work. Miss Jones is an attractive young lady with unusual social graces and financial acumen of a high order. She plays the accordion with grace and speed. I personally picked her as a teacher and my batting average as a picker is very good; more than 25 per cent, which is considerably higher than that of my predecessor. Miss Jones has many virtues; her only fault lies in her inability to teach school."

1239. *Famous last words:* "Gentlemen, I consider scholarship more important than athletics and I shall reorganize the school to that end."

—FREDERICK MOFFITT, Chalk Dust, in *Nations Schools*

1240. In these days of educational streamlining, what many a pedagog needs is a little more educational umph. Not too much, mind you, for a little umph goes a long way and overmuch is just so much jitter.

But a pinch of umph in the annual report would season the entire treatise before it goes to the dentist and doctor, there to be forever buried among the piles of debris in the waiting rooms.

A teeny bit of boop-a-doop in the entire public relations program might make life easier. A little less verbiage in teachers' meetings and a bit less profundity in convention programs would pep up many a lame idea.

—FREDERICK MOFFITT, Chalk Dust, in *Nations Schools*

1241. I am reminded this afternoon of the story of the marriage broker who had just introduced a prospective bridegroom to one of his clients. The prospective groom, taking the broker aside and hissing into his ear, declared, "You faker—you swindler—why did you get me into this mess? The girl is homely, she's old, she squints, she lisps." Interrupting, the broker declared, "You don't have to whisper—she's deaf too."

Seriously, gentlemen, I feel that we educators, taken as a group, have something in common with the prospective bridegroom. Too often we are sold, or nearly sold, a bill of goods in the form of educational theory, only afterwards to learn for ourselves through bitter experience that the theory was faulty and that we were the guinea pig for some philosophic educator living in an ivory tower.

—ARTHUR P. SILVESTER, *Bulletin, National Association of Secondary School Principals*

1242. Good advice to school administrators:

"Give me the serenity to accept what cannot be changed, give me the courage to change what can be changed, and the wisdom to know one from the other."

—REINHOLD NIEBUHR

1243. "I decided to make a scientific study of hiring teachers," writes Superintendent Sourpuss, "and so I gathered rating scales from all the schools in the country. Examination of these scales shows that an acceptable teacher, in addition to postgraduate credits at Columbia, must possess the combined qualifications of an angel, airplane hostess, clubwoman, public relations counsel, ice cream salesman, village blacksmith, glamour girl, registered nurse, beautician and child care expert, together with a sense of humor and a sweet singing voice. The rating scales don't miss a bet but obviously they are not conversant with my salary schedule.

"However, in response to my frantic summons, a few candidates appeared and I hurriedly read a couple of books on "The Technic of the Interview! Upon trying out the technic, it was quite evident that the candidates had read the same book because I was the one who was interviewed, and I was presently flunked in all qualifications heretofore mentioned, plus sex appeal. Thus thwarted, I decided on teacher selection 'in absentia' by obtaining letters of character reference. I hereby state flatly that I am an optimist, and I still do not believe that all such letter writers are prevaricators, deceivers, sockdolagers, liars or horse thieves, although I have no evidence to the contrary."

—FREDERICK MOFFITT, Chalk Dust, in *Nations Schools*

1244. In a neighborhood development the bread-man became accustomed to hearing a certain lady quiet her barking dog with the words, "Be quiet, principal, be quiet." One day he observed that she was admonishing the dog in a different manner, "Be quiet, superintendent." When asked why she was calling the dog by a different name, the lady replied, "Well, he used to sit and howl; now he just sits."

School Board

1245. The school board was discussing increments, merit raises, etc. at salary time, and there was some discussion that was quite foreign to one elderly member of the board who piped up, "Merit or single—what's the difference? Pay 'em the same."

—*Texas Outlook*

1246. A school board in Maryland decided their district needed a new school. After much discussion, the board passed this resolution:

Be it resolved that this school district shall have constructed a new school building, and be it further resolved that, in view of the increasing cost of materials, the new building shall be constructed of the materials now in the existing school building, and be it finally resolved that to avoid interruption of school functions the present school building shall be continued in use until the new school is ready for occupancy.

—WILLIAM MORGAN MacALLEN

1247.
        The school board is happy,
        The architects beam,
        For the schoolhouse looks snappy
        With windows a-gleam.

        The light is delightful,
        There's plenty of air,
        There's a view, as is rightful,
        From anyone's chair.

        But the janitor glowers
        And loudly complains
        When he spends extra hours
        On finger-smudged panes.

        And the teacher? She perches
        With fear in her bones,
        Or exhaustively searches
        For slingshots and stones.

Oh, the schoolhouse is lighter
And gayer a lot,
And schoolrooms are brighter,
If schoolboys are not.

—*Quote*

School Secretary

1248. She combines the talents of a human adding machine, cashier, telephone operator, typist, journalism counselor, nurse, public relations expert, filing clerk, printer, and information specialist.
—*Phi Delta Kappan*

1249. The president of the school board was a bit curious about a cutie just hired as a secretary by the superintendent. "Can she add, or type, or take shorthand?" he asked.

"No," said the superintendent, "but she certainly can distract."

Science

1250. Things won't change much in the completely automated office. The button that gets ahead will still be the one with the most push.
—*Changing Times*

1251. We just heard that an Ottawa man bet wrong on a recent Canadian election. His opponent held him to his bet—to eat his shirt. So the loser found himself up against an apparently unpalatable predicament. However, he appears to be of the same opinion as we: that chemistry can help us do most anything. To find a safe, palatable way of eating the shirt, the loser asked a chemist on the National Council for advice.

He received the following recipe: "Take one cotton shirt and burn it to a crisp in a very hot oven; cover the ashes. Then grill one large steak. Sprinkle shirt ashes on steak and smother with onions. Eat shirt, steak and all!"
—*Chemical and Engineering News*

1252. Someone has suggested that we humanize the scientists and simonize the humanists.

1253. At the rate science is advancing, some genius will soon invent a sound that will travel faster than planes.

1254. An eminent scientist discovered a serum which brought inanimate objects to life. He squirted some on an equestrian statue. Sure enough the rider slowly came to life and guided the enlivened horse down from its pedestal.

"Now that you have life," asked the scientist, "what will you do first?"

"Well, I'm going to catch me a pigeon and ride off with it. When I come to a place where nobody can identify the bird, there's where I'll settle down again."

1255. In these days when every citizen is expected to have opinions on the relation between government, education, and scientific research and development, surely some appraisal of the past complexities of the relation of science to society should be a part of general education.

—JAMES B. CONANT, *On Understanding Science*

1256. Science is not new: the turtle has a streamlined body, turret top and retractable landing gear; the bee has a mainspring; a daisy has a hydraulic system.

1257. Modern version of the twenty-third psalm:

Science is my shepherd, I shall not want. It maketh me to lie down in an in-a-door bed that will fold away in the daytime, creating the illusion that we have a large apartment.

It sweepeth my wife's floors, washeth her dishes, ordereth her groceries, maintaineth 70 degrees F. inside the house, 45 degrees inside the iceless ice-box, and 212 degrees on top of the gas stove.

It furnisheth her with radio music, salad recipes and the President's message while she watcheth the scientific things hum and buzz. It restoreth her school-girl complexion, waveth her hair, and maketh her seem altogether youthful.

Meanwhile, it leadeth me into strange paths of ethical conduct, where, under the guise of "service" I can continue to fleece my fellowman . . . and make money, which I need on the first of the month to keep up the bluff that we are prosperous.

Yea, though I walk through the valley of the shadow of death, I will fear no evil, for I will have my tonsils, adenoids, and vermiform appendix removed . . . for Science is with me, its test tube and laboratory findings they comfort me. It prepareth a well-filled table before me in the presence of those who are less fortunate in the scramble for place and power; it anointeth my head with Staycomb; my cup runneth over.

—*Quote*

1258. Be careful how you use the word "scum." Some scum is better than you think. It may be smarter than you are, or any of your scientific friends. It can do things our best chemist can't do.

Dr. Dean Burk of the National Cancer Institute, Bethesda, Maryland, told a General Electric Science Forum audience that algae, one-celled plants often seen as green scum on ponds, absorb sunlight and convert it by a process of photosynthesis into chemical energy more efficiently than any known man-made mechanism.

Self

1259. What lies behind us and what lies before us are tiny matters when compared to what lies within us.

—WILLIAM MORROW, *Meditations in Wall Street*

1260. An old gentleman who ran a curio shop in a city was being interviewed one day by an energetic young reporter for a newspaper which planned a feature story about the many strange and interesting things the old man had traded for and collected during his lifetime.

The reporter roved around the shop, looking at this and that and finally paused to ask the man, "And what would you say is the strangest and most interesting thing you have in the shop?" The little old man looked around at the mountain of deer heads, stuffed alligators, the mounted rattlesnakes, human skeletons, and other curios and then turning sadly to the reporter, said, "Well, I guess I am."

1261. There is only one person with whom you can profitably compare yourself, and this person is your yesterday self.

1262. If the average person were to give a commensurate kicking to the one responsible for most of his troubles, he couldn't sit down for a week.

— BUL NELSON, *Lebanon* (Ohio) *Star*

1263. A man must be able to stand alone before he is able to co-operate to any advantage.

— EMERSON

1264. It's an incontrovertible fact that nature provides food for every bird but she does not toss it into the nest.

— *Lieber's Photo News*

1265. A politician once bragged to Horace Greeley, "I am a self-made man." "That, sir," replied Greeley unimpressed, "relieves the Almighty of a terrible responsibility."

1266. Don't worry about what others will think. Have confidence in your own judgment.

1267. It's fine to believe in yourself. Just don't be too easily convinced.

1268. On a set where a young actress was throwing her weight around, Marjorie Main turned to the director and remarked, in her raspy voice: "Whenever I see a youngster who is completely carried away with herself, I'm reminded of the fly riding on a wagon who looked back and remarked, "My, my, look at the dust I'm kicking up!"

— BILL DOUDNA, Madison, *Wisconsin State Journal*

1269. If you want a thing well done, don't do it yourself unless you really know how.

1270. Definition of a quartet: four people who think the other three can't sing.

1271. I want to live with myself and so
I want to be fit for myself to know.
I want to be able as days go by
Always to look myself straight in the eye.
I don't want to stand with the setting sun;
And hate myself for the things I've done.

I don't want to keep on a closet shelf
A lot of secrets about myself
And fool myself, as I come and go,
Into thinking that nobody else will know
The kind of man I really am;
I don't want to dress myself up in a sham.

I want to go out with my head erect,
I want to deserve all men's respect;
But here in the struggle for fame and pelf
I want to be able to like myself;
I don't want to look at myself and know
That I'm bluster and bluff and empty show.

I never can hide myself from me;
I see what others may never see;
I know what others may never know,
I never can fool myself, and so
Whatever happens, I want to be
Self-respecting and conscience free.

—Anonymous

Service

1272. Life is like a game of tennis—the player who doesn't serve well usually loses in the end.

1273. It is nice to know that when you help someone up a hill, you are a little nearer the top yourself.

1274.   The latch string now is out,
Red carpet set to roll;
Please have no slightest doubt,
Your service is our goal.

—Author Unknown

1275. Engineers are working on rockets that are expected to take us to the moon. But how many of us ever find time to visit a lonely friend at the other end of town?

1276. Service! What a wonderful, challenging, stirring word! No, it doesn't take wealth, fame, or dramatic heroism to make a man great. It is all summed up in this little verse:

> Whether child or full-grown man,
> High or low estate,
> Whether rich or whether poor,
> He who serves is great.
>
> —S. V. McCarley

1277. Our most valuable possessions are those which can be shared without lessening; those which, when shared, multiply. Our least valuable possessions are those which when divided are diminished.
> —William H. Danforth, *I Dare You*

1278. To understand what to do is knowledge,
To be able to do it is skill,
To see that it gets done right is service.

1279. A youngster with a mirror was seen throwing rays of sunshine toward the upper story of a house. An old man nearby was curious and asked why he was doing it. "I'm throwing a little sunshine up in Johnny's room—he's my pal. He broke his leg last week and today is our championship baseball game and Johnny can't be with us—so I'm sending him a little sunshine to let Johnny know that we're still around."
> —C. Lease Bussard, *Optimist Magazine*

1280. The sea of Galilee and the Dead Sea are made of the same water. It flows down, clear and cool, from the Hermon and the roots of the Cedars of Lebanon. The Sea of Galilee makes beauty of it, for the Sea of Galilee has an outlet. It gets to give. It gathers in its riches that it may pour them out again to fertilize the Jordan Plain. But the Dead Sea, with the same water, makes horror; for the Dead Sea has no outlet. It gets to keep. That is the radical difference between selfish and unselfish men. We all want life's enriching blessings, we ought to; they are divine benedictions, but some men get to give, and they are like Galilee, while some men get to keep and they are like the brackish water that covers Sodom and Gomorrah.
> —Harry Emerson Fosdick, quoted in *I Dare You*

1281. Leadership and service belong together; they spiral in unison. Each involves the dynamic relationships which exist in social situations. However, there are significant differences, for leadership is always a group phenomenon. Consideration of the ideal of leadership thus invites a good look at human relations.

—Dr. WILLARD ZAHN, Dean, College of Education,
Temple University. *Phi Delta Kappan*

1282.　　　　SIGN IN A RESTAURANT

A little bit of quality
Will always make 'em smile,
A little bit of courtesy
Will bring 'em in a mile,
A little bit of friendliness
Will tickle 'em, 'tis plain
And a little bit of service
Will bring 'em back again.

Special Ability—Specialist—Specialization

1283. Janus was an ancient Roman deity who had two faces and could look both ways at the same time. You may have wished that you, too, had the ability to see clearly both the future as well as the past as you face many of the problems of the school administrator.

1284. "A history professor can no longer talk to a philosophy professor, unless they choose the common ground of the Cleveland Indians."

—W. B. WISH, Western Reserve University

1285. It is better to specialize than to cover many subjects. Perfection resides in quality, not in quantity.

—GRACIAN

1286. An intricate machine broke down, halting production in a busy factory. All the company's best machinists were called in to diagnose the trouble, but to no avail.

It was suggested that a specialist, a master mechanic, be brought in. He came, looked the apparatus over, and asked for the smallest hammer on hand. He then pecked on a critical area and said, "Now, turn on the power. It ought to work." It did.

Later, when he sent a bill for $100, the top brass were astounded at the exorbitant fee. They wrote, asking him to send an itemized statement, which he did, without reducing the amount. The itemized version read:

$1 for pecking
$99 for knowing where to peck.

Speakers—Speaking—General

1287. Let any man speak long enough; he will get believers.
—ROBERT LOUIS STEVENSON

1288. *Convention speaker:* "Those are not my own figures I am quoting. They are the figures of someone who knows what he is talking about."
—Indiana Teacher

1289. That's about all the advice I have on telling stories. If you find people still don't listen, don't be discouraged. After all, telling stories isn't everything. Remember, the giraffe can't utter a sound, and giraffes are extremely important.

1290. Androcles was a fellow, you know, who made quite a reputation fighting man-eating lions for the edification of the Caesars. One Roman Emperor noted the gladiator's system seemed to consist of whispering in the lion's ear, whereupon the beast would demonstrate a complete loss of appetite and slink away, spiritless and defeated. Androcles was summoned to the royal box and the Emperor asked, "How come?"

Androcles answered, "It's this way, sir. I merely tell him, 'As soon as you have finished your dinner, you'll be asked to say a few words.' It gets them every time."
—Papyrus

1291. Some speakers drive home facts; others drive home their audiences.
—RAY D. EVERSON, *Indiana Farmers' Guide*

1292. Boring speakers accomplish one thing, at least. They set us straight on some people we once thought were bright.

1293. After many years of giving commencement addresses, the college professor asked one superintendent, a friend of long standing, "How did you like my last speech?"

"Your last? How sensible of you," answered the superintendent.

1294. Sir Winston Churchill once said of an opponent in a House of Commons speech: "We know that he has, more than any other man, the gift of compressing the largest amount of words into the smallest amount of thought."

—Christian Science Monitor

1295. It takes a baby approximately two years to learn to talk and between 60 and 70 years to learn to keep his mouth shut.

—San Francisco Classroom Teachers' Journal

1296. When I told my wife recently how much money I received for making commencement addresses, she answered, "If you get *that much* per minute, I'll have to start listening to you when you talk at home."

—M. Dale Baughman

1297. Many people find the speech cold because they insist on sitting in "Z" row.

1298. The reason there are so few good talkers in public is that there are so few thinkers in private.

—Optimist

1299. The candidate for public office, in the midst of a campaign speech, was finding it rather tough going. Talking without notes, he paused momentarily to collect his thoughts. A prompter came to the rescue with "Talk about taxes."

"That reminds me," said the candidate hopefully, "of the tax problem. . . . There's a question of paramount importance. Some want low taxes with decreased services, and there are others who demand high taxes with increased services. And having analyzed the problem minutely, so far as I am concerned, so do I."

1300. A man accepted an invitation to be lead-off speaker at a forum. He asked the chairman how long the "leading-off" should be. Replied the chairman, "Don't muzzle the ox that treadeth out the corn."

1301. Addressing a gathering of friends recently, Representative Charles A. Halleck, of Indiana, said, "I shan't apologize for my failure to prepare a formal address. In that respect I'm like the boy who was preparing to join the army. Someone asked if he wanted to join up with the cavalry. "Heck, no!" said the lad, "when they start shooting at me, I don't want to be bothered with any horse!"

1302. The photographer of a small town weekly newspaper went to the high school to take a picture of the high school speech class in action. He painstakingly arranged all the details necessary for a good picture. The instructor at the last minute asked, "Where do you want me?" "Oh," said the photographer, "why don't you just lean against the rectum?"

1303. For solid comfort and general satisfaction an old time-worn story is hard to beat. Then the audience is a step ahead of you and knows precisely when to laugh.

1304. A good speech is like an insect. It has a head, a body, and a stinging end.

—HANOR A. WEBB, *Science Teacher*

1305. Perhaps the most famous American speech was when Eli Whitney said, "Take your cotton-picking hands off my gin!"

1306. Public speaking is a performing art. The painter exhibits his painting, the sculptor his piece of sculpture, the architect his completed building, but the public speaker must present himself as exhibit A. He is both the creator and what is created.

—VIRGIL L. BAKER, University of Arkansas

1307. According to statisticians the average person spends at least one-fifth of his or her life talking. Ordinarily, in a single day enough words are used to roughly fill a 50 page book. In one year's time the average person's words would fill 132 books, each containing 400 pages.

1308. An after-dinner speech is like a love letter. Ideally, you should begin by not knowing what you are going to say, and end by not knowing what you've said.

—LORD JOWITT, *Look*

1309. The after-dinner speaker had talked 20 minutes beyond the time usually allotted for the Lions Club dinners. Finally, as he prepared to conclude, he said, "After eating such good food, I feel if I had eaten another bite I would burst." From the far end of the table, the club heckler sounded off, "Give him another sandwich."

1310. Keeping the attention riveted on the subject while listening to some speakers after a bounteous banquet is somewhat like trying to keep the television picture focused during a thunder storm with airplanes overhead and the electric sweeper going.

1311. The role of public speaker was never really mine,
Until I moved to the country and got a party line.

1312. A bald head and my healthy appetite may have had something to do with this retort:
"He's something of a star when it comes to banquet speaking," a stranger in town commented to an old friend.
"Star!" retorted my friend. "He's more like a moon. The fuller he gets, the brighter he becomes."
— M. DALE BAUGHMAN

1313. The successful speech on any occasion is where the orator has something to say and not merely where he has to say something.

1314. Sydney J. Harris said that he has suppressed a long-felt desire to mail out a rate card giving his basic fee along with certain "extras." A few suggested charges are listed below:
"For having to listen to a committee report, $5.
"For having to listen to a treasurer's report, $10.
"For spending an hour before the talk with the program chairman, hearing all about her parakeet, $25.
"For being driven out to view local monument, $15.
"For having to sit through slides of somebody's trip to Hawaii before my talk, $50.
"For having to partake of a hotel banquet meal, $10, plus all of the bicarbonate of soda I can consume."
—*Chicago Daily News*

1315. The chairman replied in a few appropriated remarks.
—CECIL HUNT, *This Week Magazine*

1316. You can send a message around the world in one-seventh of a second, but it may take years to force a simple idea through a quarter-inch of human skull.

1317. A stand few people hesitate to take is a speaker's stand.
—CAROLINE CLARK

1318. Side comment on one speaker's lecture: "He can go down deeper, stay down longer and come up dryer than anyone I ever saw."

1319. Wit is necessary to a clever talker; intelligence is enough for a good listener.

1320. At a dinner meeting, the speaker of the evening was introduced as a live wire. It developed that he was wired mostly for sound.
—*Spectator*

1321. Time was when a man with sufficient brass could get and hold an audience. Today, however, audiences almost demand that he transform the brass into tacks with sharp points.

1322. In this world of free speech every living soul is theoretically entitled to say what he thinks. Leigh Mitchell Hodges suggests a moderate curb. Each of us should wear a button about the size of a silver dollar imprinted with the words: "What I am about to say represents one two-billionth of the opinion of the world."
—*Speakers Magazine*

1323. When it comes to a really critical matter like political leadership, we recall a fact that all of us have seen in our daily lives; the longest lectures almost always come from those with least experience.
—DWIGHT D. EISENHOWER

1324.
Unaccustomed as he is
To rise and speak,
He has notes enough to
Last through all next week.
—JOAN Y. BREWTON, *Saturday Evening Post*

1325. A hungry little fly slipped into a delicatessen shop through a door, conveniently held open by a departing patron. She settled contentedly at the meat counter and proceeded to a hearty repast. Then, filled with a glorious sense of well-being, the little fly proceeded to flit about, buzzing happily the while. This buzzing at-

219

tracted the attention of the proprietor, who brought forth a large swatter, and . . .

Well, the moral of this story is plain to see:
When you are full of bologna, keep your mouth shut!

—Quote

1326. The speaker became confused; the longer he talked, the more confused became his hearers. Finally in desperation, he declared, "If I can just get this one idea across, you'll have it in a nutshell."

1327. A student's apt comment about one of his professor's lectures: "It took Sir William Ramsay sixteen years to discover helium; the Curies thirty years to find radium; yet in just 20 minutes, he produces tedium."

1328. An old colored minister was asked to explain the secret of his amazing power as a speaker. He said, "When I preaches, first I tells 'em what I am going to tell 'em; then I tells 'em—then I tells 'em what I done tole 'em."

1329. One of the better known after-dinner speakers is he who is always making an important phone call when the waiter presents the check.

—Francis Rodman

1330. The world today needs men who can speak effectively. We have men who can build bridges or skyscrapers, who can build and fly airplanes faster than the speed of sound, who can perfect the processes of atomic fission, but we are in short supply of men who can make effective speeches, and sway men's minds.

—C. W. Scott, *Toastmaster*

1331.   His opening story made us roar,
The closing one was fine.
But of the speech that came between
I can't recall a line!

—Edmund Mottershead

1332. Notes, like the hammer and saw and axe in a Pullman coach, are emergency tools, only for use in the case of a total smash-up.

—Dale Carnegie

1333. Every prospective teacher should be required to take courses in speech and dramatics. Education is 60 per cent communication and 40 per cent inspiration.

—FREDERICK MAYER and FRANK E. BROWER,
Patterns of a New Philosophy

1334. The well is deep, and you must have something to draw with. But there is no need to make people drink out of the bucket, still less chew on the rope.

—W. R. MALTBY

1335. Before each performance, the famous magician Thurston used to stand for a minute in the wings and say, "I love this audience. I'm going to give my best to them and they are going to respond splendidly." It put Thurston over—it will do the same for you.

—WILFRED A. PETERSON

1336. Alvin Busse, well-known member of the famous Borden and Busse team of experts on human relations and effective speaking, has said: "The world's greatest speeches are made in bed . . . at home, in bed, nearly every one of us has thought of dozens of polished, witty and pointed expressions; yet when most needed they did not pop into mind."

—EDMUND MOTTERSHEAD

1337. Only a few women are classified as after-dinner speakers—most can't wait that long.

1338. The following critical expression has often been used in describing the speaker using a manuscript, "If he can't remember it, how does he expect the audience to?" I do use a manuscript, although I don't read it, and I tell my listeners, "I don't want you to remember my speech; just enjoy it and feel it."

—M. DALE BAUGHMAN

1339. Recipe for stage fright: Just before taking your feet to face the audience, close your eyes for a few seconds and imagine that every person is sitting there in his nightclothes. It will then be a snap to deliver your address.

1340. *Bill:* Very few women have any knowledge of parliamentary law."

221

Joe: "You don't know my wife. She's been speaker of the house for twenty-five years."

1341. Stage fright is an affliction that combines all the worst features of lockjaw, palsy, morning nausea, and creeping paralysis. Perhaps, the worst feature, though, is that you can't—like a sick cat—crawl under a back porch and suffer in dignity. You have to do your suffering right out in the open with lots of people watching you.

—Lucile Hasley

1342. When the occasion for impromptu speech arises, if the main discourse has been carefully composed, its style has a momentum that will carry forward with the same eloquence, just as a boat moving at high speed keeps her course and motion when the oarsmen rest on their oars.

—Cicero

1343. A common error of the amateur storyteller is that he "telegraphs his blows." The smart technique is to be well on your way before listeners realize that you are telling a story.

1344. A speech that is read is like a dried flower; the substance indeed, is there, but the color is faded and the perfume is gone.

—Paul Lorain

1345. If I am asked to stand and speak unto a group,
The blood deserts my ruddy cheek and turns to soup.
Confusion I just can't disguise, I long to flee!
O, that I were two other guys instead of me!
I can't think of a single word! I want to sneeze!
The only sound from me that's heard is knocking knees.
But when I'm seated my heart sings! I'm free from dread!
And then I think of brilliant things I could have said.

—W. L. Hudson

1346.   He keeps an audience right on its toes
from the moment he starts to spout!
He keeps an audience right on its toes—
tiptoeing out.

—Ethel Jacobson

1347. "You claim," said the superintendent to the would-be commencement speaker, "that you have every qualification of a first-rate speaker?"

"I lack only one thing," was the bland retort. "I am slightly deaf —the result of so much applause, y' know."

1348. It is deplorable that the guarantee of free speech doesn't carry the provision that the speaker must say something worth listening to.

—*Cincinnati Enquirer*

1349. The recipe for successful after-dinner speaking includes plenty of shortening.

1350. A finished speaker seldom is.

—Franklin P. Jones

1351. The easiest way to stay awake during an after-dinner speech is to deliver it.

—Franklin P. Jones

1352. He could speak for an hour without a note and without a point.

1353. A captive audience is better than one that runs away.

1354. A cannonball may sink a battleship but a load of grape-shot will only scratch the paint. I shall discuss only three aspects of teaching: drills, frills and thrills.

1355. All public speaking of merit is characterized by nervousness.

—Cicero

1356. Two minutes before I begin a speech I would rather be whipped than start; but two minutes before I finish, I would rather be shot than stop.

1357. A parrot is the only creature gifted with speech that is content to repeat what it hears without trying to make a good story of it.

1358. A good story-teller is a person who has a good memory and hopes other people haven't.

—Irvin S. Cobb

1359. The ability to speak many languages is valuable, but the ability to keep your mouth shut in one language is priceless.

1360. The important man was about ready for his speech when a news photographer was observed jockeying for a vantage point, for an action shot. The chairman, fearing that the speaker would be annoyed, called the photographer and said: "Don't take his picture while he is speaking. Shoot him before he starts."

—Toastmaster

1361. It's uncanny how much punishment the human system can take and still pull through. Standing before a microphone, you can experience everything but the ultimate coma, and yet—here's the surprise—be able to walk off the platform unaided after it's all over. Fifteen minutes later, you can even partake of a little nourishment —not, mind you, through intravenous feeding, but by actually lifting a cup of hot orange pekoe to your lips.

1362. In effective speaking some words are emphasized and some are "umphasized."

1363. Scheduled to make an after-dinner speech, a man became so nervous during the meal that he slipped out and went home. What this country needs is more introverts.

—Grit

1364. In Africa a man can't be a public speaker until he has shot an elephant; here in America a man is considered qualified if he can shoot the bull.

1365. A lot of fellows classified as after-dinner speakers are merely after dinner.

1366.   It's never so bleak
That it can't be bleaker . . .
There might have been a second speaker!

—Robert Dale

1367. Always start your speech with a statement deliberately planned to seize the listener gently by his ears.

1368. Many can rise to the occasion, but few know how to sit down.

1369. A lecturer should always arrive early and strive to look into the eyes of as many of his hearers as possible; this makes addressing them easier since it relieves the oppressive feeling usually created by a strange crowd.

1370. Veteran speakers usually gesture vigorously and walk around. A moving target is harder to hit.

—FRANKLIN P. JONES

1371.   The speaker bores you, gentlemen?
He's also boring me.
But praise him gently when he's through
He comes to us for free.

—VIRGINIA MOORE

1372. Anyone may easily become a good speaker if he but acquires the art of diluting a two-minute idea with a two-hour vocabulary.

1373. Mark Twain and Chauncey M. Depew once went abroad on the same ship. When the ship was a few days out they were both invited to a dinner, and when speech-making time came, Mark Twain had the first chance. He spoke twenty minutes and made a great hit. Then it was Mr. Depew's turn.

"Mr. Toastmaster and Ladies and Gentlemen," said the famous raconteur as he rose, "before this dinner Mark Twain and myself made an agreement to trade speeches. He has just delivered my speech, and I thank you for the pleasant manner in which you have received it. I regret to say that I have lost the notes of his speech and cannot remember anything he was to say."

1374. A young judge decided to see what he could do in the way of establishing law and justice in a small western cow town.

After he had been there a short time, he managed to get most of the townsmen, saloon keepers and all, together for a short speech.

When he stood before them to speak on the subject, "Law and Order," he paused to survey the expressions of some members of the audience. The first thing that struck him—was a ripe tomato.

—M. DALE BAUGHMAN

1375. A well-known atomic scientist was being driven to the auditorium in a metropolitan area by his chauffeur. The scientist, who was to deliver an address that evening, was rehearsing his speech as the limousine rolled along. The inspired and amazed chauffeur remarked, "Sure wish that I could speak as you do and hold the attention of large audiences." "Well, it's not too difficult," said the scientist. "Why don't you take my manuscript, look it over, and make the address tonight—I'll drive; and by the way, no one knows me here. The audience will never know the difference." The chauffeur finally consented. Strangely enough, he got along very well but was taken aback when someone in the audience called for a question and answer period. When a very technical question was addressed to him, he said, "Well, it's really very simple; just to prove how simple it really is, I think I'll let my chauffeur answer it."

Brevity

1376. After one of my speeches at which my wife was present, I asked, "How did I do?"

"Fine," she replied, "only you missed several excellent opportunities to sit down."

1377. The sexton had been laying the new carpet on the pulpit platform and had left a number of tacks scattered on the floor. "See here, James," said the parson, "what do you suppose would happen if I stepped on one of those tacks right in the middle of my sermon?"

"Well sir," replied the sexton, "I reckon there'd be one point you wouldn't linger on."

—*Rotagram*

1378. In public speaking, the greatest of all rules is this one: When you are about half done, sit down.

1379.
        I must defend your right to make
        Your point—you're welcome to it—
        But not, dear sirs, your right to take
        So awfully long to do it.

—NED WADLINGER, *Grit*

1380. The professor had a reputation for being long winded in his lectures and on this occasion was in prime condition. For nearly an hour he had droned along on his topic, the heroes of the Revolutionary War.

"Now then," he said finally, "we have disposed of the Revolution. Next, the Civil War. To what place shall we assign the heroes of the Civil War?"

One tired student, noticing that it was past the closing hour, spoke up, "One of 'em can have my place! I'm going to my next class."

1381. In Africa when a speaker talks too long at a village gathering, the listeners silence him with shouts of Imetosha! Imetosha!—Enough, Enough.

—DALE CARNEGIE

1382. Some years ago in Hartford, we all went to church, one hot, sweltering night to hear the annual report of Mr. Hawley, a city missionary who went around finding people who needed help and didn't want to ask for it. He told of the life in cellars, where poverty resided; he gave instances of the heroism and devotion of the poor. When a man with millions gives, he said, we make a good deal of noise. It's a noise in the wrong place, for it's the widow's mite that counts.

Well, Hawley worked me up to a great pitch. I could hardly wait for him to get through. I had $400 in my pocket. I wanted to give that and borrow more to give. You could see greenbacks in every eye. But, instead of passing the plate to the crowd then, he kept on talking and talking, and as he talked, it grew hotter and hotter and hotter, and we grew sleepier and sleepier and sleepier. My enthusiasm went down, down, down, down—$100 at a clip—until finally, when the plate did come around, I stole ten cents out of it. It all goes to show how a little thing like this can lead to crime.

—MARK TWAIN

1383. Spartans loathed talkativeness. Once a neighboring island was struck by a famine. An envoy was sent to Sparta to plead for help. The Spartans sent him back empty handed, saying, "We have forgotten the beginning of your speech and we understood nothing of the end."

Another envoy was sent. He took along a heap of empty bags and opening one, said, "It is empty, please fill it." All the bags were promptly overflowing. But the envoy was warned: "You need not have pointed out to us that your bags were empty. We would have seen it. It was not necessary to ask us to fill them. We would have done that. When you come again, don't talk so much."

—REVEREND FRANCIS MIHALIC

1384. It's all right to have a train of thought if you also have a terminal.

1385. A certain professor noted for the great length of his lectures surprised his class one day with a short lecture of 20 minutes. At the close of the lecture, he explained, "I regret to announce that my dog, who appears to be extremely fond of paper, last evening ate that portion of my lecture which I have not delivered."

As the professor left the room, he was approached by a student who asked, "Sir, does that dog of yours have any pups? If it has, I want to get one for my chemistry professor."

1386. Most cut and dried speeches need more cutting and less drying.

—CAROLINE CLARK

1387. I was in the bathroom shaving, getting ready for my commencement address later in the evening, when I accidentally nicked my chin a bit. My wife noticed the styptic on the cut and asked what had happened. I told her, "I cut my chin, while concentrating on my speech." Her answer was, "You'd better concentrate on your chin and cut your speech."

1388. Saul of Tarsus preached until a chap in the audience went to sleep and fell out of a window and all but broke his neck. Even then Saul may not have stopped talking. Who knows?

—DALE CARNEGIE

1389. Part of a superintendent's letter suggesting brevity in commencement addresses:

Christ's greatest speech, the Sermon on the Mount, lasted only 5 minutes; Lincoln's Gettysburg Address has only ten sentences. The whole story of creation in Genesis can be read in less time than it takes to read about traffic deaths in the morning paper.

1390.   Where is the speaker to compare
             With him who rises from his chair,

> Bows and smiles; then gains renown
> By sitting down!
> —STEPHEN SCHLITZER

1391. Advice to a long-winded speaker:
Try hard to find a good opener and a good closer; you may have to experiment and use trial-and-error methods. Now be sure they are close together.

1392. At the first meeting of my college classes, I always assure my students that I am not among those who believe that to make a lecture immortal, you have to make it everlasting.
> —M. DALE BAUGHMAN

1393.
> The coffee's cold, the sherbet wanes,
> The speech drones on and on . . .
> O, Speaker, heed the ancient rule:
> Be brief. Be gay. Be gone!
> —ISABEL DEE, *Quote*

1394. A preacher who was popular with his congregation explained his success as the result of a silent prayer which he offered each time he took the pulpit. It ran thus:
> "Lord, fill my mouth with worthwhile stuff.
> And nudge me when I've said enough."
> —*School Activities*

1395.
> I sometimes think I'll never see
> A speaker of the sort
> Who does not make it long when we
> All long to make it short!
> —S. OMAR BARKER

1396. An after-dinner speaker's words are most likely to be remembered if he forgets a few.
> —A. A. SCHILLING

1397. The history of the creation of the world as presented in Genesis can be told in 20 minutes; when you sense the opportunity to close, follow the impulse.

1398.
> I hold that speaker great
> —A truly fine narrator—

Who says, "It's getting late"
And doesn't make it later;
Whose talk is no infusion
Of long, trite platitudes,
And who says, "In conclusion"
and concludes!

—Dirck

1399. An optimist is a hopeful guy
Possessed with the delusion
That the end of a speech is drawing nigh
When the speaker says,
"In conclusion. . . ."

—Fred Baldwin

1400. A speech that's full of sparkling wit
Will keep its hearers grinning,
Provided that the end of it is close
To the beginning!

—*Sunshine Magazine*

1401. Tribal custom in a remote area of South Africa includes some regulations on public speeches. A graduate student in my class, a native of South Africa, explained that a speaker is expected to stand on one leg while addressing his listeners. When his other foot touches the ground, he must terminate his speech.

—M. Dale Baughman

Introductions

1402. The success or failure of the speaker often depends on how you offer him to the audience and the audience to him.
Let's launch speakers right:

1. *What* you say about the speaker must make the audience feel that he is important to them now.

2. *How* you say it must create suspense so that the audience is waiting for the speaker, and he is eager for the audience.

3. The speaker's name should be the final climatic words.

4. Provoke applause and stand up like a man until the speaker has taken his place.

—Bill Clark

1403. To be perfectly frank, I'm as nervous as a mail carrier on a new route; he doesn't know the dogs of the neighborhood, doesn't know whether to ring the doorbell, tiptoe through the tulips, or yell "Mail." I don't know the critics of this group, I don't know whether to ring the bell, sit down, or call for help. I think I'll call for help. (*Make introduction.*)

—M. Dale Baughman

1404. The Governor of the Virgin Islands was a guest in Washington. The toastmaster, in the introductory remarks, said the usual things and ended with "It's a great pleasure to present the Virgin of Governor's Island."

1405. "The hardest part of a lecture," insists an experienced speaker, "is waking up the audience after the man who introduces me has concluded his remarks."

—*Cracklings*

1406. Two schools claim as an alumnus our eloquent speaker this evening—Harvard and Yale. Harvard claims he was educated at Yale, and Yale claims he matriculated at Harvard.

1407. One of these days the chairman of some banquet or meeting where a speaker is to appear will break tradition and quite possibly win renown by uttering these words: "I shall now present a speaker who needs an introduction."

1408.
My nature's unemotional,
Quite stable and un-notional;
But one sort of ruction
Upsets it.

I bristle with odium
When the guy on the podium
Needs no introduction
But gets it.
—Richard F. Armknecht, *Wall Street Journal*

1409. The fifth grade English teacher assigned her class to write an essay on the life of Benjamin Franklin. One pupil, striving for brevity and conciseness, submitted this essay: "Ben Franklin was born in Boston; he traveled to Philadelphia, met a lady on the street; she laughed at him; he married her and discovered electricity."

Taking my cue from the fifth grade pupil, I intend to reveal only a few basic facts about our speaker of the evening.

1410. (*When introducing a specialist.*)

A widely known society playgirl asked her teen-age daughter to help in mailing out invitations to her third wedding.

The young lady did her share and more. When the guests presented their invitations, the society lady was chagrined to see her daughter's handwritten postscript, "Be sure and come; this is no amateur performance."

Let me emphasize that our speaker is no amateur in his profession, either.

1411. After hearing our speaker's discourse on the theme of the day, I'm sure you will feel just as Henry's father did when the lad asked, "Dad, how do fishermen mend their nets?"

Dad answered confidently, "It's very simple, Henry. They merely take a handful of holes and sew them together."

After listening to an expert on the subject of ————, the solution should appear quite simple. May I present ————.

1412. When our daughter was four years old, she rang the neighbor's doorbell and asked for a piece of cake. The lady appeared surprised and asked, "Why, what's wrong with bread and butter today?"

The prompt reply was, "Well, today's my birthday."

Now, I'm not aware that today is anyone's birthday, but it is a day when the ordinary "staff of life" is not good enough for us. We deserve and we have a special treat. I present ————.

1413. A thoughtful hostess, when she introduces two people, gives them a lead, so they won't stare blankly at each other with nothing to talk about. The introducer tries to indicate a mutual interest, a possible bond between two strangers. . . .

When you introduce a speaker, you are doing practically the same thing. You draw the audience and the speaker together so they can "communicate."

—MOLLY G. DAUGHERTY, *Farm Journal*

1414. Probably no scourge since the "Black Plague" has inflicted such suffering upon mankind as speeches of introduction.
—WALTER A. STEIGLEMAN

1415. It has been said that brevity is the soul of wit; as toastmaster I shall supply the brevity and let Mr. ———— supply the wit.

1416. Response to introduction—Thank you, Mr. Chairman, that's a much better introduction than I once received. The toastmaster said, "Some of us have heard the speaker before and others have not. Those who have not heard him are looking forward to hearing him now."

1417. Thanks for that hearty applause! When I get applause at the end of a speech, I always consider it charity; if it comes in the middle, it must be hope, but when it comes before the speech, it proves you have faith.

1418. Nervous speaker bothered by microphone paraphernalia: "These microphones are like cuspidors. They're no good if you don't hit 'em dead center."

1419. *Response to introduction:* "Now I know how a pancake feels when it has been immersed in a pitcher of sweet maple syrup."

1420. *Response to introduction:* "A machine has been invented that will unwrinkle raisins and blow up foods to as much as 30 times their true size. It must have been invented by the man who introduces public speakers."
—ZULA BENNINGTON GREENE, *Capper's Weekly*

Openers

1421. Speaker, clearing his throat: "I'll make some loud noises from the throat sound like deep messages from the brain; when I'm through you'll probably think it has been twin cylinder exhaust from a one cylinder engine."

1422. It's always a problem to know just what to do at a time like this; one never knows whether to let the audience continue to enjoy themselves, or to start with the speeches.

1423. "Temporarily, the sense of hearing is considerably dulled by eating," asserts a physician. Kindly nature does the best she can to protect us against post-prandial oratory.

—Grit

1424. I feel like the man who had just inherited a harem—I know what to do but I don't know where to start.

1425. (*When the audience is small.*)
Socrates once appeared to speak in Athens and found only a smattering of the citizens present.

Not at all perturbed, he remarked, "Altogether there are only 14 present; however, I am certain that I am privileged to speak to the 14 most intelligent people in all Athens."

1426. Thanks for that enthusiastic applause. However, since you haven't yet heard anything, I must necessarily attribute it to RFC— relatives, friends and charity. Since I'm away from home, it must be the latter, charity.

1427. (*When the applause is meager.*)
Thanks for that enthusiastic applause. It sounded exactly like a caterpillar crawling across a Persian rug.

1428. An inquisitive oldster asked a youngster selling newspapers what the papers cost him.

"Two cents," answered the lad.

"What do you sell them for?"

"Two cents," was the answer.

"Goodness, son," said the man, "you can't make any profit doing business that way. Why do you sell papers for what they cost you?"

"Oh," answered the newsboy, "I do it because it gives me a chance to holler all I want to."

(If you're getting paid for your speech, you can comment that you're better off than the newsboy since you're making a profit and getting a chance to holler all you want to.)

1429. There are three things difficult to do: climb a brick wall leaning toward you, kiss a girl leaning away from you and, make a speech.

1430. Ogden Nash, the humorist, was addressing a midwestern women's club, and began with a heartfelt comment: "Ladies, I have

234

100 good reasons for speaking to you today. Ninety-nine of them are monetary."

1431. Before I got up here to talk, only two people knew what I was going to say. Me and the Lord. Now only the Lord knows.

1432. Three things matter in a speech: who says it, how he says it, and what he says—and of the three, the last matters the least.
                                                                —Lord Morley

1433. The newly elected president of the Junior Chamber of Commerce was speaking in dedication of a new baseball diamond for the youth of his city. "Fifty years ago," he began, "the place where I now stand was wilderness." Unable to recall the following lines of his speech, he repeated, "Fifty years ago where I now stand was wilderness." Again, his mind was a blank. And then he exclaimed, "I wish to hell it was now and I was in it."

1434. All work and no plagiarism makes a dull speech.
                                                                —Banking

1435. (*When you're speaking away from home.*)
A woodpecker sharpened his beak on sassafras saplings and niggerhead rocks in Brown County, Indiana. He migrated to California and was amazed when he saw his first giant redwood. He went to work on one when lightning struck the tree and split it all the way down.
"Woody" was knocked to the ground unconscious, defeathered and otherwise disheveled; when he regained consciousness, he surveyed the damage and remarked, "It certainly is remarkable what a fellow can do when he's away from home."

1436. I feel very much like the lean and lanky Hoosier boy, nearly six feet and ten inches tall, who applied for a job as a life guard. He met some of the qualifications but reluctantly confessed that he couldn't swim to do any good. When asked how he thought he could help save a life, he pointed to his long, gangly legs and insisted, "But I can wade to beat hell!"
Now, I may not be able to swim along with my subject, but at least, I'll wade right in.

1437. An Arkansas farmer bought a mule. He beat him over the head with a club to make him work; no results. The mule seller happened along and said, "Put down that club. He's been beaten so much now, he ignores it. Now watch me." He bent down, picked a daisy and started tickling him under the chin. The farmer asked, "How's that going to make him work?" "Don't hurry me," said the mule seller, "this is just to get his attention; it's something he doesn't expect."

1438.   Of what has preceded, it can be said,
These things are being done,
Of what is to follow, it can be said,
These are some of the things we hope for.

1439. The late Charles Dalton used to measure boredom in an audience by counting, as he sat on the platform, the number of movements a person made per minute. If the speech was intensely interesting, hands or legs were shifted only about once in 60 seconds. But if the speaker droned on and lost his grip, there might be as many as 10 signs of restlessness every minute.

1440. It's quite possible that one of Daniel's remarks when he was thrown into the lions' den was "Well, after this banquet there will be no speech."

1441. A child came home from his first day at school quite perturbed. He explained that his teacher had told them that they would be put into the furnace. Dad, of course, was somewhat alarmed and asked the teacher for an explanation. It seems that she had announced, "If you miss two weeks of school, you will be dropped from the register."

(I hope my remarks this evening are not that misleading.)

1442. For me to appear on the program after ————(predecessor) is like hearing a millpond frog croak after hearing the heavenly angels sing. ————(predecessor) will be the first to deny that he is an angel, just as I might be the first to deny that I am a frog. Nevertheless, the simile holds in the present predicament and the predicament's yours as well as mine.

—JOHN A. SCHINDLER, *Bulletin, National Association of Secondary School Principals.*

1443. This will be a little longer than my usual after dinner speech —just six words, "Leave them, dear, I'll do them." Lest you suspect that I'm a henpecked husband, let me illustrate. The other evening I wanted some hot water—I demanded hot water! I got hot water! This incident proves that I'm boss at our house. I sure do hate to wash dishes in cold water!

—M. DALE BAUGHMAN

1444. One speaker on the program, heckling the other before his speech: "Tell them all you know. It won't take longer than 10 minutes." The speaker came back with, "I'll tell them all we both know; that won't take more than 15 minutes."

1445. It's a real pleasure to speak in this beautiful auditorium this evening. I presume you know the etymology of the word auditorium. It is derived from two Latin words: audio—to hear, and taurus—the bull.

1446. For you who are over 16 years of age, I have some jokes; for you who are under 16 years of age, I have some anecdotes and illustrative stories. And for you who are just 16 today, "Happy Birthday!"

1447. At the outset let me assure you that I am properly humble in the presence of such an assemblage. I cannot guarantee that I will say anything of importance. I am sure of this, however; you haven't traveled far to hear it. I am comforted and assuaged by the knowledge that you don't expect much from me.

The last joke I heard can safely be told here: Two small boys were cornered by a billy goat; seeing what was going to happen, one said to the other, "Say your prayers." He did, in these words, "Lord, make us grateful for that which we are about to receive." Now, I make no apologies for that which you are about to receive.

—M. DALE BAUGHMAN

1448. Unusual candor was shown by the toastmaster who rose after the dinner and said, "Gentlemen, it is high time we got the bull rolling."

1449. Perhaps I should mention that I am noted more for my nonsensical nuggets than for my scholarly comments or intellectual gems. To allay any suspicions you might harbor that I am what a pupil of mine once described as "an old piece of china, a cracked pot with a loose lid," I shall plunge immediately into the slipstream of my address. Let me hasten to add, however, that the blueprints call for some sparklers here and there.

—M. DALE BAUGHMAN

1450. In the Orient, speeches at public dinners are delivered before the banquet commences. Now we have a better understanding of what is meant by the wise men of the East.

1451. Statement in a biology textbook: "The human jaw is said to be growing smaller." In view of the manner in which it is constantly exercised, that is a statement difficult for many of us to believe.

1452. Biblical history reveals that Samson killed 10,000 men with the jawbone of an ass; today many men talk themselves out of promotions, public favor, and return engagements with the very same weapon.

1453. Crime records indicate that a murder is committed somewhere in the U. S. every 40 minutes. It is perhaps mere coincidence that this is the length of the ordinary after-dinner speech.

1454.
        Every rose has its thorn,
        There's fuzz on all the peaches,
        There hasn't been a banquet yet
        Without some lengthy speeches.

1455. The speaker-to-be inquired of the chairman, "How long shall I talk?" The chairman answered cheerfully, "Why, take as long as you like—we all leave at 8:30."

1456. The Egyptians have a saying that there are three things difficult to hide—love, smoke, and a man on a camel. I can easily add a fourth—the strange affliction known as stage fright, now being experienced by your speaker.

—M. DALE BAUGHMAN

1457. Pappy Waldorf, retired California football coach, was being honored at a dinner and when he got up to make the principal address, he said: "I've belonged to this club for two years but this is the first meeting I have attended. What's more I will say it will be the last unless you improve the caliber of your principal speakers."

1458. I like to tell stories and I have found that most people not only enjoy them but learn more easily through the medium of anecdotes and broad illustrations than in any other way.

As to what the unimpressed minority may think, I don't care.

—ABRAHAM LINCOLN

1459. "Ladies and gentlemen," said the after-dinner speaker, "before I begin my address, I have something important to say."

1460. It is a poor speech that offends no one; that neither makes the listener displeased with himself nor with the speaker.

1461. The mind is a wonderful thing, it starts working the minute you're born, and never stops until you stand up to speak in public.

1462. The community dinner was over at last and the patient members of the audience who had survived the long address of the principal speaker breathed a deep sigh of relief.

"The speaker was all right," the toastmaster's wife whispered to her husband, "but it seems to me that he could have put more fire into his speech."

"I feel the opposite way," answered her toastmaster husband, "in my opinion he could have put more of his speech into the fire."

1463. Words of advice from Dale Carnegie to those who make speeches.

"Fill up the barrel,
Knock out the bung,
Let nature caper."

—*How to Develop Self-Confidence and Influence People by Public Speaking,* Dale Carnegie, Pocket Books Inc., New York. (By permission of National Board of Young Men's Christian Associations.)

1464. Pleased with what I thought was a most successful speech, I once asked my wife as we left the auditorium, "Did you notice how my voice seemed to fill the auditorium?"

"I surely did," she agreed. "I also noticed that some of the audience left to make more room for it."

1465. One writer authority says "the toastmaster is like the flour in a plum pudding—he is necessary to hold all the other good things together, but the moment he predominates and thrusts himself forward at the expense of the plums, the citrons, and the spices, he becomes a nuisance—and he spoils the pudding." Believe me, I don't want to spoil the pudding.

—Toasts and Stories for Every Occasion

1466. The toastmaster is the man at a dinner party whose duty it is to inform you that the best part of the entertainment is now over.

—Sunshine Magazine

1467. As the after-dinner speaker sat down to his meal, he coughed. His upper plate fell to the floor and broke.

The guest at his side realized his plight, dug into his pocket and came up with a new set. The speaker-to-be tried them. They were too big. The man supplied another set. They were too small. The third set was a perfect fit.

The speaker got along perfectly with the borrowed teeth, and returned them with thanks.

"By the way," he inquired, "are you a dentist?"

The helpful guest shook his head. "No, I'm an undertaker."

—Morris Past

1468. I don't advise you to start talking until you have begun thinking. It is no good opening the tap if there is nothing in the tank.

—Clarence B. Randall, quoted in *Executive's Digest*

1469. One way to interest an audience is to startle them at the very beginning, just as the writer sometimes startles his readers. Hal Boyle tells of a news friend who suggested starting every column with "A human skull rolled out on the table." Another said to start with—"Take your hands off me, the duchess cried." The latter has three things that interest people most—sex, money, and high society, the writer claimed.

1470. And sometime when *you* have the misfortune to be the speaker, tell this one about the young tenderfoot lawyer from the East who adventured into a wild and woolly Western cattle town and hung out his shingle. In the fullness of time he was invited, with some misgivings, to address a Chamber of Commerce meeting. He was scared to death, and showed it by giving a pretty gosh-awful performance. His self-confidence was not restored to any great degree when, at the conclusion of the meeting, three grimfaced cattlemen arose and with a conspicuous display of ropes and guns, made directly for the speaker's table. The young lawyer was all for beating it by a convenient rear exit, but an elder and more experienced head counselled him. "Jest you set still, son. They ain't nobody a-goin' t' harm you. Them fellers is a-comin' fer the Program Chairman!"

1471. A rustic approached the station agent in a small village and asked for arrival and departure times of all westbound, eastbound, northbound and southbound trains.

The agent obligingly gave him this information: "The next eastbound train arrives at 2:00 P.M., the next westbound train leaves at 4:00 P.M., the next train north arrives at 6:00 P.M., and the southbound train just left."

"Good," said the rustic, "I guess it's safe to cross the tracks now."

Now that I've been properly introduced and have responded to the introduction, I think it's safe to cross the tracks and launch into my subject.

1472. Try as I might I cannot help being reminded of that novel soap advertisement, "Use Lumpo soap. It doesn't cleanse, it doesn't bubble, it hardly lathers, but it is good company in the tub."

Here I am about to make a speech, but I can't inspire, I can't amuse, and it is questionable that I can inform; but I'll do my best to be company in the tub.

—M. Dale Baughman

1473. The new school secretary was in conference with the principal. "Miss Smith," said he, "you are a most attractive young lady. Furthermore, you dress neatly, you have a pleasant expression, and your voice is pleasing to the ear."

"Really?" replied the young office girl, "but you shouldn't pay me so many compliments."

"That's quite all right," said the principal, "I only wanted to cheer you up before discussing your skills in punctuation and spelling."

1474. (*When you are called upon unexpectedly to say a few words.*)

241

I appreciate the opportunity and honor of talking to you on this occasion, even if only briefly, but I must admit that I am inadequately prepared to express my thoughts. Actually, Mr. Chairman, my situation is much like Jonah's at the time he said to the whale, "If you hadn't opened your big mouth, I wouldn't be in this hole."

—M. Dale Baughman

1475. It's real comforting to know that you do not expect too much of this speech. "Uncle Jim," the town patriarch, after much protest, finally agreed to his first operation, but he insisted on one final question. "Doc," he said, "how long after you give me the anesthetic will it be before I begin to know something?"

"Uncle Jim," replied the surgeon, "now isn't that expecting a great deal of an anesthetic?"

Now, I really can't say how long it will be before you begin to know something about ——— and I trust that it won't have an anesthetic effect.

1476. The depth and breadth of my subject is indeed discomforting. Quite frankly, I feel just like grandpa as he explained his ignorance of the game of golf. "There's one contest I don't know a gol-durned thing about! Why, I wouldn't even know which end of the caddy to pick up."

I'm not at all sure which end of my subject to pick up first.

1477. Mr. Chairman, I appreciate your fine introduction but I always remember that flattery, like perfume, is to be smelled, not swallowed. To you in the audience thanks for the kind reception you have given me. Let me give you early assurance that I plan no lengthy and profound address—on the contrary it will be much like the junior high school boy's composition.

The English teacher cautioned against flights of fancy, imitation and help from others as she assigned a composition to her junior high school pupils. "Instead," she instructed, "simply be yourselves and say what is in you."

Jack Smart took her advice and submitted the following composition: "This is not an imitation; this is not copied; I have in me my gizzard, stummick, lungs, heart, two popsicles, one apple, one licorice stick, some peanuts, and my dinner.

Like Jack, I shall simply say what is in me and let it go at that.

—M. Dale Baughman

1478. The theme of my subject is not new nor has it suffered from lack of attention by orators and writers. As I attempted to organize and record my thoughts on this matter, I thought of the rural dweller who lived by a frog pond. The noise from the pond grew increasingly louder until the farmer decided to get rid of the frogs and make a profit at the same time. He finally convinced the hotel chef to order four dozen frogs' legs. A while later he delivered five pairs of frogs' legs to the chef who demanded to know why the order was so short. "Well, it's this way," said the rustic, "the noise from my frog pond was so terrific that I concluded that there were at least a hundred of them. I caught five frogs and the noise stopped."

My topic may have hundreds of frogs croaking about it, but when we get to the bottom of the pond, there are only a few fundamentals worth expanding.

1479. Unaccustomed as I am to public speaking, I know the futility of it.

1480. My speech will be like the latest Paris fashion; long enough to cover the subject and short enough to be interesting.

1481. I want it clearly understood that I am not going to make a long speech—you look a little tired already. One reason I'm not going to make a long speech is that the other day I was talking down in Houston, Texas. I had been going only about an hour and a half and I wasn't near through, when three fellows down at a table in front pulled out six shooters—they just scared me to death. I started stuttering around and one of them said, "Don't worry, preacher, these aren't for you, they are for the guy who invited you."
—WILLIAM ALEXANDER, Minister, First Christian
Church, Oklahoma City

1482. I seem to be having a little trouble getting this speech started—it certainly isn't because I didn't prepare for it. I started this day right; I stood under a cold shower before breakfast for ten minutes—next time I might even turn on the water.

1483. One of your own teachers recommended me for this speaking engagement. When I came into the auditorium today, I saw him and asked, "Why did you recommend me to speak on this important occasion?" "Well," he said, "you gave me an 'A,' didn't you?" "Yes," I said, "but didn't you have any other reasons?" "Well," replied the young teacher, "I couldn't think of any."

—M. DALE BAUGHMAN

1484. There are two basic types of speeches: The comprehensive insurance speech—it covers everything; the Bikini bathing suit speech—it covers only the essentials.

—M. DALE BAUGHMAN

1485. One of my first speaking assignments was to the parents and players at a junior high school basketball banquet. One of the parents offered me a check for $7.50 which I refused, commenting that it might be used for team equipment.

"Would you mind," asked the parent, "if we include it in our special fund?"

"Certainly not," I said. "But I'm curious. What is the special fund for?"

"To help us get better speakers for our banquets."

—M. DALE BAUGHMAN

1486. Advice to scared speakers: "Draw yourself up to your full height, look your audience straight in the eyes and begin to talk as confidently as if every one of them owed you money. Imagine that they have assembled there to beg you for an extension of credit."

—DALE CARNEGIE

1487. "My good friend," boomed the political speaker, "I'm pleased to see this dense crowd here tonight."

"Well," said a voice from the back of the hall, "don't be too pleased. We ain't all dense."

1488. Thank you very much, I appreciate that very kind introduction. I am frank to say that it makes me feel more or less like that old mother cow who was contentedly chewing her cud on a high plateau while her little bull calf ran closer and closer to the 2,000-foot cliff. He would run up and look over and run back; run up and look over and run back; run up and look over and run back; one time he went a little too close and down and down he went, 2,000 feet to the rocks below. The old mother cow, still contentedly chewing her cud, rose leisurely to her feet licking her big red lips with her big red tongue, ambled over the cliff, looked down and said, "My, a little bull goes a long way."

—WILLIAM H. ALEXANDER, Minister

1489. Formula for an after-dinner speech:
Take three large breaths.
Compliment the audience.
Outline what you are not going to talk about.
Mention points you will touch on later.
Use two familiar quotations.
Mention points you will not have time to cover.
Refer to what you said first.
Tell a funny story.
Compliment the audience.
Compliment the city, state and nation.
Sit down amid tumultuous applause.

—*Pipe Dreams*

1490. A murderer, sentenced to the gallows, was asked by the warden just before the execution, "Do you have a last request before we spring the trap?"

Being a golf enthusiast, the murderer replied, "Yes, I'd like to try a practice swing."

Please consider my first story a practice swing.

1491. I'm afraid, too, that Lincoln spoke the truth about Commencement speakers when he said, "The world will little note, nor long remember what we say here."

—GERALD POOR, *Clearing House*

1492. A speaker of considerable renown and also of considerable conceit once appeared at the appointed place and found only a very small audience. He was sarcastic and caustic as he asked the chairman, "Well, don't the people of the town know I'm here?"

"Well, I don't know," answered the confused chairman, "it might have leaked out."

1493. A little boy who was very fond of molasses found a barrelful of the delicacy and helped himself to some each day until the barrel was almost empty. To get the last bit he tiptoed and reached down, down, until he toppled in headfirst. He finally managed to extricate

245

himself, staggered to the mirror and surveyed himself. When he saw the gooey mess, he implored, "Oh, Lord, give my tongue strength to live up to this occasion."

1494. In my opening remarks I feel compelled to admit quite frankly that what you are about to hear is not original with me—it was not necessarily preceded by creative thought. The situation is not a little like that of the experience of the traveling man with the only railroad in my home county back in Indiana. The railroad in question was well known; well known, that is, for never being on schedule with its passenger trains.

The traveler was a salesman who had been trying for some time to sell my Dad a bacon slicer for his general store. On one occasion as he stepped from a musty coach at the end of his journey down from Indianapolis, he offered a cigar to the conductor with this re-mark, "Old-timer, please accept this as a slight token of my ap-preciation." "What's the occasion?" asked the surprised railroader.

"Well, I've made the Indianapolis to Brown County run several times," said the traveler, "and this is the first time this train ever made it exactly on schedule."

"Listen, Mr. Salesman," retorted the conductor, "I'm right fond of good cigars but I can't accept it—my conscience would never let me rest. The truth is—this ain't today's train. This is yesterday's train."

In one sense of the word the gist of my speech is yesterday's train.
—M. Dale Baughman

1495. A speaker was invited to make a Memorial Day address. On the invitation this program was listed: talk by the mayor; recitation of Lincoln's Gettysburg Address; address by a high school boy; your talk, and then the firing squad.

1496. Many public speakers know how to say nothing, and if done with enthusiasm, it is often applauded.

1497. Making a speech is like going to the dentist. No matter what the dentist advertises, the event is never quite painless.
—Margaret L. Jones, *Dun's Review and Modern Industry*

1498. My grandfather once told me that there are three things that rise slowly: an old man with a cane, bread in a cold room, and a schoolboy on a cold winter morning. May I add a fourth? A humble speaker in the presence of such an assembly of educated hearers.

—M. Dale Baughman

1499. Formula for a successful sermon or a successful speech:

"Begin low, go slow, rise higher, take fire, and sit down in the storm." I heard about one young minister at a church ice cream social who began low, went slow, rose higher, took fire and sat down in the ice cream freezer.

—M. Dale Baughman

1500. In the beginning let me tell you something about the nature of my remarks. I have something old, something new, something borrowed, but never blue.

1501. Let your voice say to your audience, "I like you; I am glad to have the opportunity to speak to you," while your words bring them the speech you have prepared.

—Toastmaster

Relief Devices, Transition, Recoveries

1502. I could say something funny here, but I don't want to change the mood you're in.

1503. I'm not reminded of a story but here in my notes it reminds me to tell one.

1504. Take your time. I don't explain 'em—I just tell 'em!

1505. I'm confused—if you are, there's only one conclusion to be reached. This speech must be profound.

1506. There's one thing about being a poor speaker; you don't have to worry about having an off-night!

1507. You might as well laugh—they won't get any better!

1508. No individual laughing, please—just in groups.

1509. (*When they laugh.*) It's a relief to know that this is an audience, not a jury.

1510. Well, I didn't expect laughs, but frankly, I did anticipate some intellectual nods.

1511. (*When the response is not encouraging.*) My, you're stubborn out there!

1512.   I find his sense of humor greatest
Who laughs the longest at my latest.

                                              —LOYD ROSENFIELD

1513. When several long-winded speakers have preceded you:
At this time I'm reminded of that well-known slogan, LSMFT—
Let's stand, my fanny's tired!

1514. Upon taking a drink of water while speaking: I remember talking at a high school athletic banquet when my mouth became dry and I took a drink just as I did now—the team wit from back in the rear remarked in a loud voice, "First time I ever saw a windmill run by water!"

1515. After telling a good story: "Go ahead and laugh—it's good for you. I told that little story to my secretary the other day, and she laughed so hard—she fell right off my lap!"

1516. When a story evokes only mild laughter: "Now that the hysteria has died down, I'll move on to my next gem—please observe that one joke follows another. After all, what other method is there? It's extremely difficult to tell two at a time."

1517. Finishing up a fiery speech of inspiration, the speaker concluded, "I'm just like a cork; you can't keep me down; though I may be pressed below the waves, I rise again; you will find that I always rise to the surface again, gentlemen!"

From back in the audience came an impatient voice, perhaps from one with whaling experience, "Yeah, you *have* to come to the surface—to blow!"

1518. When much laughter follows a good story: "I hope all you good laughers hang around; there's some mighty weak material coming up."

1519. On one occasion while lecturing to my class at the University of Illinois, during a heavy rainstorm, I remarked, "Well, I guess I've kept you overtime." "Go on, sir, it's still raining outside," encouraged one talkative student.

                                         —M. DALE BAUGHMAN

Hecklers

1520. In my introductory remarks I once was explaining to the audience something of my background and early boyhood in Brown County, Indiana. "Now, I wasn't born in a log cabin, but my folks moved into one just as soon as they could afford it—I started out in life as a barefoot boy"—just then a voice from the rear sounded out, "Brother, none of us was born with shoes on."

—M. DALE BAUGHMAN

1521. Speakers who have trouble holding an audience might remember the story of the speaker who complained, "There are so many rude interruptions, Mr. Chairman, that I can hardly hear myself speaking."

"Don't let it bother you," came a voice from the rear. "You ain't missin' nothing!"

—*Louisville Courier-Journal Magazine*

1522. Sitting at the table just in front of the speaker was a man whose almost constant coughing, sneezing and nose-blowing created more than just a mild disturbance. The speaker's threshold of annoyance was low. When he could stand it no longer, he suggested in a low voice, "Perhaps the open air might be good for your cold."

From the afflicted one came this answer, "This is no ordinary cold—I'm just allergic to hot air."

1523. In the days of the Old Testament it was a miracle if an ass spoke. How times have changed!

1524. Tommy Upton of the Washington Senators squelched a heckler near the bench this spring by telling him this story in soft tones: "You know, when I was a boy, my father had a jackass on our farm and he used to bawl me out for teasing that jackass. He warned me that when that jack died, he'd come back to haunt me in some form. You know, I never believed my father until today."

—*Washington Post*

1525. An inebriate in the audience interrupted the speaker in the midst of his address by crowing like a rooster. Looking at his watch with complete nonchalance, the speaker exclaimed, "Morning already! Impossible! I could never have believed it but the instincts of lower animals are infallible."

1526. One speaker squelched a "hissing" heckler by this direct method: "There are only three things that hiss—a goose, a snake, and a fool. Identify yourself!"

Closers

1527. Toastmaster's final words: "If I've forgotten anything or anybody, it's entirely unnecessary.

—M. Dale Baughman

1528.   I love a finished speaker,
I really and truly do,
Not one who's necessarily polished,
Just one who knows when he's through.

1529. At this point I'll demonstrate my terminal facilities by relating the story of the little boy who ate a green persimmon. He came dashing into the kitchen where he exclaimed to his astonished mother, "Help me! Help me! I'm closin' up!"

1530. I'm now reminded of Lady Godiva's remark as she neared the end of her historic ride, "I'm drawing near my clothes."

1531.   One thing a speaker should remember for sure,
The mind can absorb no more
Than the fanny can endure.

1532. Second wind is what a public speaker acquires when he says "And now in conclusion."

1533. Advice to speakers: In the old farmer's words, "When you're through pumpin', let go the handle."

—*Horizons*

1534.   The effective speaker—
STANDS up to be seen,
SPEAKS out to be heard,
SITS down to be appreciated.

—Nan Johnson

1535.   There are speakers who please me,
To whom I'll allude:
They say, "Now, in conclusion"
And promptly conclude.

—Edward A. Lawrence, *Rotarian*

1536. An orator has to have a copious vocabulary in order to dilute a 2-minute idea sufficiently to fill a 30-minute speech.

—Nuggets

1537. Feeling a possible minor cold coming on, I asked my wife to take my temperature. Quite by accident she picked up the barometer instead of the thermometer. After three minutes were up, she withdrew the instrument and read confidently, "Dry and Windy." I sincerely hope that is not your appraisal of my remarks here this evening.

1538. There are three essentials, in addition to good content and good delivery, of a successful speech. Rule 1—Be sincere, Rule 2—Be brief. Rule 3—Be seated. Having observed Rules 1 and 2, I will now use Rule 3 and be seated.

1539. From all indications you have listened well and patiently. Undoubtedly, there are those among you who do not agree with some of my proposals and conclusions. That is well and good but remember the story of curbstone Johnny. He was crying loud and long when a kind old lady offered her sympathy, "There, there, little boy, I wouldn't cry like that if I were you."

The sullen weeper looked up and barked, "You cry your way, old lady, and I'll cry mine."

1540. (*The question period at the end of some talks can be devastating.*) As a salvage device, if you don't shine, use this story.

Some of my answers may have been unsatisfactory and less complete than you desired. The maid for a well-to-do family quit when she reported for work one morning and found two alligators in the bathtub. It seems that the lady of the house had put them there temporarily upon their arrival from friends in Florida, and then had forgotten them in her haste to go shopping. When the maid quit, she left this note: "Madam, I came to work at the usual time but I have quit. I will not work around alligators. I would have told you this before, but for some reason I did not expect the question ever to come up."

I, too, would have been better prepared, but I did not expect some of these questions to come up.

1541. *Professor to class:* "Well, I see that Will back there in the last row is using his red lead. When he scribbles through one of my lectures with green lead, I know that I may continue. When he switches to red lead, that's a good sign I should stop.

1542. A flashy and verbose politician gave his all in his efforts to sway the audience. When he had finished, he asked a crony, "Well, did I deliver my message well?"

His friend answered enthusiastically, "Yes, quite well."

"I'm glad," said the politician, "for there was nothing in it."

Sports

1543.   I think that I shall never see,
A coach so good that never he
Does have to worry for his job,
Or try to please the supporting mob
Of fans and students and business men.
They have a ten-game winning streak
They lose but one—who is up the creek?
Though they had lost to a better team
It is the coach that's off the beam!

—IRVING THOMPSON

1544. At football games, other players are far outnumbered by quarterbacks; two on the field of play; four on the bench; and 75,000 in the stands.

1545. Though Mickey Mantle has been around for six years, he's still inarticulate and runs like a thief from after-dinner speaking chores. But he is not without a sense of humor. At a big blow-out in St. Petersburg, Larry McQueen, the toastmaster, announced there would be no speeches. Then in the next breath he called upon Mantle for a few words.

Mickey brought his bat around fast. "When Mr. McQueen said there would be no speeches," he said, "I tore mine up."

—*Scholastic Coach*

1546. There's an unusual guest book at the Burlington, Iowa, hospital. It's called the "Anxious Guests' Book." I recently read some of the comments scrawled by fathers-to-be during or after their hours of waiting.

"This is my last one—I promise!"
"The cannons can really boom—it's a boy!"
"I ordered a shortstop, but it seems she'll have to play
with the Bloomer Girls."

—Des Moines Register

1547. It would be interesting if political parties would take a tip
from the world series telecasts and let the candidates tell where their
lather comes from.

—RAYMOND DUNCAN

1548. A young pitcher who had been having a good season in a
Class D league went into a bad slump every time he faced a veteran
batter of an opposing team.

To an associate he glumly confided: "I gotta get out of this league,
if I want to keep pitching. Every time that guy comes up I throw
him my best fast ball—I put everything I have on that pitch—and do
you know what happens?"

"What?" asked the sympathetic friend.

In a voice vibrating with anger, the young pitcher confided: "He
spits tobacco juice on my fast one every time it goes past the plate!"

—Wall Street Journal

1549. A brash rookie stepped out of the batter's box after a called
strike and asked Umpire Moriarty, "How do you spell your name,
Sir?"

The puzzled but unsuspecting umpire gave it to him, letter by
letter.

Sighed the rookie, "Just as I thought; only one "I".

—CLEON WALFOORT, *Eagle*

1550. Jocko Munch, the famous minor league catcher, was in a
terrible batting slump when his club booked an exhibition game
with a nearby insane asylum. In one of the early innings, one of the
inmates jumped out of the stands, set up near the first base line,
made nine imaginary pitches, and returned to his seat. The fellow
repeated his performance for three straight innings.

Jocko turned to one of the attendants and asked, "What's that guy
think he's doing?"

The attendant explained, "He imagines he's a pitcher who's pitching a no-hit game."

"If I don't get a hit in this game," replied Jocko, "he'll have a catcher tomorrow."

—Scholastic Coach

1551.   Come baseball time and I'll defend
This proposition to the end;
A diamond is a boy's best friend.

—CHARLES LEE

1552. Baseball coach to Freshman candidate: "Now, suppose you just go through the motions without trying to hit the ball." "But," objected the intellectual rhime, "that's precisely the difficulty I'm trying to overcome."

1553.   In winter when it's cold out,
Appears the baseball holdout;
In spring when it's warm out,
He gets his uniform out.

1554. Win or lose (and when he was manager of the Chicago Cubs, it was mostly lose) Charlie Grimm always has kept his sense of humor. One time, when the Cubs were digging deep in the barrel for new talent, one of Grimm's scouts excitedly phoned him from somewhere in the sticks.

"Charlie," he shouted, "I've landed the greatest young pitcher in the land. He struck out every man who came to bat—27 in a row. Nobody even got a foul until two were out in the ninth. The pitcher is right here with me. What shall I do?"

Back came Grimm's voice, "Sign up the guy who got the foul. We're looking for hitters."

—JOE MILLER, *Eagle*

1555. Dee Williams, former Cub catcher, silently watched one of his teammates jawing away at Umpire Charlie Berry. Naturally the player lost the argument and everybody started moving back to their positions. It was then that Dee turned to Berry.

"Charlie," he said quietly, "answer me one question: How do you get your square head in that round mask?"

—Scholastic Coach

1556. A baseball manager can shuffle his batting order 362,889 times using nine players; it's no job for a man who can't make up his mind.

1557. There was the old sports writer, for instance, who was asked by a cub, "Is that the West where the sun is setting?" The veteran replied, "If it isn't, you have one helluva story, son."

1558. John Kieran, the erudite, one-time sports writer of the New York Times, was asked to speak at Yale, but some students objected to the compromise with intellectualism in allowing a sports writer to address a group of old Eli's sons . . . So Kieran made his entire speech in Latin.

1559. Johnny Hero, the quarterback of the home town team, was leading his forces in a 6–0 victory over the invaders. Only a few seconds were left when he heaved a pass which was intercepted and run back the length of the field for a touchdown and subsequent point after touchdown. Thus, victory was turned into defeat in a single instant. Later, Johnny was getting his hair cut; the barber opened up on him and finally asked in desperation, "Why did you do it?" Johnny answered rather slowly, "Well, I guess if I had three days to think about it, I wouldn't have done it either."

1560. Colorful scouting report from Steve Belichick of Navy after watching North Carolina: "When Tatum's men warmed up at one end of the field, they tilted it."

1561. Football season: the short warm-up period between spring practice and the winter bowl games.
—HAROLD COFFIN

1562. Indiana University football coaches couldn't help but be impressed by one glowing letter from an alumnus about a prospect he had in mind.
"He's lean and mean," the letter ran, "and in the summer he hunts rattlesnakes for fifty cents a pound."

1563. Hurricane Jackson, heavyweight boxer, had this to say after he was beaten on a TKO by Champion Floyd Patterson: "My legs were lazy. I kept trying to unlazy them, but they just stayed lazy."

1564. It is unfortunate for high school and college basketball coaches that in a few skyscraper centers the head is to the body as the attic is to the house—the highest part and sometimes the most empty.

1565. One may wonder if Thanksgiving wasn't originated by parents whose sons had survived the football season.

1566. Football was once an illegal sport. In 1349, Edward III issued a proclamation which forbade its being played because people were neglecting their archery for this more exciting game. In those days it was very different from our modern organized game, for there were no set rules and no referee. Goals were sometimes several miles apart and any device could be used by players to get the ball. Consequently, broken shins and fractured skulls were common.

Football seems to have been a favorite pastime on the Eve of Lent. In some places, every able-bodied man was compelled to take part in this "game of the year" and often it lasted nearly all day.

1567. One coach's comment on their anticipated trip to the Rose Bowl: "It's a long way to go just to agitate a bag of wind."

1568. I played football in school, and I was known as Neckline Hope. I was always plunging down the middle, but never really showing anything.

—Bob Hope

1569. *Football season:* Time of the year when girls whistle at men in sweaters.

1570.
The football season's on the wane,
December doth approach,
The frost is on the pumpkin,
And the blast is on the coach.

—Author Unknown

1571. According to former line coach Pat Boland of the Iowa Hawkeyes, a football player taking an anatomy test wrote: "The anatomy is divided into three parts—the head, the chest and the abdomen. The head houses the brain and eyes; the chest houses the lungs, heart and liver; the abdomen houses the vowels of which there are five—A, E, I, O and U.

1572. It was a wet and miserable day, and the Notre Dame backs were having a hard time handling the soggy and slippery pigskin. The field captain called time and sent a back to the bench.

"What's the matter?" snapped Coach Hunk Anderson.

"We need rosin in there!" gasped the back.

Anderson leaped to his feet and his eye swept up and down the bench. "Where's Rosin?" he barked. "Get that guy in there!"

1573. A glossary of football terms:

Interference:	Cheering so loud it prevents me from hearing how Notre Dame is doing on my portable radio.
Quarterback:	What I don't get from the program salesman, who never has change.
Forward Pass:	What I complete every few minutes with the bottle the fellow in back of me hands me for his friend, the fellow in front of me.
Substitution:	Whatever they sell for coffee.
Clipping:	Charging me $5 each for end-zone seats.
T-formation:	A method of hiding the ball from the spectator.
Sustained drive:	The three-hour 50-mile crawl home.

—LOYD ROSENFIELD, *New York Times Magazine*

1574. Did you hear the one about the football coach who was collared by an angry rooter after losing a game by a big score? "How many students are enrolled in this university?" asked the old grad politely.

"About 17,000," replied the coach.

"Is it asking too much to put two of them in front of the ball-carrier?" snarled the old grad.

1575. The housekeeper in Football Coach Forest Evashevski's Iowa City home is devoutly religious. After the Rose Bowl victory, fans presented Forest with a Cadillac. He drove the car home, pulled in front of his house and strolled to the front porch. The housekeeper was watching. "What do you think?" Evy questioned. The housekeeper stood silently for a few moments and said, "Just remember, the same people who praised Jesus also crucified him."

1576. *Fran Allison, actress:* "Golf is just a lot of walking, broken up by disappointment and bad arithmetic."

1577. When we were first married, my husband would work in the garden, but now he goes out to play golf. It's a case of diamonds, hearts, spades—and now clubs.

—*Pandorama*

1578. Golfer: A guy who can walk several miles toting a hundred pounds or more of equipment, but who has Junior bring him an ash tray.

1579. Golf is like taxes—you drive hard to make the green and then wind up in the hole.

1580. At the last home talent golf tournament the club secretary caught one of the entrants driving off about a foot in front of the teeing mark.

"Here!" he cried indignantly, "you can't do that. "You're disqualified!"

"What for?" demanded the golfer.

"Why, you just drove off in front of the mark."

The player looked at the secretary with pity. "Go back to the clubhouse," he said tersely, "I'm playing my third stroke."

1581. The golf shark married a girl with a passion for auctions. In his sleep he hollered "Fore!" His bride countered with "Four-Fifty."

1582.
A capital golfer was G:
He drove from a capital T,
And the words he let fall
When he missed the ball
All began with capital D.

—*Penn Punch Bowl*

1583. *Wife, at 2 A.M.:* "Where have you been?"
Husband: "Playing golf."
Wife: "After dark?"
Husband: "Yes, we were using night clubs."

—Gus Schrader, *Cedar Rapids Gazette*

1584. Overheard in the locker room of a men's club—one fat man to another: "I'm in such bad shape that I can't even do the exercises to get into shape again."

—*Milwaukee Journal*

1585. Politics, race, creed, color, and religion all are equal on the playing field. Sports is a common ground on which men and women of all nationalities and many different backgrounds may meet.

—Avery Brundage

1586. The wife of the famous athlete had broken her wristwatch, so she called out to her husband: "Tom, there's only one way I can time your egg—run out and do the mile."

1587. A champion track man was once asked his recipe for winning races. "Well, it's simple," he said, "the thing to do is take the lead at the start and improve your position throughout the race."

1588. *A coach's advice to his athletes:* "Boys, you can't fly with the owls at night and keep up with the eagles in the daytime."

1589. In Italy referees have the power to arrest spectators who boo, hiss or otherwise show annoyance.

1590. Coaches are doing quite well financially these days, I hear; I have just learned of a coach who started poor at the age of 20, and retired with a comfortable fortune of $50,000.

This was accumulated through industry, economy, conscientious effort, perseverance and the death of an uncle who left him $49,990.

1591. The maharajah of an interior Indian province decreed that no wild animals could be killed. Soon the country was overrun by man-eating tigers, lions, panthers and boars. The people could stand it no longer and gave the maharajah the heave-ho. And this was the first instance on record where the reign was called on account of game.

—Philnews

1592. "Honest, coach, a fellow just gave me this cigarette to hold while he stepped into the library for a moment."

—Parke Cummings

1593.
There is a fellow that I know
Born just about as long ago
As I and with me, bound to grow,
The boy inside o' me.
Sometimes I wish he were not there,
For when in games I'm not quite fair,
He says to me, Stop! Is that square?
That boy inside o' me.
It really does no good to hide
A thing from him because I've tried,

> And I'm so glad I'm on his side,
> That boy inside o' me.
>
> *—Sunshine Scrapbook*

1594. A Chinese student defined an American University as follows: "An American University is a vast athletic association, where, however, some studies are maintained for the benefit of the feeblebodied."

—Indiana Telephone News

1595.
> I think that I shall never see
> A satisfactory referee,
> About whose head a halo shines,
> Whose merits rates reporters' lines;
> One who calls them as they are
> And not as I should wish by far.
>
> A gent who leans not either way,
> But lets the boys decide the play;
> A guy who'll sting the coach who yaps
> From Siwash High to old Millsaps;
> Poems are made by fools like me,
> But only God could referee.
>
> *—Author Unknown*

1596. Roger Counsil of Wood River, Illinois has been named Southern Illinois University's most valuable athlete for the year. He was considered too heavy for most of his specialties—diving, the trampoline, tumbling and the pole-vault. But he made out all right, never losing a diving event in 26 dual meets over the three years.

"Actually," Counsil remarked on receiving the award, "my only talent is for going up and coming down."

1597. A wrestler had spent a long evening with friends at the village inn. They showed him a quick way home across the fields, forgetting that the local bull was loose.

The bull attacked, but found itself gripped by the horns and lugged about the field until it managed to free itself and bolt.

"Pity I had those last two drinks," said the wrestler. "I ought to have got that chap off his bike."

1598. Told that mummies 8 feet tall have been exhumed in the West, a basketball fan figures the boys struck a prehistoric Y.M.C.A.

1599. Intercepted during an Amateur Athletic Union raid on University mailboxes was this interesting letter, relayed to us by an entirely unreliable impeachable source:

Dear Coach Broadshoulders:

Remember our discussion of your football men who were having troubles in English? I have decided to ask you, in turn for help.

We feel that Paul Spindleshanks, one of the most promising scholars, has a chance for a Rhodes Scholarship, which would be a great thing for him and for our college.

Paul has the academic record for this award, but we find that the aspirant is also required to have other excellence, and ideally should have a good record in athletics. Paul is weak. He tries hard, but he has troubles in athletics.

We propose that you give some special consideration to Paul as a varsity player, putting him if possible in the backfield of the football team. In this way, we can show a better college record to the committee deciding on the Rhodes Scholarships.

We realize that Paul will be a problem on the field, but as you have often said—cooperation between our department and yours is highly desirable, and we do expect Paul to try hard, of course.

During intervals of study we shall coach him as much as we can. His work in the English Club and on the debate team will force him to miss many practices, but we intend to see that he carries an old football around to bounce (or whatever one does with a football, during intervals in his work).

We expect Paul to show entire good will in his work with you, and though he will not be able to begin football practice till late in the season, he will finish the season with good attendance.

Sincerely,
Howdoyou Like Themapples, Chairman,
English Department
—*Daily Illini*

1600. *Mr. Newrich was advising his son's tutor:* "There's no sense in teaching the boy to count over 100. He can hire accountants to do his bookkeeping."

"Yes, sir," murmured the tutor, "but he'll want to play his own game of golf, won't he?"

—*Man's Shop*

1601. Very few football teams simply go out on Saturday and WIN games, but according to the sports writers teams went out and clipped, captured and bested; dropped, downed, drubbed, dampened, and drowned; edged, nipped, notched, and knocked; overpowered, routed, ripped, rapped, wrecked; romped, rambled, and rumbled; surprised, topped, toppled, turned on, and upset opponents.

1602. The real measure of an athlete is not what he can do in comparison to others but against his own best self.

1603. It's not the size of the dog in the fight, it's the size of the fight in the dog.

1604. An athlete's size is determined by the size of the thing it takes to get his goat.

1605. There's an old story about the farm-boy who was so fast that when he went hunting, his father made him run alongside the rabbits and feel them to see if they were fat enough before picking them up to take home.

Glenn Cunningham once said, "I have done that myself. I can't outrun a jackrabbit. But I can out-last a young one. He jumps away at a 40-mile clip, and then rests. I just run along until he finally wears out and I grab him up."

—EARL RUBY, *Louisville* (Kentucky) *Courier-Journal*

1606. A man had two cats and two exit-holes in the door because when he said "Scat!" he meant "Scat!"

A coach can save a lot of precious minutes if the boys come on the run when he blows his whistle instead of playing around. This "Scat" technique teaches alertness and hustle.

1607. Young Elroy Hirsch snaked through the woods of his native Wausau, Wisconsin, switching a football from arm to arm as he sidestepped and dodged the trees on the way to school. He often put on a sudden burst of speed, trying to outdistance his own shadow.

Elroy never got away from his shadow. Neither was he ever tackled by a tree. He grew up to become the pass-catching, touchdown-scoring right end of the professional champion Los Angeles Rams.

1608. The substitute: He is the person who waits upon the bench with his hand upon his cane, watches every play, listens to all the cheers, always hoping to get in. He watches his teammates execute plays which he has helped to work, during practice, to perfection. For months he's had the lowly place of submerging himself in loyal desire that teamwork might be made complete, and yet he has not heard his name in the crowd's acclaim. The crowd sees him waiting for his chance, the chance perhaps that will never come, but nevertheless he gives his best. He is content when thousands laud his teammates, but let us remember that successful teams were never built without the "Sub" who prays, hopes, works, and waits.

1609. My legs are the weakest part of me; I run more from the hips up than from the hips down. That is how it has to be with everybody—you go where your heart takes you, not your legs. . . . A handicap can become a great blessing if you keep a strong heart and run like a man, not a jackrabbit.

—GLENN CUNNINGHAM

1610. It was a quiet baseball afternoon more than 50 years ago in the community of Lowndesborough, Alabama, when umpire Sam White called one against a local hero named Frank McCoy. McCoy appeared displeased. So were the home town fans.

A voice came from the grandstand, "Kill the umpire!"

So Frank swung his bat at Umpire White's head—and did just that.

Thus was the pattern handed down by baseball forebears to present-day times, when an umpire is a figure of lonely but lofty eminence, fortified by regal tradition against the slings and arrows of outraged baseballers.

1611. Plug thinking produces plug players. If you have thoroughbred players, they must think noble thoughts.

1612. Good guarding is like making love. You must keep close to your opponent.

1613. They say he certainly looked like a prize fighter or star athlete over in his corner or on the field or floor before the fight or game started, but in this particular fight, as the bell rang, he just couldn't take or stand those body punches and about the middle of the third round he just passed out of the picture. Stamina, ability to take punishment, and all those vital requisites were totally lacking. Pre-battle appearance didn't count for much after the fight began.
Moral: It's performance that counts!

1614. I don't believe in baiting an opponent. It is cheap. I do think every player should look at his opponent and say to himself, "I'm your guard. You're going to see a lot of me tonight. In fact, you'll be sick of me before the evening is over."
—Author Unknown

1615. Description of a team with dissension: They are combatable teammates.

1616. Napoleon, being asked the importance of morale, said, "Three to one in favor of morale as against material."

1617. A great athlete had this to say, "If I ever have any ability, don't give me all the credit. I am entitled to precious little. My success has been made possible by all who have contributed to making basketball the great game that it is—the coaches, fans, officials, my teammates and especially the reserves who have made it possible for me to practice day after day and develop my talents. I am but a drop in the bucket compared to the ocean of mankind that has made my performance possible."

1618. The newspaper Soviet Sports indicated that American "futbol" is a rough, bad game that cripples players both physically and spiritually. The Russians previously described "beizbol" as a "beastly battle, a bloody fight and mayhem and murder."

1619. Ralph Beard, former All-American basketball player at the University of Kentucky, was generally hailed as the country's No. 1 player one year. However, at the end of the season, the squad chose Alex Groza as the team's most valuable player.

1620. If the baseball code permitted substitutions after each play, as football rules once allowed, maybe I could win more games. I have it all figured out. On defense I would use my crack fielders. Then at bat I could send in some of my lumbering sluggers, who are not much good for anything else.

As soon as a batter reached first, I could substitute one of the school's sprinters. He would speed to second on a flashy steal, eliminating the need to sacrifice. The next sub, say, gets a stingy single, sending the sprinter to third. I now put in another rabbit on first, and send in my one and only perfect slider to run for the man on third. The next batter gives way to a dead-eye bunter.

Now I pull a real fast one. I have the rabbit on first steal second, then signal for a fake squeeze play. The batter pulls a perfect fake, keeping the catcher behind the plate, and my wonderful slider crosses the dish in a cloud of dirt.

After picking up a batch of runs, we go on defense again—with my defensive team taking the field, of course. Not liking the looks of the opponent's heavy slugger, I let my pitcher run up a 1 and 1 count, then put in a little runt who has a nasty habit of putting the ball low on the outside corner. He does that and the count runs to 1 and 2. Now I substitute a fast-ball artist, who delivers that bullet of his and the mighty slugger goes down swinging.

How about it, men. Couldn't we have some fun with a free-sub rule?"

—C. H. STREET

1621. A woman called the sports department of the Arkansas Democrat and asked, "What was the date of the golf tournament held in Texarkana?" They looked it up and told her. "Thanks," she said, "I just wanted to figure when to expect my baby."

1622. Astronomers have often speculated about a baseball game on the moon. Each team would need dozens of outfielders, some stationed more than a quarter of a mile from the batter's box, because when the batter connects the ball will fly 1500 feet or more.

Since the base-running batter is so light that he can take a 30-foot stride, it's only three steps to first base and 12 for a circuit. The poor pitcher would have to rely on his straight ball, because there is no air on the moon; he couldn't pitch a curve. On the other hand, his shortstop would be able to jump 20 feet into the air to snag an infield fly.

The average Dodger fan wouldn't have much fun at the moon baseball game; he couldn't holler at the umpire.

For that matter, the catcher would have to talk to the pitcher in sign language even when they went into a huddle. Same old reason; there isn't any air.

—Science Yearbook of 1948

1623. Lefty Gomez used to tell about the plot he and Bill Dickey designed for slugger Hank Greenberg. Explained Gomez, "When I got two strikes on Hank, Dickey was to step out of the catcher's box as if to receive the pitch-out. If Hank relaxed, Bill was to jump back in time to receive a fast one over the plate for the third strike. In answer to the inevitable question, "How did it work?" Gomez would sorrowfully answer, "How do I know? I never could get two strikes on the guy."

1624. Years ago a college in Kentucky awarded an honorary degree to that great horse, the late Man o' War. A professor, who had been at the college for many years and had seen many of these honorary degrees awarded with little discrimination, was discussing the affair with friends.

"Do you, as a scholar," he was asked, "feel annoyed at seeing an honorary degree awarded to an animal, even so distinguished a one as Man o' War?"

"Not at all," the professor replied. "This is the first time they've granted the honor to an entire horse."

1625. Bernie Bierman had a classic answer to the frequent question, "How do you get such big men for your Minnesota football teams?" "It's like this, friend. When I go driving along country roads, I look for boys walking behind plows. When I see one, I stop and ask him the way to Minneapolis. If he leaves the plow and points the way in the usual manner, I thank him and drive on. But if he picks up the plow and points with it, I just load him in the car and head straight for the registrar's office."

1626. Football games are something like necking parties. The only difference is the height at which the tackles are made.

1627. I was exhorting one of my usually good defensive players to a better effort. "You can't let your man run loose to score. Your teammates are working hard to get a few points. They need your support!"

"So do I, Coach," replied the boy. "Mine's home; I forgot it when I packed my gear this afternoon."

—Joseph Zaleski

1628. Oh, yes, he's a great fighter! The last fight he had was a couple of weeks ago. The man was several pounds heavier than he was, and several inches taller. But it didn't frighten him in the least. And he succeeded in knocking the man down. The fellow arose but he immediately bowled him over again. The third time the man arose, he not only knocked him down, but broke his crutches and took all his pencils away from him.

1629. College football makes hardy young people. You can't sit three hours on cold concrete, eating cold hamburgers and peanuts and be a weakling.

1630. One year when the youngsters of a certain Illinois village met for the purpose of electing a captain for their baseball team for the coming season, it appeared that there were an excessive number of candidates for the post, with more than the usual wrangling.

Youngster after youngster presented his qualifications for the post, and the matter was still undecided when the son of the owner of the ball-field stood up. He was a small, snub-nosed lad, with a plentiful supply of freckles, but he glanced about him with a dignified air of controlling the situation.

"I'm going to be captain this year," he announced convincingly, "or else Father's old bull is going to be turned into the field."

He was elected unanimously.

—Fenimore Martin

1631. *Baseball fanatic:* "Take the average person and if you ask them, they'll tell you a baseball has 108 stitches, which shows how wrong people can be, for I'm here to tell you there's 109 stitches, there being one stitch inside that can't be seen."

1632. To put is to place a thing where you want it. To putt is a vain attempt to do the same thing.

1633. *Star Athlete:* "What's my temperature, Doc?"
Doc: "Hundred and three."
Star Athlete: "What's the world's record?"

1634. "I've got on a pair of golf socks."
"Golf socks?"
"Yeah—eighteen holes in 'em."

1635. Discussing his tennis technique, a stout, amiable, bald man panted, "My brain immediately barks out a command to my body. 'Run forward, but fast!' it says. 'Start right now! Drop the ball gracefully over the net and then walk back slowly!' "
"And then what happens?" he was asked.
"And then," replied the stout man, "my body says, 'Who—me?' "

1636. Every time the novice golfer swung his brassie, he missed the ball and hit an anthill killing scores of ants. The ants were wild with fright because each swing annihilated hundreds of them. Said one frightened ant to another, "Brother, let's get on the ball—it's the only safe place I know."

1637.
I think that I shall never see
A thing more ugly than a tree;
The certain tree I have in mind
My golf ball always stops behind.

1638. A crisis arose and a young pitcher was at home alone for the first time with his three-months-old son. He put in a frantic call to his battery mate, the father of three children.

The catcher instructed, "First, place the diaper in the position of a baseball diamond, with you at bat. Next, fold second base over home plate; now place the baby on the pitcher's mound, and finally pin first base and third base to home plate." Another victory.

1639. Perhaps the funniest story in the memory book of the Harlem Globetrotters concerns the night in Montana when they got caught in a blizzard. Their old Ford went off the road into the side of a sheep-herder's cabin. The team, the sheep-herder and nine sheep were stranded in the cabin for three days . . . 14 people and nine sheep in a room 20x13.

"I lost my taste for mutton right there," said owner Abe Saperstein.

1640.   You can pitch a no-hit game,
But it's just another loss
If the errors of your teammates
Put opponent's runs across.
You might be a brilliant runner
Pass and kick with easy grace,
But you'll miss the winning touchdown,
If a teammate's out of place.
In the sporting world or business,
In the office or a mill,
Nothing can produce a winner,
Like a little teamwork will.

—Author Unknown

1641. A football coach, who was named Coach of the Week, explained how his team of lightweights, spearheaded by a 114 lb. quarterback, sprang the upset of the year after a winless season.

"I got myself a whole new backfield. I picked the four skinniest youngsters on the squad and that's really what did the trick. You know, I had the weakest offensive line in the whole state but I had some big boys in the backfield. My line wasn't big enough to open big holes to run through, so I figured, we are opening teenie-weenie holes, so why not use teenie-weenie backs to run through those teenie-weenie holes. It worked, and we scored three touchdowns with my 4 by 6's. Not a back was over six inches wide and four inches thick. I measured 'em. It was a perfect fit."

1642. In the early morning of human existence, on a bright spring day, a cave boy full of animal energy came out of his cave and saw a coconut, and having nothing better to do gave it a kick. Another cave boy happened to be coming out of his cave at the same time and seeing the coconut rolling toward him gave it a kick toward the place from whence it came. Thus or in some such way began the game of ball among homo sapiens. . . .

One English writer points out that the game of football dates back at least 600 years in the British Islands and states that in all probability the game was played by the Roman Legionnaires 2000 years ago. Among the early Saxons Shrove Tuesday was a day set aside for football. This special event dated back to a great victory

269

in battle that the Saxons won over the Danes; and tradition states that the ball used that day was the head of a dead Dane.

—WILLIAM H. BATESON, *School Activities*

1643. Baseball fans who have been driven slightly daffy by their wives' impressions of the great American game may be more tolerant with the Mrs. after this glimpse of the diamond through Chinese eyes.

Our Allies in the Far East have been viewing the American boys clouting homers and stealing bases for a number of years, and they've become slightly confused. For instance, the Chinese believe that the pitcher is duty bound to try to hit the bat with the ball. If he succeeds in doing so he is properly punished by the batter who runs like a fiend to all four bases. On each of these bases stands one of the pitcher's friends waiting to stop the runner by preventing the ball from hitting him. But if one of the pitcher's friends seems likely to miss catching the ball, the runner will then slide under him and take cover.

The catcher dons a hideous mask in order to disconcert his own pitcher. Should the batter be foolish enough to allow himself to be hit by a pitched ball, he is put in disgrace. He is not permitted to stand at bat any longer but must humbly trot to the base in a crippled and painful state. Should the next batter connect with the ball, the runner is doubly punished by being compelled to dash to the next base.

The roar of "Ding How" emanates from the stands when the ball has failed to touch the bat in three swings.

Pelting the umpire with pop bottles is not part of the Chinese reaction to the game. Instead, they pay homage to the star player—by tossing firecrackers his way.

—BEN GOULD

1644. Definition of a football player: A contortionist, because he is always going around his own end.

1645. Golf is a game in which a ball 1½ inches in diameter is placed on a ball 8,000 miles in diameter. The object is to hit the small ball, not the large one.

1646. Comment of a football coach after watching his team work out the last time prior to the opening game: "I wouldn't let my mother-in-law run behind that line!"

1647. A school administrator must solve many problems and make many decisions. He needs courage to do both.

Weak men do not make good umpires. At least one major league umpire, Charlie Moran, regards himself and his decisions highly. He makes it clear that he's boss. One might say that he has a confident bearing. In one close play at home, runner and catcher waited for Moran's decision. The ump hesitated, and the catcher barked, "Well, is it safe or is it out?" Moran snapped back, "Till I call it, it ain't nuthin'."

1648. The football team had fumbled all evening; when a sub, warming up in front of the bench dropped a ball, it was too much for an old grad, now a rabid fan: "Send him in, Coach," he yelled from the stands, "he's ready."

1649.
> The football team of Yarvard
> Once played a ladies team.
> The guards and tackles made 'em blink,
> The center was a dream.
> And Lo! the ladies beat them
> by 24 to 9
> For Yarvard lost 200 yards
> For holding in the line.

1650. The golfer stepped up to the tee, raised his club carefully and let drive. The ball soared over the fairway, bounced high onto the green, and rolled into the hole. The delighted golfer began to wave his clubs and shout.

"What's the matter?" asked his wife. "Have you gone crazy?"

"I've just made a hole in one," he yelled.

Catching his enthusiasm, his wife said, "Do it again, won't you? I didn't see it."

Statistics

1651. Statistical thinking will one day be as necessary for efficient citizenship as the ability to read and write.

—H. G. WELLS

1652. An economist is a man who begins by knowing a very little about a great deal, and gradually gets to know less and less about more and more until he finally gets to know practically nothing about practically everything.

Whereas, a statistician, on the other hand, begins by knowing a very great deal about very little, and gradually gets to know more and more about less and less, until he finally gets to know practically everything about nothing.

—United Benefit News

1653. Statistics, like chloroform, lull many people to sleep in blissful ignorance. Commenting upon this human frailty to rely too much upon the logic of statistics, Dr. Jay B. Nash of New York University gives us the following story:

An inebriate lay at night in a hotel which had a sprinkler system in the room as a fire safety device, and under the glass on the dresser were the statistics of how many people had slept with peace in the room, the hours of sleep and all the other details. After reading this several times he sauntered off to bed saying,

Now, I lay me down to sleep, statistics make my slumber sweet

If I die, I am not concerned

I may get wet, but I won't get burned.

Look behind statistics! Find out how they're made up and on what definitions they are based. Don't take them at face value.

—Ben Solomon, Youth Leaders Digest

1654. The statisticians have now found that nine out of every ten women are knock-kneed. And all the time people have thought that statisticians never had any fun.

1655. You should use statistics as a drunk uses a lamp post—for support rather than illumination.

—Schoolmaster

1656. Statistics are like a Bikini bathing suit. What they reveal is suggestive, but what they conceal is vital.

1657. If all statisticians were placed end to end, they would undoubtedly reach a confusion!

1658. A statistican is a man who draws a mathematically precise line from an unwarranted assumption to a foregone conclusion.

Strategy

1659. *High school junior to recruiting officer:* "But you can't turn me down—I've proposed to three girls, told my principal what I think of him, and sold my car!"

1660. The man wondered why it was that his friend had so much luck with the used cars he bought. He never seemed to have any trouble with them. So one day he asked him how he always managed to choose so wisely.

"I don't understand it," the man said. "After all, you know very little about cars."

"That's true," admitted the other, "but I've got a system. You see, I get a car on approval and then right away drive to another used car dealer and tell him I want to sell it. In the next minute he's telling me everything that's wrong with it."

—Mark Jetty

Student Masterpieces

1661. The assignment for the sixth grade hygiene group was a composition on anatomy. One promising lad submitted the following masterpiece:

"Your head is kind of round and hard, and your brains are in it and your hair on it. Your face is the front of your head and where you make faces and eat. Your neck is what keeps your head out of your collar. It's hard to keep clean. Your shoulders are sort of shelfs where you hook your suspenders on them.

Your stummick is something that if you do not eat often enough it hurts, and spinach don't help none. Your spine is a long bone in your back that keeps you from folding up. Your back is always behind you no matter how fast you turn around. Your arms you got to have to pitch with and so you can reach the batter. Your fingers stick out of your hand so you can throw a curve and add up rithmatick. Your legs is what if you have not got two of, you cannot get to first base. Your feet are what you run on, your toes are what always get stubbed. And that's all there is of you, except what's inside, and I never saw it."

—Pharmagraph

1662. The teacher, in the last week of school, was trying almost desperately to give her class an impression of fractions which would last through the summer. She told them they could think of fractions at home as well as in school and gave such examples as "half a sandwich," "a quarter of a pie," and "tenth part of a dollar." At that point one little boy "caught on" and proudly contributed, "My father came home last night with a fifth."

1663. The judges of a school essay contest felt one nine-year-old's composition on the subject of "Manners" had special merit and awarded him first prize. Here it is in full: "I have good manners. I say good night and good morning and hello and good-by, and when I see dead things lying around the house, I bury them."

—Scholastic Teacher

1664. A third-grade teacher carefully explained that a group of sheep is a *flock* and a group of quail a *bevy*. Then she asked for the names of groups of other animals. When she came to camels, a child timidly suggested, "A carton."

—Joseph Charles Salak, The Instructor

1665. My fifth-graders were discussing the different meanings the word "boom" could have. The children mentioned booms made by explosions, log booms, and the like.

"Then," said Roger, "there was the one that Clancy lowered."

—Aurel Weiford, N.E.A. Journal

1666. Then there was the little girl who asked, "What's a butter dream?" She had joined in the singing of the round, "Row, row, row, your boat, gently down the stream; merrily, merrily merrily, merrily, life's a butter dream," or so it had sounded to her.

—Alice S. Clark

1667. A teacher reading to her class, came across the word "unaware." She asked if anyone knew the meaning. One pupil timidly came up with this definition:

"Unaware is what you put on first and take off last."

—Texas Outlook

1668. The high school Literature teacher assigned tardy pupils to examine Shakespeare's works for references to the alarm clock.

"Silence that dreadful bell." (*Othello*)

"Methought I heard a voice say 'Sleep no more.'" (*Macbeth*)

"A plague upon this howling." (*Tempest*)

1669. The high school seniors of our school were putting on their annual dramatic production. The comely heroine, in one dramatic scene, seeking a respectable job in a large city, was at last forced to ask the hotel keeper for employment. According to the script, the young lady was told that her help was not needed, whereupon she was to drop to her knees with a final plea of desperation: "Oh, master, couldn't you use a waitress?" Rehearsals had been perfect, even at this critical point, but on the eventful night, the hopeful young actress became somewhat confused: "Oh, waiter," she cried, "couldn't you use a mistress?"

1670. A first-grader, asked to discuss local news stood up before his classmates and reported: "Last night Mommy had a baby, and now I think my Aunt's coming down with it."

1671. *Part of an essay:* In *mid-evil* days the country was organized on the old *futile* system. A *pheasant* with a gun was equal to a noble on a horse.

—Hoyer Grams, *Sunshine Magazine*

1672. A first-grade teacher was looking over the shoulder of a little boy who had drawn a picture of a church. The steeple was tall and above it was a horrible black mass. "What," asked the teacher, "is that above the church steeple?" "The cost," replied the child." "The cost?" queried the teacher. "Yes," said the boy. "That's what my Dad keeps saying is higher than the church steeple."

1673. "The parts of a letter," wrote one of my third-grade boys recently on a test, "are hello, middle, goodbye, stamp."

—Katherine McCaskill, *The Instructor*

Stunts

1674. If you're the speaker or the master of ceremonies at a large gathering where members of the audience are sitting in rows of chairs, you can often find an opportunity to try this amusing stunt:

Ask the audience to stand and engage in some simple exercise, such as thumb wiggling—suddenly command each one to turn around and shake hands with the person behind him. Surprise and slight confusion result when each finds the other has turned around and there is no one to shake with.

1675. The occasion may arise where you wish to pep up the audience. If so, remember the old gimmick used in sales clinics here and there: Ask the audience to follow you as you thrust your fist forward with an explosive punch, accompanied by the words, "Boy, do I feel good!"

1676. Einstein's formula for success: $X + Y + Z$ equals SUCCESS: in the formula X stands for hard work and Y stands for play. Someone always asks, "Well, what does the Z stand for?" "Oh, that," you say, surprised, "represents when to listen."

1677. You may startle some hearers when you make the statement that teachers should be given a raise every week. You go on to explain that you do not refer to this kind of raise—$raise; but rather you mean this kind of raise—*PRAISE!*

1678. Here is an interesting experiment that has proved very rewarding to me on many occasions: Ask members of your audience to write, quickly, names of two wild animals, two colors, two flowers, two pieces of furniture, and two carpenters' tools.

In any group the great majority always write lion and tiger, red and blue, rose and violet, chair and table, hammer and saw.

You can remark, "This proves that human nature is about the same all over."

1679. It's time to plant for success—(this can be used when speaking to youth groups.)

First plant five rows of peas: preparedness, promptness, perseverance, politeness, and prayer.

Next to them plant three rows of squash: squash gossip, squash criticism, squash indifference.

Then plant five rows of lettuce: Let us be faithful, Let us be unselfish, Let us be loyal, Let us love one another, Let us be truthful.

No garden is complete without turnips: Turn up for church, turn up for smiles, turn up with new ideas, and turn up with determination.

—Illinois Parent Teacher

1680. CHAMP or CHUMP—It's up to "U."

1681. Did I hear you say that you work too hard?

366	Let's start with 366 days in the year: you sleep eight hours
− 122	per day, which is one-third of the day. One-third of 366
244	days is 122 days. This leaves 244 days. You allot one-third
− 122	of the day for rest and recreation. This takes off another
122	122 days, leaving only 122 days. There are 52 Sundays
− 52	which are not work days. Subtracting 52 more days leaves
70	70.
− 26	Every Saturday you get a half-holiday which means we
44	can subtract 26 more days, leaving now only 44 days.
− 28	Undoubtedly, you allow one and one-half hours daily for
16	lunch and coffee breaks; this amounts in one year's time
− 14	to 28 days. Subtracting lunch and coffee time, there are
2	16 days left, but nearly everyone gets 14 days vacation a
− 2	year and when this is subtracted only 2 work days are
0	left. When Christmas and New Year's Day are subtracted, you actually find that you don't work at all.

1682. "She told me that she loved me," sounds harmless enough and is a complete sentence. But, University of South Dakota English professor, Sherwood Cummings, says one word, "only," used before each word in the sentence gives it seven different meanings. The word trick is used to teach college freshmen the importance of placing modifiers correctly in a sentence.

—Phi Delta Kappan

1683. The instructor drew a line on the blackboard and turned to his psychology class. "I'm going to ask each of you to estimate the length of that line." Rapidly he polled the class. Estimates ranged from 53 inches to 84 inches. The instructor put them down. Then he totaled them and divided the result by the number of students in the class. The average estimate, he announced, was 61⅙ inches, although no one had given that exact figure.

Then he measured the line. It was 61¼ inches long. It's a practical example of the old saying that "Two heads are better than one."

—Property

1684. It isn't true that optimists are more popular than pessimists. Ask ten persons to name the Seven Dwarfs, and nine of them will remember Grumpy and only two of them can recall Happy.

1685. Do you know, or care to know, the algebraic equivalent of the Greek letter Pi? Pi is used to denote the ratio of the circumference of a circle to its diameter. The numerical equivalent is 3.1415926. To recall this fact, if you should be quizzed remember this sentence: "May I have a large container of coffee?" The figures correspond to the number of letters in the words of that sentence.

1686. A high school principal achieved a life-long goal when he bought a $75 suit for $20. He put it on; going down the street he met a colleague who looked him over and caustically remarked, "What's wrong with that suit?" "Why, nothing—I just bought it at a real bargain!"

"Well," said the friend, "for one thing, the lapels don't match—one is higher than the other."

The principal went back for alterations, but the salesman informed him that there were no free alterations on a $75 suit marked down to $20. He suggested, "Just hike up one shoulder like this." (*Demonstrates.*) The principal followed instructions and went out on the street again with one shoulder up. He chanced to meet another acquaintance who immediately noticed his new suit and complimented him on it; however, he remarked, "The sleeves appear to be a little short."

Back went the principal again for alterations, but just as before the salesman was uncooperative; no free alterations on a "sale" suit. "Just draw your arms up into the sleeves a little," he advised. (*Demonstrate.*)

The principal tried it and went out in better spirits. He encountered another old friend who also commented on the suit but observed that the trousers were too long. Again the uncompromising clerk gave more advice, "Just hike them up a little in the crotch." (*Demonstrate.*)

278

This time he came out with one shoulder high, arms pulled up into his sleeves, and trousers pulled up high in the crotch. (*Demonstrate.*) An old lady looked him over carefully and exclaimed, "Look at that poor crippled man, but what a beautiful suit he has on!"

Success

1687. Success comes before work only in the dictionary.

1688. . . . Pay dirt is not all "pay." It abounds in losses, failures, tragedies. It is a testing ground of character and competency.

In football it is the place where opposition stiffens in answer to the chant of "Hold that line." It is the place where the untrained and the untried are most likely to grow tense from the strain and make mistakes. It is the place where the individual who cannot stand success thinks the rest of the trip will be "easy sailing." In this territory, the borderland of victory, both overconfidence and overeagerness beget fumbles and blunders.

—GLENN LONG, *Healthways*

1689. Success is not a commodity to be bought in stores, nor is it a talent bestowed only upon a fortunate few.

1690. Do your best.
Lives of great men all remind us
When we think the matter over,
That they passed where lots of grind was,
Ere they got into the clover.

—*Optimist*

1691. Every man has an equal chance to become greater than he is.

—*Sunshine Private Press*

1692. The conditions of success are always easy—we have to toil awhile, endure awhile, believe awhile.

—*School Musician*

1693. If you want to be not only successful, but personally, happily, and permanently successful, then do your job in a way that puts lights in people's faces. Do that job in such a way that, even when you are out of sight, folks will always know which way you went by the lamps left behind.

—KENNETH McFARLAND, *Bulletin, N.A.S.S.P.*

1694. The best counsel I can give is the advice of a friend in writing to a young man who had just been promoted: "Keep on doing what it took to get started."

–John L. McCaffrey, *Houston Times*

1695. William Green, 23, a student at the Royal College of Art, revealed his painting technique. First, he puts a large, fresh white canvas on the floor; then does the following in the order named:
1. Pour paint and a tint of printer's ink on it.
2. Jump up and down on the paint, dance on it, and skip over the surface.
3. Ride over the canvas on a bicycle, skidding to scatter the paint; later use the bicycle to spread it around further.
4. Soak the canvas in paraffin.
5. Shovel sand on the painting to give "added texture."

His paintings sell for up to 100 pounds. ($280.)

–*United Press*

1696. A Successful Man:
> A man who can afford a man
> To mow the lawn and dig the weeds
> So he can take the weekend off
> And play a round or two of golf
> And get the exercise he needs.

–George Starbuck Galbraith

1697. Behind every successful man can usually be found three people: his wife and Mr. and Mrs. Jones.

1698.
> This thing called success
> Consists, I have found,
> In making mistakes
> When no one's around.

–Stephen Schiltzer, *Saturday Evening Post*

1699. The man who is afraid of making a big mistake will never make a big success; more opportunities are lost by over-preciseness than through carelessness.

–Sydney J. Harris

1700. I certainly wasn't born with a silver spoon in my mouth; just a rickety wooden ladder which I have tried to climb.

–M. Dale Baughman

1701. Advice given to me by an Uncle was this: Continue to work toward the top of the ladder; you'll find the top steps aren't as crowded as the bottom ones, since there are fewer folks at the top.
—M. DALE BAUGHMAN

1702. The world is filled with people who have worked hard but have little to show for it. Something more than hard work is necessary; it is creative thinking and firm belief in your ability to execute your ideas. The successful people in history have succeeded through their thinking. Their hands were merely helpers to their brains.
—CLAUDE BRISTOL, *The Magic of Believing*

1703. It all depends on what you call success. But when you're picking the school kid most likely to succeed, don't overlook the one whose dog waits longest outside the school door.
—BURTON HILLIS, *Better Homes and Gardens*

1704. A young man starting out today should analyze his own problems, prepare himself, perfect his thinking—and be ready and willing to face the inevitable failures and discouragements. I would not depend too much on a fairy godmother pointing out the Road to Success. I would be more inclined to do some surveying and map-making of my own.
—CHARLES KETTERING, *Short Stories of Science and Fiction*

1705. Wealth, notoriety, place and power are no measure of success whatever. The only true measure of success is the ratio between what we might have done on the one hand and the thing we have made of ourselves on the other.
H. G. WELLS, quoted by WILLIAM H. DANFORTH in *I Dare You*

1706. Success is getting what you want out of life without violating the rights of others.

1707. Abraham Fuller, English scholar: "The real difference between men is energy. A strong will, a settled purpose, and invincible determination, can accomplish almost anything; and in this lies the distinction between great and little men."

1708. The secret of success can be stated in nine words: Stick to it, Stick to it, Stick to it.

281

1709. Some day, I hope to enjoy enough of what the world calls success so that somebody will ask me, "What's the secret of it?" I shall say simply this: "I get up when I fall down."

—Paul Harvey

1710. Many a wife has helped her husband get to the top of the ladder. Then she left him standing there while she decided whether the picture would look better there, or somewhere else.

1711. Do you know how to fail? If you do, then you will know also the secret of succeeding, for the two are forever locked together. On a thousand gridirons, coaches each fall prepare their charges to take the field of battle in the grand sport of football. Do you know the first lessons those candidates for the team will be taught? Not how to make a touchdown—that is easy. The first thing they must learn is to fall down, and for days the coaches will be teaching their teams how to be tackled, how to fall limp so as not to be hurt, how to expect to fall and then rise again and press onward toward the goal.

—Rev. William E. Phifer, Jr., *Christian Observer*

1712. The most difficult part of getting to the top of the ladder is getting through the crowd at the bottom.

1713. If you don't care to have your face stepped on, don't try to climb the ladder of success.

—*Cincinnati Enquirer*

1714. All that stands between the high school graduate and the top of the ladder is the ladder.

1715. In picking a life career for yourself, pick a tough one. Then you won't have too much competition.

1716.
I eat my peas with honey,
I have done it all my life;
They do taste kind of funny,
But it keeps them on my knife.

1717. The father of success is work. The mother of success is ambition. The eldest son is common sense.

Some of the other boys are perseverance, honesty, thoroughness, foresight, enthusiasm and cooperation.

The eldest daughter is character. Some of the other sisters are cheerfulness, loyalty, courtesy, care, economy, sincerity and harmony.

The baby is opportunity.

Get acquainted with the "old man" and you'll be able to get along pretty well with the rest of the family.

—Try Square

1718. God gave us two ends; one to sit on and one to think with. Success depends on which one we use the most. Heads we win, tails we lose.

1719. The formula for success is simply putting the right people in the right jobs and then sitting on the sidelines and being a damned good cheerleader.

—A. MARSHALL JONES

1720. Women can never be as successful as men; they don't have wives to help them.

1721. In the lexicon of youth there is no such word as "fail." Remember the story of the boy who wanted to march in the circus parade? When the show came to town, the bandmaster needed a trombonist, so the boy signed up. He hadn't marched a block before the fearful noises form his horn caused two old ladies to faint and a horse to run away. The bandmaster demanded, "Why didn't you tell me you couldn't play the trombone?" And the boy said, "How did I know?—I never tried before!"

—WALT DISNEY, *This Week*

1722. A survey of 900 successful men—not just moneymakers, but ones who have made the world better by their work—showed that 300 started life as farmers' sons, 200 sold or carried newspapers, 200 started as messenger boys, 100 started working in factories, 50 began at the bottom in railroad work. Only 50 out of the 900 had well-to-do parents to give them a start.

—*Highways of Happiness*

1723. "My son just graduated from agricultural college," said the proud father.

"Did he win any honors?" asked an interested friend.

"Yes," said the father, "he was voted the most likely to sack seed."

283

1724. The successful man was asked the secret of his accomplishments. His reply was: "Good judgment!"
"Where did you learn good judgment?" he was asked.
"From experience."
"And from where did you gain your experience?"
"From poor judgment."

1725. Triumph is just umph added to try.

1726. The first step to a bigger success always has been: success where you are now.

1727. The most successful man is the man who holds on to the old just as long as it is good and grabs the new just as soon as it is better.

—Robert P. Vanderpoel, *Think*

1728. Those with a deep religious conviction have the inner poise and strength to succeed in football or in life.

—Bud Wilkinson, Football Coach, University of Oklahoma

1729. Whatever theology, you will find it hard to disagree with the colored preacher who told his congregation, "There's an election going on all the time. The Lord votes for you and the Devil votes against you, and you casts the deciding vote.

1730. Those who succeed are not necessarily extraordinary—the rest of us haven't exerted ourselves enough.

—*Manning* (Iowa) *Monitor*

1731. A successful man is one who makes more money than his wife can spend. A successful woman is one who can find such a man.

—*Chattanooga* (Tennessee) *News-Free Press*

1732. One way to assure yourself fame and a place in history is to invent a Christmas tree which will evaporate on December 26th.

—Francis O. Walsh

1733. The man who brags about sitting on top of the world might well remember that it turns over every 24 hours.

1734.   Who works his brain a little more
             And works his jaw a little less
             Is he whose lips will be the first
             To taste the sweetness of success.

—Inez Clark Thorson, *You*

1735. You don't have to climb the highest mountain to succeed. Still around are several molehills which haven't yet been scaled.

1736.   Remember this maxim
          In life's rugged pull;
              You can't hit the bull's-eye
          By shooting the bull!

1737. You'll never get to the top if you make a practice of blowing yours.

—North Carolina Education

1738. You don't have to lie awake nights to succeed. Just stay awake days.

—Healthways

1739. Life is like a cafeteria. There are no waitresses to bring success. You must help yourself.

1740. Luck is something that usually comes to a fellow who has been working hard for years making a place to receive it.

—Harold Helfer

1741. A prominent salesman, now retired, summed up his success in three simple words: "and then some."

"I discovered at an early age," he said, "that most of the difference between average people and top people could be explained in three words. The top people did what was expected of them—and then some. They were thoughtful of others; they were considerate and kind—and then some. They met their obligations and responsibilities fairly and squarely—and then some. They were good friends to their friends—and then some. They could be counted on in an emergency—and then some."

1742. The rung of a ladder was never meant to rest upon, but only to hold man's foot long enough to enable him to put the other somewhat higher.

—Thomas Huxley

1743. Success is for those energetic enough to work for it, hopeful enough to look for it, patient enough to wait for it, brave enough to seize it, and strong enough to hold it.

—Food for Thot

1744. To succeed in this modern age of the atom, the jet, and the satellite, you need also a big charge of gumption, guts and go. Even then, the only way you can avoid losing your shirt is to keep your sleeves rolled up.

—EUGENE BERTIN, *Pennsylvania School Journal*

1745. Remember when a $10,000-a-year man was a success? Now he's a plumber's helper.

—MAURICE SEITTER

1746. It's a shame that when success turns a person's head it does not also wring his neck just a little.

1747. What is it that brings one man success in life, and mediocrity or failure to his brother? It can't be mental capacity. There is not the difference in our mentalities that is indicated by the difference in performance.

The answer is, some men succeed because they cheerfully pay the price of success, while others, though they claim ambition and a desire to succeed, are unwilling to pay that price.

The price of success is . . .

To use all your courage to force yourself to concentrate deeply and constantly; to study it from all angles, and to plan ahead.

To have a high sustained determination to achieve what you plan to accomplish not only when conditions are favorable to its accomplishment, but in spite of all adverse circumstances which may arise.

To refuse to believe that there are any circumstances sufficiently strong to defeat you in the accomplishment of your purpose.

—Source Unknown

Supervision—Supervisor

1748. *Lines to a supervisor:*

Get ye up from the paper-and-memo morass,
Eschew the executive chair;
Go help out the lass who is "losing" her class,
Your real job is waiting you there.

—FREDERICK MOFFITT, *Nations Schools*

1749. The supervisor is no hermit soul living on an intellectual

Olympus. He is a social being who participates actively in the affairs of men. His interest in people makes him an acceptable member of any group of which he may be a part, whether it be a professional group with interests similar to his own or a lay group with many and varied interests which he can share or can learn to share.

—*Leadership Through Supervision*, 1946 Yearbook, A.S.C.D.

1750. There is another conception of supervision, something like the view of the athletic coach (heard most often in a losing season) that his job is not so much to teach football as to build men. Analogously, the supervisor sees himself as one who inspires his teachers, lifts them above themselves, reinvigorates their flagging spirits.

—*Leadership Through Supervision*, 1946 Yearbook, A.S.C.D.

Tact

1751. Tact is the ability to fleece the flock without making them flinch.

1752. A man has tact who won't change his mind but will change the subject.

1753. The plumber was instructing his new assistant on the niceties of the trade: "Above all," he said, "you must exercise politeness and tact." The assistant allowed as how he understood about politeness but "what was tact?" "Well, son," he replied, "it's this way. If you walk into a bathroom to fix a pipe and a young lady is in the tub you close the door quickly and say, 'Beg your pardon, Sir.' The 'Sir'—that's tact."

Taxes

1754. Being the burden they are to most people, taxes pop up as frequent and unpleasant topics. No wonder, then, why so many were interested in hearing about the discovery of a South Pacific island where there are no crimes, policemen, beggars, fights, taxes— or inhabitants.

1755. The general property tax is one of the worst taxes known. It puts a premium on dishonesty; it reduces deception to a system;

it presses hardest on those least able to pay; it imposes double taxation on one man, and grants immunity to the next. Its abolition must become the battle cry of every statesman.

—Professor Seligman, Columbia University

1756. Rule for taxation: The art of taxation consists of so plucking the goose as to obtain the largest amount of feathers with the least possible amount of hissing.

—J. B. Coleman

1757.   My bill for taxes riled me some—
          Since it was more than I expected—
          But he to whom I raved was calm—
          And collected.

—Archer T. Spring

Teacher—Teaching

1758. As long as the public believes that anyone can teach, the public will believe that anyone can criticize teachers.

—Arthur F. Corey, *Ohio Schools*

1759. You can lead a teacher to curriculum planning but you can't make him think.

1760. A torn jacket is soon mended; but hard words bruise the heart of a child.

—Kavanagh

1761. There is no final way to judge the worth of a teacher except in terms of the lives of those he has taught.

—Editorial, *Peabody Journal of Education*

1762. A Texas lad rushed home from kindergarten and insisted his mother buy him a set of pistols, holsters and gun belt.

"Why, whatever for, dear?" mother asked. "You're not going to tell me you need them for school?"

"Yes, I do," he asserted. "Teacher said tomorrow she's going to teach us to draw."

—*Minneapolis Tribune*

1763. In our profession the slogan should be "dig in or dig out."

1764. You don't have to live in a big town to do big things in education.

1765. The teacher who is satisfied with average results will never be a top-notcher.

1766. No one has any right to find life uninteresting or unrewarding who sees within the sphere of his own activity a wrong he can help to remedy, or within himself an evil he can hope to overcome, or within another a life he can assist to greater heights.

1767. "Professor," said the curious student, "will you attempt to explain to me the Theory of Limits?"

"Well, young man, let us assume that you have called on an attractive young lady. You happen to be seated at opposite ends of the living room. You move toward her half the distance; then you move half of the remaining distance toward her; again you decrease the distance between you by 50 per cent. Continue this for some time. Do you get the idea? Theoretically, you will never reach the girl. On the other hand, you will soon get close enough to her for all practical purposes."

—Source Unknown

1768. A professor who had taught for many years was counseling a young teacher. "You will discover," he said, "that in nearly every class there is a youngster eager to argue. Your first impulse will be to silence him. I advise you to think carefully before doing so. He probably is the only one listening."

1769. The teacher is a composite. A teacher must have the energy of a harnessed volcano, the efficiency of an adding machine, the memory of an elephant, the understanding of a psychiatrist, the wisdom of Solomon, the tenacity of a spider, the patience of a turtle trying to cross the freeway in rush-hour traffic, the decisiveness of a general, the diplomacy of an ambassador, and the financial acumen of a Wall Street wizard. She must remember always that she teaches by word but mostly by precept and example.

—*Jackson* (Mississippi) *News*

1770. A teacher can never truly teach unless he is still learning himself. A lamp can never light another lamp unless it continues to burn its own flame. The teacher who has come to the end of his subject, who has no living traffic with his knowledge but merely repeats his lessons to his students, can only load their minds; he cannot quicken them. Truth not only must inform but must inspire. If the inspiration dies out, and the information only accumulates, then truth loses its infinity. The greater part of our learning in the schools has been wasted because, for most of our teachers, their subjects are like dead specimens of once living things, with which they have a learned acquaintance, but no communication of life and love.

—RABINDRANATH TAGORE, *Phi Delta Kappan*

1771. Because a man lives, does it mean that he grows? At a boys' school, a new headmaster was chosen from among members of the faculty. After the appointment was announced, a teacher approached the chairman of the selection committee with a gnawing question.

"I accept the fact that I wasn't picked for the headmastership," he said forthrightly, "but can you tell me why I wasn't at least considered for the post? It seems curious. After all, I've had twenty years' teaching experience here."

"That's not quite the way we looked at it," came the reply.

"In your case, the board felt that what you've had is *one* year's experience repeated twenty times."

—*Guideposts*. Copyright, 1955, Guideposts Associates, Inc.

1772. A great teacher is not one who imparts knowledge to his students, but one who awakens their interest in it and makes them eager to pursue it for themselves. He is a spark plug, not a fuel pipe.

—M. J. BERRILL

1773. A sad faced little fellow, sits alone in deep disgrace;
> There's a lump arising in his throat and tears drop
> down his face.
> He wandered from his playmates; he doesn't want to
> hear
> Their shouts of merry laughter, since the world has
> lost its cheer.
> He has sipped the cup of sorrow
> He has quaffed the bitter glass
> And his heart is fairly breaking—the boy who didn't
> pass.

> In the apple tree the robin sings a cheery little song,
> But he doesn't seem to hear it, showing plainly some-
> thing's wrong.

Comes his faithful little spaniel for a romp and a bit
of play.
But the troubled little fellow bids him sternly "go
away!"
And alone he sits in sorrow with his chair a tangled
mass
And his eyes are red with weeping—the little boy who
didn't pass.

Oh, you who boast a laughing son, and speak of him
as bright;
And you, who love a little girl who comes to you at
night,
With shining eyes and dancing feet with honors from
her school,
Turn to that lonely lad that thinks he is a fool
And take him kindly by the hand, the dullest of his
class
He is the one who most needs help—the little boy who
didn't pass!

—Author Unknown

1774. It was still early when I reached school, one morning recently. I was surprised to see a youngster hovering near the door.

"It's locked," he offered disconsolately as I tried the knob. I began to fumble for my keys. Immediately he brightened.

"You're a teacher!" he announced with both surprise and pleasure.

"What makes you think that?" I asked, amused and not a little pleased to think that my station in life should be regarded with such delight.

He hesitated not a moment, but said softly and with respect, "You have the key."

I was promptly humbled as well as overwhelmed at the magnitude of that simple statement, of the implication and the responsibility involved by merely having a "key."

This was perhaps the most pertinent statement directed toward me in my entire teaching career. It started me thinking. . . .

—SUSAN SCHILLING

1775. Beginning teacher, walking into principal's office after two weeks of teaching: "Gimme that inspirational speech again. I'm gettin' kinda discouraged."

1776. If the teacher and the group leader . . . present a pattern of conformity, we will be building a generation who will be easy fodder for fascism.

—Dr. Nathan E. Cohen

1777. A qualified teacher possesses educational qualifications that look good to the class.

—J. K. Kincaid, *Phi Delta Kappan*

1778. A court in Dortmund, Germany counseled music teacher Siegmar Schroeder to use psychology instead of beatings to implant music appreciation.

For emphasis the court gave the 41-year-old teacher an eight month suspended jail sentence and fined him $119 on a charge that he regularly beat his 10- and 11-year-olds for inattention.

1779. The teacher can light the lantern and put it in your hand, but you must walk into the dark.

—William H. Armstrong

1780. Paying no attention to the red traffic light, the whizzing cars, or the policeman's outraged whistle, the little old lady marched across the street. Brakes squealed, horns blasted and the cop strode angrily up to her. "Say, lady," he growled, "didn't you see my hand raised? Don't you know what that means?"

"Well, I should hope I do," snapped the lady. "I've been teaching school for 25 years."

—*Texas Outlook*

1781.   Men must be taught as if you taught them not,
And things unknown proposed as things forgot.

—Alexander Pope

1782. Common sense is the most uncommon thing in teaching.

1783. "As I teach my pupils," said my teacher-friend, "I try to remember one oft-stated axiom: "There is nothing so unequal as equal treatment of unequals."

—*Phi Delta Kappan*

1784. He who plants a tree does well; he who fells and saws it into planks does well; he who makes a bench of the planks does well; he, who, sitting on the bench, teaches a child, does better than the rest.

—DEAN FARRER, *Christian Leader*

1785. Teaching in America is a 24-hour job, twelve months of the year; sabbatical leaves are provided so you can have your coronary thrombosis off the campus.

—JACQUES BARZUN

1786. Thrust into a strange world, a good teacher is the best thing that can possibly happen.

A teacher is Courage with Kleenex in its pocket, Sympathy struggling with a snow-suit, and Patience with papers to grade. Teachers spend twelve hours a day searching for truth and the other twelve searching for error.

They are indispensable, invincible, and nearly inexhaustible. A teacher really does not mind sniffles, squirmings, stomach aches, spills, sloth and sauciness. Neither does she disintegrate before tears, trifles, fights, futility, excuses, parents who spout, little boys who shout, and little girls who pout.

Most of all, a teacher is somebody who likes somebody else's children—and still has enough strength left to go to the P.T.A. meeting. Thank heaven for teachers.

—Selected—*The Gleaner,* Publication of Dept. of Education and Psychology, Kansas State Teachers College

1787. "I've taught ten years," said Mr. Q.
"Without a problem rising."
And when he fully atrophies,
'Twill not be at all surprising
To see him stand at the gates of hell
On his harp string improvising.

But Mr. X was problem wise;
He constantly *assigned* them,
Can't take time he huskily said,
"To let the students find them.
By pre-planned teaching we can put
Their problems all behind them."

1788. The farm bloc of a state legislature was resisting the request for a raise in salary for the teachers of its small agricultural college. Finally, a faculty committee traveled to the capital to make a personal plea. "The work is easy," grumbled one farmer-representative. "I don't imagine you fellows teach more than 10, 11 hours a day."

"Sir," replied the faculty spokesman, "we teachers are a lot like one of your bulls. It's not the amount of time we spend. It's the importance of what we do."

They got their raise.

1789. A good teacher is one who can show children how to be smart—without being smart-alec.

—DAN KIDNEY

1790. It's distressing, some of the things I've seen done in names of either authoritarian or progressive teaching. The great teachers of all ages have used the sound methods that the majority of our teachers are being taught to use today.

—LAWRENCE DERTHICK, U.S. Commissioner of Education

1791. Frank M. Kahout, local vice-president of Minneapolis Federation of Men Teachers received the following note (as an excuse for tardiness):

"Dear Teacher, Please excuse John for being late. His Uncle died last night and we had a hard time waking him up this morning."

—RALPH C. RAMSTAD, *Minneapolis Federation of Men Teachers News Bulletin*

1792. ". . . It seems that the home, the church, the business world, the state have turned to us alone to train the citizens of tomorrow in everything from the use of a toothbrush to the choice of a vocation and the casting of an intelligent vote. The classroom teacher must welcome the American infant of four or five, take off his overshoes and mittens, amuse him, and teach him correct table manners and an infallible code of morals. He must be taught how to dance and how to say the blessing at the family table. He must be taught to be clean and to treat the rights of others with respect. . . .

He must, under the supervision of teachers, be guarded against all diseases, protected from all germs, inspected by dentist and oculist and physician. He must, as he progresses, be taught more of literature, history, and science than college professors used to know, yet he must be as accurate and rapid in his calculations as the adding machine. He must be correct in speech, no matter what sort of language he hears out of the classroom.

He must be polished and broad-minded, alert, shrewd, and keen, no matter what his years and temperament. He must be honest and steady, despite his heredity. He must be a skilled workman. He must become an intelligent, reliable citizen. If he does not develop into such a paragon of perfection under the influence of his teachers, who have him a few hours a day for nine months for eight or nine years, it is proof that his teachers have been negligent and that the school is a failure.

After dismissal, when all the youngsters have been buttoned up, booted, and spurred, and sent to the home which complains that school hours are too short, his teacher must refresh herself by meetings with supervisors, by calls upon all the homes represented in her school, by joyous attendance of the parent-teachers association, by inspection of the home gardens, by reading a paper at the club, by showing a lively interest in the civic league, by singing in the community chorus, by teaching a Sabbath-school class, and by taking a correspondence course in the university lest she become stale and rusty. She must always be dressed neatly and in good taste, and be sweet, sympathetic, and charming in manner!

And in return for these things she shall be rewarded with a wage less than that which the brickmason receives! The classroom teacher is by all odds the rarest bargain the public sees."
—Taken from an address presented at the N.E.A. Convention, 1917. Speaker Unidentified

1793. It was a September Saturday in 1940; I was 20 years old and ready to begin my second year of teaching. Another county institute had just drawn to a close and all the teachers of Brown County, Indiana had been given their teaching assignments for the coming school year; all but two, that is. Looking first at one another and then at the two brown envelopes lying there on the front pew of the church, Boward Hock and I stood there, perplexed but amused.

Large brown envelopes containing instructional materials and miscellaneous directions from the county superintendent of schools had been picked up by the teachers as they left the Nashville Methodist Church which always served as the meeting place for the annual pre-school county institutes. Written in bold letters on one of the two remaining envelopes was the word, "Branstetter"; on the other appeared the designation, "Helmsburg Junior High School." Branstetter was a one-room rural frame school building, housing grades one through six, while Helmsburg Junior High School, a village consolidated school, was to be housed in a new modern brick building near the high school.

Breaking the silence, Boward queried, "Which one is yours? Do you know where you're going to teach?"

"I don't know which envelope is mine," I replied. "Neither do I know where I'm going to teach. Is it the same with you?"

When he answered "Yes," it was time for a good laugh in spite of the fact that each of us viewed our own plight with a great deal of seriousness and apprehension.

As we reflected on our amusing predicament, that of uncertainty as to our teaching assignments, we suddenly became aware of a figure in the doorway. The township trustee, putting in his first appearance of the day, poked his head in and beckoned us to come outside. Expecting to learn of our assignments at last, we eagerly went outside where we found the czar of township schools in an obvious dilemma.

Shifting from one foot to another and looking neither of us in the eye, he sheepishly admitted, "Boys, I haven't decided who should teach the rural school and who should be assigned to the consolidated junior high school." Perhaps it should be explained why the three of us stood there, two in tense expectation and one in torturing indecision, long after the meeting had ended. In 1940 in my home county there was no shortage of teachers; actually, there were more teachers than positions. Traditionally, final selection and appointment of teachers by township trustees was based largely on familial and political relationship; my rival and the trustee had in common some very strong political ties. Consequently, he found it most difficult to make his decision concerning our appointments— since there existed between the township trustee and myself a familial relationship. Really, there was little, if any, reason for him to make a choice based on the factors of training and experience. In these respects, the candidates were nearly equal.

Former schoolmates and teammates, now rivals, both Boward Hock and I had insisted on teaching in the new consolidated junior high school, avoiding like the plague any thoughts of assuming the role of a rural schoolmaster for grades one through six. It was easier to teach just grades seven and eight, we thought, and besides, the junior high school position carried with it athletic coaching responsibilities, an added assignment which each of us considered not as a duty but as a privilege.

This particular elected civil official, a successful realtor with less than six years of elementary education, knew no more about the operation of schools than I did about the realty business, and that was little, very little. Lacking both the training and experience for decision making in school matters, he stood there in a definite and obvious quandary. Suddenly, he pulled a quarter from his pocket, looked straight at me and barked, "Call it," and he tossed the coin into the air. Before the coin had reached the peak of its ascent, there flashed through my mind the open water bucket, the outhouse, the red-hot coal stove, the coal shed, the coal bucket, the oiled floors, the carved initials, the worn-out blackboards, the cloakroom odors of peanut butter and egg sandwiches, and the natural ventilators which admitted wind, rain, and sunshine with equal ease.

Racing through my mind, too, as the tossed coin started downward in its flight, were the many advantages of the new consolidated school, one year's assignment to which depended on the flip of a coin. "Call it," he had said. What a basis for making teacher assignments! What a manner of getting a job! Should I "call it"? "Heads," I called hopefully, just before the flipped coin bounced on the ground. It wasn't heads and it didn't stand on edge.

Now that I am engaged in the activities of teacher training, an area which requires broad and varied experiences, the real significance of that flip of a coin looms before me. My year as the teacher, janitor, and nurse for grades one through six in that rural school was an experience of immeasurable value.

—M. DALE BAUGHMAN

1794. Our job, the fascinating task of every alert, growing teacher, is to take a lot of live wires and see that they're well grounded, so as to avoid future short circuits and blown fuses. But we need to do even more than teach them good habits and basic skills they will need for success in college.

—Source Unknown

1795. To the average teacher, getting the very most out of her pupils is just about as difficult as trying to smuggle daylight past a rooster.

—M. Dale Baughman

1796. Don't be a 2 x 4 teacher, one who always stays between the two covers of the textbook and within the four walls of the classroom.

1797. Two salesmen were crossing the water and noticed a woman leaning against the rail of the ship.

"I'll bet she's a school teacher," ventured one.

"I know a school teacher when I see one," returned the other. "I'll bet you five dollars that she is not."

The other man covered the bet and stepped up to the woman. "I beg your pardon, but will you answer a question for us? Are you a school teacher?"

"No," she replied feebly. "It's that I am seasick that makes me look the way I do."

1798. A young man once had difficulty learning how to diagram a sentence. The teacher explained the point in question again and again and finally asked, "Don't you understand that, now?" The boy's puzzled expression did not change and he continued to stare at the blackboard. "Sure I understand it—I just don't see no future in it." Before a state department of education can render any real service to a school system, the *classroom teachers*—not just the superintendent of education—must see the future in it. . . .

—Frank Philpot

1799. . . . It reminds me of a story my Dad used to tell about the teacher who was teaching a class of little girls. She was trying to tell them about what all had been discovered recently that was not here years ago—the telephone, the radio, and so on. She asked, "What is here today that wasn't here forty years ago?" A bright little eight-year-old jumped up and hollered, "Me!" and she's right. That

is the most important thing that's here today that wasn't here forty
years ago.

—WILLIAM H. ALEXANDER

1800. A young teacher, very insistent that he should have a few
days off, was asked the reason by the superintendent, a former Navy
officer.

"My wife is expecting a baby," he replied.

"Listen, young man, remember this," advised the superintendent,
"you are only necessary at the laying of the keel. For the launching
you are entirely superfluous."

1801. Some people say a teacher is made out of steel,
Their minds can think, but their bodies can't feel,
Iron and steel, and hickory trees,
Frowns and gripes, from 8:00 to 3:00.

You teach six full hours and what do you get?
Another day older and deeper in debt.
You pay your dues in this and that,
Then for 24 hours your billfold is flat!

I was born one morning when it was cloudy and cool.
I picked up my register and headed for school.
I wrote 84 names on the home room roll
And the principal said, "Well, bless my soul."

You teach six full hours and what do you get?
Cuts and bruises and dirt and sweat.
I got two black eyes and can hardly walk.
When I turned my back, then came the chalk!

I got 84 kids and 42 seats,
Sixty are talking while 24 sleep,
I can hardly get 'em all through the door,
If I don't watch out, they'll send me more.

You teach six full hours to 84 brats,
And all of them yellin' like dogs and cats,
They're cutting on seats and writing on walls,
Hugging and kissing in the upstairs halls.

The last bell rings and I start for the door,
My head's a-ringing and my feet are sore.
I taught six full hours, my day is made—
But I still have 300 papers to grade!

You teach six full hours and what do you get?
Another day older and deeper in debt,
I'd go to St. Peter, but I just can't stay,
I gotta come back for the P.T.A.

—Author Unknown

1802. As a final suggestion, for whatever it may or may not be worth, I suggest that you be prepared to be a contortionist: Keep your back to the wall, your ear to the ground, your shoulder to the wheel, your nose to the grindstone; keep a level head, and both feet on the ground. At the same time keep your head in the clouds, on the alert for a silver lining.

—CARL C. BYERS, *Superintendent's Bulletin,* Parma, Ohio

1803. Before 1900 about one-fourth of all the teachers in the U.S. had not finished even a high-school course; one-fourth more had not more than a high school education; one-fourth more had only two years beyond the high school; the remaining one-fourth were college graduates, most of them with no professional training.

—FREDERICK E. BOLTON, Dean Emeritus, College of Education,
University of Washington, *U.S. News and World Report*

1804. Teachers generally today can do everything that teachers generally were able to do 50 years ago. No great secrets of teaching once known have ever been lost. Meanwhile, we have made some genuine improvements in textbooks, audio-visual aids and standardized tests, to name only a few developments which have made our teachers more effective rather than less so in the past 50 years.

—DAVID G. SALTEN, Supt. Long Beach, N. Y.
U. S. News and World Report

1805. Recently a New Jersey teacher, who supplements his salary by operating a bulldozer during vacations, made an application for credit to purchase a home, stating that he was a teacher. It was turned down. The teacher resubmitted the application, this time putting down his occupation as bulldozer operator. It was promptly approved.

1806. Overheard in a teachers' workshop in which the theme was "Teacher Load": "Teachers could do a better teaching job if they were unloaded." "Do you want to adopt the emotion?"

1807. We must train our teachers as a sculptor is trained, not as a physicist. They must think like poets, not like statisticians. For they are dealing not with things, like the chemists, nor with bodies, like the physicians, nor yet with minds alone, like the psychologists. To them and to us is reserved the splendid privilege of fashioning and nurturing those coruscating iridescent entities called personalities, transient as the glancing sunbeam but more lasting than the granite of our hills. It is at once the most precious and most dangerous duty entrusted by mankind to men.
—Max Rafferty, "A Chronicle of Masks," *Phi Delta Kappan*

1808. A young woman took a job as a private tutor, but suddenly left it. Asked why she had resigned, she said, "Had to. Backward child. Forward Father."
—*North Carolina Education*

1809. If teachers can accumulate degrees and write books, well and good, but the first requisite should be their ability to inspire youth.
—Eleanor Roosevelt

1810. *Unidentified teacher, commenting upon a lethargic pupil:* "The only difference between this girl and the Sphinx is that she moves when the bell rings."

1811. Much of teacher's work is according to an educational fad, fashion, or even a fetish, and like styles in other areas, these change from season to season and probably more often than do the "hair-do's," skirt lengths or cuts of clothing. Like other changes of styles, some of the educational "hairdo's" seem very freakish.
—O. C. Miller, *The Democratic Way to Better Schools*

1812. When I was six years old, I started to a one-teacher school including several grades. The only thing I can remember from that first year at school is that one of the big boys knocked the teacher down with a book. Although I was perhaps not as bright as the average six-year-old, I knew that was no way to treat a book.
—C. R. Van Nice, *Teacher Teamwork with a Problem Public*

1813. The superior teacher stimulates and inspires his students to live at the highest possible level. He nurtures the self-realization of each individual, helping him to develop a sound, satisfactory philosophy of life and effective living habits. He makes the acceptance of civic and social responsibilities a natural corollary to community citizenship. He promotes physical and mental well-being and is constantly alert to the needs for guidance and the discovery of special talents and interests in his students.

—F. EARL WILLIAMS, *Bulletin, N.A.S.S.P.*

1814. *One gossip to another:* "I'm entertaining two locust teachers in my home."

The other, amused, remarked, "That must have been a slip; didn't you mean local?"

"No, I said locust and I *meant* locust."

"But locusts—they're insects that come in swarms, and eat everything in sight, and . . ."

"Don't I know it!" snapped her friend, "and I'm entertaining two of 'em in my home this week!"

1815. What a student learns in a course is dependent not only upon the objectives of the course, the teaching methods employed, and the learner's ability and effort, but also upon the frequently overlooked factor of better teacher-student relations.

1816. Nothing is really impossible, teacher, except some of the pupils you encounter.

—Kiwanis Magazine

1817. A good teacher knows his subject, is enthusiastic about it, and is eager to pass on his knowledge to the students in a way to arouse their interest. A good teacher is characterized by sincerity, and a great teacher also by humility.

The classroom, filled with a captive audience of idealistic and trusting young men and women, is the last place in the world where one may justify cynicism, irrelevancies, unpatriotic utterances, or that cheap substitute for wit sometimes called smart-aleck-iness.

—WALTER C. LANGSAM, School and Society

1818. A teacher needs:
> The education of a college president.
> The executive ability of a financier.
> The humility of a deacon.
> The adaptability of a chameleon.
> The hope of an optimist.
> The courage of a hero.
> The wisdom of a serpent.
> The gentleness of a dove.
> The patience of Job.
> The grace of God, and
> The persistence of the Devil.
>> —Author Unknown

1819. Great teaching has always been associated with a personality—a personality that is capable of interpreting living realities—of opening new avenues of light and understanding—and of assisting men and women to use their own powers to the fullest degree.
>> —Lucy Gage, *Educational Leadership*

1820. The teacher is the lowest on the totem pole. If the school's faults are to be corrected, the teacher will have to be moved to the center of the stage. She does the teaching—the important part of the work of the school.
>> —O. C. Miller, *The Democratic Way to Better Schools,*
>> Exposition Press

1821. College teacher: One who talks in other people's sleep.
>> —*Chaff*, University of Illinois Student Magazine

1822. A beginning math-science teacher put the following ad in the paper: "My service for hire—start haggling at about $4500."
   A superintendent responded with this message: "Bring own cigarettes and coffee—this may take time."

1823. *Superintendent of a blackboard jungle school:* "Do you want a $4,000 or a $5,000 job?"
   Teacher: "What's the difference?"
   Superintendent: "Well, we provide a bodyguard for the person who takes the $4,000 job."

1824. How to get rid of a teacher:

1. If a parent, remark about the teacher's finesse in handling Johnny—if an administrator or supervisor, look him straight in the eye and say something praiseworthy about teaching skill and professional zeal. The effect will be so novel that an ordinary teacher will die of over-exertion in a few weeks.

2. Raise his salary. He's been eating so little so long, he'll eat himself to death.

1825. A merchant became curious when week after week, a local teacher came in and bought several brooms. Finally, he sought an explanation.

"Well," said the teacher, "I'm selling them to my neighbors and friends for a dollar each."

"Look, man," protested the merchant, "you can't go on doing that. You're paying me $1.25 each for the brooms."

"That's right, I know," conceded the teacher, "but it beats teaching."

1826. The battle-scarred administrator inspired his corps of beginning teachers with his first-of-the-year messages—a challenge to "poke their heads over the parapet, and awaken the sleeping giants" in their pupils.

To the dismay of the neophytes, he gave the same talk at the next meeting, one month later. After the same forceful presentation had been given the third time, a spokesman for the group blurted out, "Don't you have more than just one pep talk?"

"Certainly," he said quietly, "I have many, but you haven't done anything about the first one yet."

1827. There are only two classes of teachers, so far as compensation is concerned—those who are underpaid, and those who have no business in the classroom. It is impossible to place a cash value on the influence of a good teacher. By good teacher we do not necessarily mean those of high academic training, desirable as the training may be. The good teacher is a pleasant, understanding person who not only is skilled in the art of presenting subject matter but one who just as skillfully, by precept and example, leads children into desirable habits and attitudes.

—ROBERT E. McKINNEY, Speech to Southern Division, Illinois Education Association

1828. A teacher is like the storage battery in an automobile—constantly discharging energy. Therefore, he needs frequent recharging to forestall running dry. This is where educational leadership comes in.

1829. The citizens in my native Brown County were considering an increase in teachers' salaries which would mean also a tax increase.

Truck farmer West Arthur expressed the general sentiment of the voters when he explained, "Well, most are in sympathy with it, but few are in favor of it."

—M. DALE BAUGHMAN

1830. An angry, red-faced art teacher half-dragged an equally red-faced junior high school youth into the principal's office. The principal sized up the situation, observing that the offender's face was painted red with tempera paint.

He asked the youth for an explanation. The youth replied, "She told us to paint a familiar face."

1831. The teacher's business is to see to it that every child at some time, in some way, in some subject, achieves a marked success and that some time he gets an honest gauge of himself by failure.

—DR. WILLIAM H. BURHAM, *Instrumentalist*

1832. A little boy during his first day at school attracted the teacher's attention with his display of weeping.

"What's wrong, Billy?" asked the teacher.

"I don't care much for school and I guess I have to stay with it until I'm sixteen," protested the lad.

"Don't let it worry you," suggested the teacher. "I have to stick with it until I'm 65."

1833.   One bleak fact will confront you,
          And briefly shred plans to rubble:
          For each pupil with a spark of genius,
          There'll be ten with ignition trouble.

—BETH BLUE, Indiana Teacher

1834. I am convinced that we shall never be able to make teaching a profession if we say to young people that after 15 or 20 years of service, they will receive only $1500 or $2000 more than they received as beginners.

—PAUL MISNER

1835.

I am neither old nor antique,
I was tutored well in Greek,
But I cut my second dentals,
On the good old fundamentals,
And I'm puzzled by what you meant
And the way you captured each student.
Can't you tip me off this fall
As to how you get 'em on the ball
Just to ease my nightly domework
Doing little Willie's homework.
Thank you for all the bother,
I remain—A baffled father.

Teacher's response to the above:
Thank you for your kindly letter,
Sorry we don't know you better.
Methods change in school you know;
Otherwise we couldn't grow.
Homework shouldn't be a bother;
It's for Willie, not for father.

—*Idaho Parent-Teacher*

1836. Butcher Jack Russell saw a pistol in math teacher James Pletcher's pocket when he stopped in his shop in Utica, a suburb of Detroit. A patrolman nabbed Pletcher when the teacher's car stalled in traffic. "Come out with your hands up—and no funny business," ordered the patrolman. Searching Mr. Pletcher, the patrolman found the gun—a water pistol. "I have a dozen like them at home," the math teacher explained. "I've been confiscating them from my students."

—*Education Summary*

1837. It is tragic that teaching is more concerned with what is around us but makes little effort to relate what is around us with what is inside us.

—EARL S. JOHNSON, *Chicago Schools Journal*

1838. Teachers come in assorted sizes, weights, and colors. They have various interests, hobbies, religions, and beliefs, but they share one creed: to help each child to reach the highest possible degree of personal development.

—JANE C. BUTLER

1839. A teacher is like a doctor; half the value of his care lies in the confidence with which one approaches him.

—STEPHEN WEST, *Etude*

1840. To a small child's way of thinking, a school teacher is just someone who is trying to find out what he doesn't know.

—KAY INGRAM

1841. We must not assume that only classroom teachers teach. Indeed, if we define a teacher as one who guides students into ways of rich living, then the only difference between parents and "school" teachers is in the kind of teaching which they do. The school is especially equipped to do certain specialized kinds of teaching, to give continuity and system to learning experiences that the average parent cannot. The school, too, can build group morale and responsibilities. But the home is more often where the heart is—and emotions are very important parts of the educative process.

—EDGAR DALE, Professor of Education, Ohio State University

1842. Some of the best teaching I have seen has been done by competent coaches in the athletics programs of our secondary schools. The reason is easy to find; the coach wants to teach his subject matter, and he wants to teach the boy. Unless he teaches the subject matter and the boy, he will not get acceptable results on the field, on the court, or in the pool.

—EUGENE YOUNGERT, Superintendent, Oak Park, Illinois, *Bulletin, N.A.S.S.P.*

1843. The candidate for heaven rapped at the pearly gates. "Who's there?" asked St. Peter. "It is I," replied the candidate. "You go to hell; you're an English teacher."

—A. J. WALKER, *English Journal*

1844. The good teacher knows, and can tell people about it in a persuasive manner.

1845. A teacher, noticing that one little boy always used a black crayon for his drawings of horses, cows, barns and whatever else, became very disturbed about the state of the boy's mind and called a meeting with the child's parents, the school principal and a psychiatrist.

They finally got to the root of the trouble. It was his only crayon.

1846. The young man paused as his eyes caught the words on the bulletin board: "Take life as you find it, but don't leave it so." At length he commented to himself: "Therein lies the summation of my responsibility as a teacher. If I can change the lives of those who come under my tutelage, so they may live more abundantly, I shall not have taught in vain."

—M. FERN SLUSHER, Moline, Illinois

1847. There seems to be an erroneous notion that once you become a teacher all you have to do is enclose yourself within four walls and a Great White Father in an ivory tower will administer to your every want and need.

—CARL J. MEGEL, President, American Federation of Teachers, addressing annual convention

1848. It is nothing short of a miracle that modern methods of instruction have not yet entirely strangled the holy curiosity of inquiry.

—ALBERT EINSTEIN

1849. I believe that the American teacher is the most solid supporter of democracy, and that education ought to be teacher-centered as well as child-centered. Teaching can never be mediocre or it becomes self-defeating. Teaching must be great, yet greatness has many dimensions. It is not a possession, but a pilgrimage. It is measured by consequences—its influence on the lives of students and on culture.

—FREDERICK MAYER, Professor of Philosophy, University of Redlands, *Phi Delta Kappan*

1850. Superintendent to teacher asking for a raise: "Of course, you're worth more than you're getting, Morton. Why don't you let up a bit?"

1851. What is teaching? To stimulate, encourage, and direct learning is the soul and substance of the art of teaching.

—BAGLEY-KEITH

1852. A teacher's prayer:

O God, Thou who has ever brought all life to its perfection by patient growth, grant me patience to guide my pupils to the best in life. Teach me to use the compulsion of love and of interest; and save me from the weakness of coercion. Make me one who is a vitalizer of life and not a merchant of facts. Show me how to overcome the forces that destroy by harnessing the urges that lead to the life abundant.

Give me such a sense of value that I may distinguish the things that last from those that pass, and never confuse mountains with molehills.

Grant me insight to overlook the faults of exuberance because I can see with prophetic eye the possibilities of enthusiasm.

Save me, O Lord, from confusing that which is evil with that which is only immature.

May I learn the laws of human life so well that, saved from the folly of reward and punishment, I may help each pupil of mine to find a supreme devotion for which he will give his all. And may that devotion be in tune with Thy purpose for Thy world.

May I be so humble and keep so young that I may continue to grow and learn while I teach.

Grant that I may strive not so much to be called a teacher as to be a teacher; not so much to speak of Thee; not so much to talk about love and human service but to be the spirit of these; not so much to speak of the ideals of Jesus, but in every act of my teaching to reveal his ideals.

Save me from letting my work become commonplace by the ever present thought that, of all human endeavors, teaching is most like the work that Thou hast been doing through all the generations. Amen.

—Chaplain Wallace Grant Fiske, OCS, AAFETTC,
Florida Association, District Convention

1853. Teaching school is like milking cows. What you do today must be done again tomorrow. Repetition is inherent in all work. The routine in the classroom can be dull for students, too. As one of the youngsters in "Fripsey Fun" put it, "It's the best dull year we have had yet!"

Day after day, teachers experience the same forgetting of 7 x 8.

The same dress on the bulletin board cries for change; the same pile of dust under the radiator has been ignored by the same custodian. Teaching is repetitious but so is housekeeping and hog-raising.

Since we are compelled to spend most of our lives doing the routine things we must find a glow in doing what must be done.

One thoughtful lady, when asked how she was getting along, replied, "Oh, I'm just coasting along in a happy rut." She made a "happy rut" out of the routine of housekeeping, cooking and child care.

Our personal rut may be rugged, deep, and sometimes discouraging—but it need not be miserable.

Rossini said, "Give me a laundry list and I will set it to music." A roomful of children has more inspiration than a laundry list. There is great satisfaction in being satisfied with what we are.

If our cows won't stay milked, it is not the fault of the cows. The Lord made all of us for a purpose. Make our rut "a happy rut." "It may level out and then we can start a new one!"

—*Curriculum Bulletin,* East Peoria Public Schools, Illinois

1854. *School teacher:* "I've met some school administrators who were enthusiastic about hard work. Believe it or not, it was just my luck that all of them happened to be men I was working for at the time."

1855. In these days of urgent need, it is as important for the teacher to support his profession as it is for the citizen to support his country.

1856. All great teachers have been great because of their moral leadership of the people.

1857. *Teacher to lethargic pupil:* "Are you working hard on your history course?"
Pupil: "Yes, I'm constantly on the verge of mental exertion."

1858. An old riddle asks, "How far can you go into the woods?" The answer is, "Halfway—for after that you start to come out."

The first months of teaching are often months in which the experience is similar to that of going deeper and deeper into the woods. About this time of the school term you ask, "How far can

you go into the woods?" And the answer is that about this time of the school term, halfway, is when you start to come out.
—CLARA COCKERVILLE, Ass't. Superintendent, Armstrong County Schools, Kittanning, Pennsylvania

1859. A doctor works with intricate skill for many hours to perform an operation which will save the life of his patient. . . .

A teacher counsels with a child in trouble long after the classrooms are silent and the school corridors are deserted. . . .

An artist observes his surroundings with a keen eye and selects from life about him the heightened patterns of form and color. . . .

A teacher quickens the minds of children to the presence of beauty in the city, on the farm, on a hillside near their home—in a painting, a poem, a thought. . . .

1860. Teaching is to a significant degree an art, and the better the teacher, the more this is apparent. Some of the most significant influences of the fine teacher are very subtle in nature and rest largely on the personal relations of teacher and pupil. . . .
—HOLLIS CASWELL, N.E.A. Journal

1861. When I die, I hope it will be my good fortune to go where Miss Blake will meet me and lead me to my seat.
—BERNARD M. BARUCH

1862. They ask me why I teach and I reply, "Where could I find more splendid company?"
—GLENNICE L. HARMON

1863. What every conscientious teacher yearns for is only that his pupil's mind shall hold within it some ideas that are clearly his own.
—DR. NATHAN PUSEY, President, Harvard University

1864. We ought to recognize the teacher's nobler role as parent substitute.
—FULTON OURSLER

1865. The only crown I ask, dear Lord, to wear is this—that I may help a little child.
—MARION B. CRAIG

1866. School boards consider teachers' salaries at the wrong time of the year. If they'd wait until about mid-way in the summer vacation, every mother in town would wholeheartedly favor any raise.

—DON P. RADDLE, Sparta, Wisconsin, Herald

1867. If a school teacher in St. Joseph, Missouri hadn't put a comforting arm around me one day and made me welcome in my little world, I might well have done something foolish and desperate.

—IRVING BEN COOPER, New York Judge

1868. A good teacher is so rare the rumor of him spreads like a scandal.

—JOHN ERSKINE

1869. After they have had a professor around a while, the students come to accept him as they do leaky plumbing.

—MAX LERNER, Columnist

1870. Anyone who teaches in a metropolitan high school today is either a saint, or just insensitive.

—DR. FRANK BAXTER, University of Southern California

1871. To be sure, we must integrate the curriculum. But what good is this if the professor's mind remains perched on its gaunt pinnacle or secluded in the lab?

1872. Ponce de Leon set out to find wealth (youth was what he called it) in a fountain whose magic waters would guarantee bright eyes, bounce and stamina for eternity—or at least a flat stomach after 40.

Like the Spanish explorer, teachers want health and youthful vigor, but too many of them do too little about it; and yet health is a prime requisite for successful teaching.

—FRED V. HEIN, N.E.A. Journal

1873.   Praying for strength, I greet a class,
          Whose special feature is their mass;
          A sea of faces follows me,
          Expecting love, security.
          My task ahead is large indeed;
          To serve each pupil's private need.
          To teach them well. This is my hope.
          Where am I now? End of my rope.

> For how can they learn properly?
> There's hardly classroom space for me!
> —GENE FUSCO, *N.E.A. Journal*

1874. Make your instructions clear. Present them in simple terms that cannot be misunderstood. Don't cover too many ideas in rapid sequence. Give one idea at a time and make sure he understands it. Don't tell him what *not* to do—that may be the only thing he will remember. Consequently, he may do it instead of the thing you want him to do.

> —RICHARD WETHERILL

1875. There's satellites, rockets and electrical sockets,
> New germs to uncover and stars to discover;
> A trip to the moon is enticing and might be;
> Living on Mars is entirely likely.
> Obsessed with the technical whirl they call progress,
> I'm literally batty but must not regress;
> Evolution, I love thee, but you're hard on the creatures
> Who keep up with your pace, the poor science teachers.
> —*Passing Marks*, San Bernardino, Calif. City Schools

1876. In the honor system the professors have the honor and the students have the system.

> —HAVILAH BABCOCK, Professor of English, University of
> South Carolina

1877. The world seldom notices who teachers are; but civilization depends on what they do.

> —LINDSAY J. STILES, *Wisconsin Journal of Education*

1878. A teacher who is able to direct the hidden springs of energy into a constructive path on the part of his students, who is able without distortion or drama to give a fuller life to the people he is guiding, is indeed a great man.

> —Anonymous Donor of Merle M. Hoover Scholarship,
> Columbia University

1879. In September, parents mop their brows, heave sighs of relief, and gasp: "Thank heaven! There they go, our children to school." Meanwhile, the teachers—after a calm and collected summer—whisper (a lot of them are still afraid to talk out loud): "In the name of heaven, here they come—the brats—after three months of intensive training!"

> —VICTOR F. HOFFMAN, *Cresset*, Valparaiso University

1880. Unfortunately, teachers are often made fun of by cruel cartoonists and thoughtless motion picture and TV experts. Teachers are subject often to unfavorable conversation in the home and in social groups. Young people are aware of all of this and when somebody suggests that they consider teaching as a career, too many of them are likely to smile and say: "Who wants to be a teacher?" But I repeat, prestige must first be established before an adequate supply of teachers will be available, and only the public can guarantee prestige.

—H. CLAUDE HARDY in the *New York State Education*

1881. Educators, however, are not mere messenger boys or service station attendants for society. They should question and re-examine old and new values. Surely, one of the basic contributions of the good teacher should be to create a spirit of honest inquiry and reflection in their students. This process certainly should begin in the high school and be continued through college.

—MARK STARR, *North Central Association Quarterly*

1882. I suppose every teacher receives some interesting if not convincing excuses from parents of absentee pupils.

I remember this one from the parent of a first grader who had missed an entire day. Next morning he handed me this excuse which read, "Please excuse Billy's absence yesterday. He got wet in the A.M. rain and had to be dried in the P.M. sun."

—M. DALE BAUGHMAN

1883. "How can we ever show our appreciation?" gushed the superintendent to the band teacher who had won all his contests. "Sir," replied the victorious bandmaster, "ever since the Phoenicians invented money, there's been only one answer to that question."

1884. A schoolteacher once said to me, "I've got only six more years of this work. Then I'll start living." There's something wrong when we think of our work as a painful prelude to the pleasure of living.

—RALPH W. SOCKMAN, *Arkansas Methodist*

1885. Teaching is for many of us the most important profession of mankind. It is a creative one, requiring strength, experience, and imagination. If a beginning teacher has physical and emotional strength, experience will come. And only a person with imagination should teach.

—Evelyn Adlerblum

1886. Jobs are like icebergs; seven-eighths of them are invisible from the surface.

—Robert Weaver, *Family Weekly*

1887. An executive develops a team of men and women capable of producing goods and service needed by a community.

A teacher fashions an harmonious group of children capable of saying: "This problem concerns us. We will try to solve it."

—*The Teacher's Letter*

1888. Teachers who became actively engaged in community affairs should be aware of their double identity and double responsibility: (a) to the community, and (b) to the school system which they represent. This awareness should lead them to realize that they can serve their schools and communities best by being both good, livable human beings and alert, informed schoolmen.

—*The Teachers Letter*

1889. The nearsighted school teacher was rapidly losing his temper. "You at the back of the class—what was the date of the signing of the Magna Charta?"

"I don't know."

"Well, then, can you tell me what the Gordon Riots were?"

"I don't know."

"I taught that last Friday. What were you doing last night?"

"I was out drinking beer with some friends."

The school teacher gasped, and his face went almost purple. "You have the audacity to stand there and tell me that! How do you expect to pass your examination?"

"Well, I don't. I'm an electrician, and I just came in here to fix the light."

Television

1890. A teacher in Carmel, California, claims that according to a fifth-grade pupil, the U.S. time zones are, from west to east: "Pacific, Mountain, Central and Ed Sullivan Time."

—Television Age

1891. Research shows that pupils in the elementary school spend on the average more than 20 hours per week televiewing while the average for high school students is between 14 and 17 hours.

—Paul Witty, Editorial, *Reading Teacher*

1892. Give children more heroes and fewer villains. Let us have done with extolling characters who are simply more cagey, or more crafty, than the next one.

—Dr. Martha M. Eliot, Children's Bureau Director, Edison Foundation

1893. The day before last year's eclipse of the moon, my teacher-husband announced to his sixth-grade class that they should be sure to watch the total eclipse at 9 o'clock the following evening. He described it as one of the most wonderful shows that Nature would ever offer them, and stressed the fact that it would be free to everyone to enjoy.

When he had finished, a world-weary eleven-year-old asked resignedly, "What channel will it be on?"

—Dorothy Gonsalves

1894. A new candy, especially designed to be eaten while watching television, has been put on the market. It has a "hi-fi taste" and the sound it gives off is variously described as a crunch, a crackle, or something resembling an audience in a movie house.

1895. We parents are often squelched by our children by things that they say after we have finished reprimanding them. Here is one good example. Last Sunday the boys' television antenna broke on their portable TV; so, remembering an extra set of rabbit ears stuck someplace in the basement, I proceeded to search for them. All the while, my little girl, Marcea, followed me around chattering all the way. Finally she asked what I was looking for, to which I replied, "Rabbit Ears." "What do you want rabbit ears for, Daddy?" was her next question. This, I thought, was a silly question, so I replied, "For goodness sake, Marcea, what do you think I want rabbit ears for?" Noticing the inflection in my voice, she held her head down and shyly looked up at me and asked, "For rabbits?"

—Robert Youman, *Johnson County* (Indiana) *News*

1896. Educational television offers many opportunities, far more than radio ever did. The profession of college teaching can easily get into a rut. The shortage of staff, combined with the undesirable alternatives that lie before us, should compel us to seek ways out of the rut. Our goal today is to educate all young people who are capable of profiting by a college education under the best qualified faculty we can secure. To this end television offers great possibilities, and we in the profession will be wise to exploit them to the utmost.

—J. PAUL LEONARD, former President, San Francisco State College, now President, American University, Beirut, Lebanon

1897. In Washington County, Maryland, there's a TV set in every schoolroom, so I'm told. I think they've got something, for with the national kid population skyrocketing we'll never end the teacher shortage under our present system. The ideal as of 1960 probably will be—not a professor on one end of a log and a student on the other—but a professor on one end of a coaxial cable and 50,000 or more students on the other.

—Author Unknown

1898. The TV repairman was trying to locate the trouble in a friend's set. The six-year-old came dashing home from school. "I'll bet," he said, "if you'd clean out the dead cowboys from the bottom of the set, it would work again."

—*Cappers Weekly*

1899. We read where a fellow, without a TV set, cut a hole in the wall to his neighbor's apartment, and every night he would watch the wrestling matches. It was two weeks before he found out they didn't have a TV set either.

Temper

1900. There is far too much temper and far too little mental in the temperamental.

1901. Hitting the ceiling is the wrong way to get up in the world.

1902. Funny thing about temper. You can't get rid of it by losing it.

1903. Behold, there were five little sparrows, living happily in a tree. Sammy Sparrow came winging home with the news that a truck had overturned and there was plenty to eat. They went, and there were dried prunes and nothing but prunes all along the way. They ate prunes until they could eat no more. To rest they flew over and sat on a farmer's plow handle. Revived a bit, Sammy Sparrow started to fly due north, but in mid-flight he was overtaken with convulsions and fell dead. Henry Sparrow started the opposite way, but he, too, fell and died in agony. The other brothers started east and west, but met the same grim fate. Alicia Sparrow, who was the brains of the family, flew straight up but perished. Lest you suspect that someone had "strychnined" those prunes, those brave sparrows sacrificed themselves to teach us a lesson crucial in this business: "On days when you are full of prunes, don't fly off the handle."

Theory

1904. One of the tragedies of life is the murder of a beautiful theory by a brutal gang of facts.

1905. Theory may be fine to raise our hopes, but it's practice that raises our wages.

Thought

1906. Children may be kept swinging on the gate of sense when they are fully prepared to make easy and fruitful excursions into the garden of thought.

—Dr. E. E. White

1907. A train of thought is of little value unless it carries some freight with it.

1908. Thinking is a most important and most neglected art. One of the criticisms I would suggest against our present system of education is the lack of training in the art of thinking.

—David Sarnoff, President, RCA. *Wisdom*

1909. Whatever your present environment may be, you will fall, remain, or rise with your thoughts, your vision, your ideals. You will become as small as your controlling desire; as great as your dominant aspiration.

—JAMES ALLEN, *Weekly Unity*

1910. A prominent educator made this statement: "The process of thinking draws the blood from the feet to the head." This is a possible explanation of why we sometimes get cold feet when we think twice about a certain proposition.

1911. According to many so-called teachers, meditation consists only of reciting pollyanna affirmations. And this is supposed to work like magic. Nothing of the kind! The tremendous power of the subconscious mind is not that easily reached. A great deal *more* than the reciting of affirmations is needed.

—EDWIN J. DINGLE

1912. You can't stop people from thinking—but you can start them.

1913. Do not ever try to think a thing out of existence, for the more you think of it, the deeper it becomes embedded in your consciousness.

1914. The Edisons and the Marconis were the long range thinkers of yesterday. WANTED: Some long range thinkers today!

—WILLIAM H. DANFORTH, *I Dare You*

1915. The human tongue is only inches from the brain, but when you listen to some folks they seem miles apart.

1916. There have been only a few thousand thought cultivators in the history of the world. It has been said that except for about 1500 of these thinkers living in the last 3,000 years, we might still be living in caves.

—CHARLES KETTERING, *Short Stories of Science and Invention*

1917. For as many years as I can remember, it has been announced as an important aim of education to make students think and to train them in thinking habits. In view of how little we have known about the psychology of thinking, this is a little like attempting to train a pupil in a sport concerning which no one knows the rules. If we have succeeded at all in training students to think, we have done it like the wrestler who proceeds on the catch-as-catch-can basis.

—J. P. GUILFORD, University of Southern California

1918. Think like a duchess, act like a duchess, talk like a duchess; curbstone English keeps you in the gutter.

—BERNARD SHAW

1919. Wishful, even hopeful thinking, without *discipline, force* and *firmness*, does more harm than good. Even our modern psychologists recognize that. Yet not one in a thousand exerts mental discipline and power to concentrate, sufficient to make effective use of the tremendous powers of the sub-conscious mind, which, authorities are now agreed, are almost *without limit*.

—EDWIN J. DINGLE

1920. Negative thinking is merely the absence of Positive Thinking. Negative Thinkers are passive. They are not "against" anything—just firmly disinterested.

1921. Our private statistician says a person will exert himself 176 times as much to put something in an empty stomach as in an empty head.

1922. Food for thought, like any other food, should be attractive and appetizing.

1923. Thoughts are like magnets, in that positive and negative forces are involved.

1924. We have millions who are afflicted with mental laziness—those who are satisfied. They are the easy thinkers. When a new thought is given them, they find it much easier to agree than to question it. And that is dangerous, especially if the idea is a bad one.

—CHARLES F. KETTERING, *Short Stories of Science and Invention*

1925. No man who thinks in terms of catching mice will ever catch lions.

1926. Thinking is a habit like piano-playing, not a process like eating or sleeping. The amount of thinking you can do at any time will depend primarily on the amount of thinking you have already done.

1927. A shallow thinker seldom makes a deep impression.

1928. One who travels thoughtfully adds another dimension to his life.

1929. Teach them to look at a matter from every side before they announce their conclusions.

Teach them to observe, to be accurate and careful in their observations and statements.

Teach them to search for truth and to be able to recognize it.

Teach them the meaning of cause and effect.

Teach them not to be superstitious.

—Teacher Training Officer

1930. A conservative is a man who acts impulsively after thinking for a long time.

—HERBERT V. PROCHNOW

1931. Be careful of your thoughts—they may break into words at any time.

1932. Some people become lost in thought only because it is unfamiliar territory.

1933. Men are ruled by their thoughts and men rule the world. Thoughts are real—they are far more powerful than the most potent chemicals that are mixed and can be much more explosive.

Thoughts are the blueprints for action—they are the parents of deeds. As we are controlled and completely governed by our thoughts, far greater care should be given to what we put into our minds than to what we eat or wear.

In the final analysis, you alone are responsible for your thoughts. You alone decide upon the choice of thinking that completely controls your life. You decide whether your thoughts are to be constructive or destructive or whether they will be translated into good or evil actions.

—ROY KEATON, *The Lion*

1934. A farmer on a special shopping errand for his young son finally ventured into the pet shop and asked the price of the parrot. He was more than amazed when he discovered that the price was one hundred dollars for this small bird.

He had an idea. He brought from his farm a turkey and offered it to the keeper of the pet shop, saying, "I only want two hundred dollars for it."

"You must be mad," observed the merchant.

"Why, it makes sense to me," said the farmer. "If one hundred is a fair price for that tiny parrot, then my turkey must be worth at least three hundred."

"Wait a minute," insisted the shopkeeper, "the parrot can talk, what can your bird do?"

"My bird is a philosopher," said the farmer. "He thinks."

1935. Mullah Nasr-ed-Din, a 12th century Persian humorist, was a practical joker. He originated a rumor that bread would be given away at 5:00 A.M. next morning to all the villagers. The village buzzed and people rose early—but at 5:00 A.M. there was no bread. An hour later there was still no bread. One old-timer, wise to Mullah's ways, realized what had happened and started up the hill to Mullah's abode.

He met Mullah hurrying down. "Where are you going, Mullah?" he asked. "To the village to get some bread," replied Mullah. "But it's your own joke," reminded the old-timer. "I know," said Mullah, "but I got to thinking about it and decided there might be something to it."

1936. . . . These original thinkers seem to have many things in common. First, there is the desire and ability to create—to do something original—something no one has ever done or been able to do before. Second, there is the quality of persistence, the urge to keep going until it is finished—regardless of surroundings, poverty, or health. Third, there is that dissatisfaction which seems to be the standard equipment of these men. Regardless of how outstanding their work appears to the world, they themselves are never satisfied with it and are sure if they had it to do over they could have done a better job.

—CHARLES KETTERING, *Short Stories of Science and Invention*

1937. As a man thinks—so is he not, unless he puts *power* in his thought. One lecturer after another, one new thought book after another, tries to tell you that holding the right thought can accomplish *anything*. Nonsense! Thought without *force* behind it can actually be harmful. True, mind-power can do almost anything. But it must be mind-*power*. Holding the right thought is only the *first step*. He who depends on thought alone is deceiving himself.

—EDWIN J. DINGLE

Time

1938. "Yesterday is a canceled check. Tomorrow is a promissory note. Today is the only cash you have—spend it wisely."

1939. There are only a handful of things that actually *have* to be done in this world, and there is time for all of them. The trouble is that most of us get to *doing* so many things that we have no time to *be*.

—JOAN YOUNGER

1940. Men spend their lives in anticipation, in determining to be vastly happy at some period or other, when they have time. But the present time has one advantage over every other; it is our own.

1941. To do a great and important work, two things are necessary—a definite plan, and not quite enough time.

—*Nuggets*

1942. Time flies, all right, but during working hours it often seems to be bucking head winds.

—LUKE NEELY, *Saturday Evening Post*

1943. The longer the fiddle, the brighter the blaze. Time is not for burning.

1944. Time: You can't save it, you can't borrow it, you can't loan it, you can't leave it, and you can't take it. We can do only two things with it: (1) use it, and (2) lose it.

1945. Recently, the newspapers told of a man who refused a million dollars for an invention he had evolved in his spare time. Of course! Most of the world's great men have achieved their true life work, not in the course of their needful occupations, but—in their spare time. Think it over, and you will see how true it is.

—ALBERT PAYSON TERHUNE, *The American Magazine*

1946. There's a proverb which says "whatever you have, spend less"; this includes time, which should be used, not spent.

1947. According to a study made by a University of Wisconsin psychology class, if you live to be 70, you will have spent one year on the telephone, about 20 years sleeping, 2 months signing paychecks for 20 solid years of work done, 5 years shaving and dressing, 5 months tying shoes, 2½ years in bed, 2½ years smoking, 7 years in sports, and 3 years just waiting on something or somebody. They don't say where you will have spent the rest of your time.

—*Northwestern Bell*

1948. While on a motor trip with a friend through Georgia, I met a local character who spent most of his time on the porch of a "fork-in-the-road" settlement in the turpentine region.

His slowness of speech and deliberate actions caused me to ask him the why and wherefore of his outstanding characteristics. "Wal, son," he drawled, "hit don't pay nobody to be in a hurry. You allus pass up more than you catch up with."

—Millard Miller, *Country Gentlemen*

1949. There is nothing wrong with wanting to get somewhere. Most people have plans for progress in their work or homes or family. It is a tragic mistake, however, to hurry so much to "get somewhere" that we miss all our opportunities for happiness today. You will never again be as young as you are today. Do you have time for children? They may no longer be children when you think you have time.

—Rev. Malcolm E. Nygren

1950. Time wasted is existence; used, it is life.

1951. Time passes quickly. There is nothing we can do about it except to see that, as far as possible, it passes fruitfully. If in passing it lays up its store of good deeds done, noble ambitions clung to heroically, and kindness and sympathy scattered with a lavish hand, there will always be given to it a permanence and enduring quality that nothing can take away. Take time to look—it is the price of success. Take time to think—it is a source of power. Take time to play—it is the secret of perennial youth. Take time to read—it is the source of wisdom. Take time to be friendly—it is the way to happiness. Take time to laugh—it is the music of the soul.

—Author Unknown

1952. When John Erskine was 14 or 15 years old, his music teacher asked him how long he practiced each day. "Four or five hours," came the answer. "Four or five hours at a stretch?" asked the teacher. The pupil nodded. "I was afraid of that," the teacher said. The warning that followed, John Erskine never forgot. His teacher pointed out that as he went about earning his own living, he would seldom have as much as five hours at a time to practice.

He who would build a productive life must cherish the shortest snatches of time, for therein lies opportunity.

Tolerance

1953. When our PTA honored Miss Bestwick, retiring teacher, someone asked where she learned to be so tolerant. In her first year, she explained, when a mole on a little boy's neck turned out to be a spot on her eyeglasses.

—Burton Hillis, *Better Homes and Gardens*

1954. The only thing harder to inherit than money is a tolerant attitude.

—Hal Boyle

1955. Tolerance is that kindly feeling we have for people who don't agree with us but who admit we *could be right*.

1956. Tolerance: That uncomfortable feeling that the other fellow may be right after all.

—*Personnel Adviser*

Tradition

1957. A great factory was in flames. Clouds of smoke billowed skyward and sparks and flames mounted to the heavens as part of the roof collapsed. Thousands stood in awe, helpless.

A cry went up. "Tons of T.N.T. are stored in that building; unless the fire is stopped, there will be an explosion that will wreck the neighborhood! Somebody do something quickly!"

The fire department sped through the streets, sirens shrieking. The crowd breathed a sigh of relief.

But a little knot of citizens stood at a street corner holding a conference. "Only Bill Brady, the fire chief, knows how to get at the fire and put it out," said one. "He has been a good chief and has saved hundreds of thousands of dollars' worth of property. But he has served as chief eight years. There is a tradition that no fire chief ought to serve longer than that, so he ought to be fired. Let us go at once, pull him from his car and take his authority away from him."

"That's right," agreed another. "Bill has got to go, and right now. We ought to put Charley Clatterwood in his place. Charley never fought a fire in his life; he has had no experience, but everything we know has been done well he says has been done all wrong. He says he himself would make a good chief, so we ought to put him in charge of fighting this fire right now."

"You're right," said another. "It is true that Charley has been working in that rival factory. Those people would be glad to have their competition destroyed right now by this fire. But we have to dismiss good old Bill and put Charley in charge this instant. You see, there is tradition—or something."

—Origin Unknown

1958. One cold snowy morning an old man was seen, dressed in his nightshirt, vigorously chopping kindling. His neighbor, amazed at the brevity of the old man's clothing in such severe weather, asked, "How come?"

The old man never missed a lick in his chopping as he replied, "For the last 70 years, I have always dressed by a fire, and I'll be dad gummed if I'm gonna stop now."

—*Capper's Weekly*

Trouble—Troubles

1959. Warning! Following are the names of the seven Mischievous Misses who are responsible for most of our troubles: Miss Information, Miss Quotation, Miss Representation, Miss Interpretation, Miss Construction, Miss Conception, Miss Understanding. Don't listen to them! Beware!

—William J. Boetcker, *Forbes*

1960. Thomas Carlyle, great man that he was, could easily be upset by some trifling happening. A neighbor of his had a rooster that would start crowing about 4 o'clock every morning, when the author, having had a strenuous day and evening, wanted to sleep late. Being so greatly disturbed by the rooster, he went to his neighbor to complain.

"Does the crowing keep you awake?" asked the owner. "No," replied Carlyle, "it is not his crowing that keeps me awake; it is my lying there expecting him to crow."

—W. G. MONTGOMERY, *Weekly Unity*

1961. The greatest mistake is to feel sorry for ourselves and to think that our problems are large and everybody else's are small. We are surrounded by trials and tragedies. How fortunate we are. Our hardships cannot be compared with those visited upon the men of the armed forces on the battlefronts of the world. According to Socrates, "If all our misfortunes were laid on one common heap, whence everyone must take an equal portion, most people would be content to take their own and depart."

—Source Unknown

1962. The tractor of an Oklahoma farmer broke down in the mud one day. He went to his barn for chains and a shovel. As he crossed the field a neighbor called, "Having a little trouble, Charlie?" He replied: "Nope—no trouble at all. I don't call anything trouble I can fix."

1963. It is not the things we don't know that gets us into trouble —it is the things we know for sure that are not so.

1964. If you could kick the person responsible for many of your troubles, you wouldn't be able to sit down in comfort for six months.

1965. Troubles, like babies, grow larger by nursing.

1966. Whenever you are tempted to tell your troubles to other people, remember that half your listeners aren't interested, and the rest are glad you're finally getting what's coming to you.

1967. It's the little things that really trouble you—you can sit in comfort on a mountain, but not on a tack.

1968. When you say that you've troubles as great as my own,
I'm forced to admit that it's true;
But consider the fact that mine happen to me,
While yours merely happen to you.

1969. One way to keep happy is to learn to enjoy trouble.

1970. Most of us carry our own stumbling block around with us— we camouflage it with a hat.

1971. *Joe:* "You look very downcast."

Jim: "Yes, my wife has been away for six weeks, and she's just come back."

Joe: "Why should that make you sad?"

Jim: "Well, I told her that I spent all my evenings at home and today the light bill came. It's fifty cents."

Truth

1972. According to Hindu law, lying is justified in only two cases; in saving a person's life and in paying a compliment to a lady.

1973. When the truth is in your way, you are on the wrong road.

—Josh Billings

Understanding

1974. If you don't understand pre-adolescent youth, please don't misunderstand them.

1975. If you can't understand children, don't brand them!

Vacation

1976. The one book that really tells you where you can go on your vacation is your checkbook.

—Imogene Fey

1977. Anyone who says you can't take it with you never saw a car packed for a vacation.

Verbosity

1978. Shoe shine for 15 cents: "Pedal habiliments artistically lubricated and illuminated with ambidexterous facility for the paltry remuneration of 15 cents per operation."

1979. A home economist was giving a cooking demonstration before a group of farm women. "Take an egg," she explained, "and carefully perforate the basal end. Duplicate the process in the apex. Then, applying the lips to one of the apertures, by forcibly exhaling the breath, discharge the shell of its contents."

Aunt Cassie, age 85, turned to a neighbor. "Beats all how different this new-fangled way is," she said. "When I was a girl, we just poked a hole in each end and blowed."

—*W.O.W. Magazine*

1980. An old saying, "A rolling stone gathers no moss," dressed up in new clothes: "A mass of concentrated earthly material perennially rotating on its axis will not accumulate an accretion of bryophtic vegetation."

1981. A precocious five-year-old son of a professor asked his father what was the exact meaning of the verse beginning, "Humpty-Dumpty sat on a wall."

"In simple terms," said the professor, "it means Humpty-Dumpty perched on a vertical, solid structure; losing his equilibrium, he dropped from a higher to a lower level. Even the potentate's equestrians failed to succeed in assembling the fractured particles. Is that clear, son?"

"Absolutely," replied the son, "the lack of clarity in these alleged Mother Goose rhymes is amazingly apparent to one with an intellect above the moronic level."

1982. If some college professors I've heard in meetings receive "wordage" as salesmen receive "mileage," they would be wealthy beyond imagination.

—M. Dale Baughman

1983. Many a tourist to my native Brown County, Indiana, has been completely astonished at the literacy and lucidity of one of the highly educated old-timers there. Not infrequently, touring city dwellers have commented to him as he sat in his porch swing sucking on his corn-cob pipe, "Doesn't it get pretty lonesome around here?"

Preceded first by a well-aimed spit and then a shift of his corn-cob pipe he delivers his surprising philosophical reply, "Solitude exists only as a temporary function of the mind's reaction to one's surroundings, inoculating those affected with considerable success. Being indigenous to this primeval forest and having suffered from claustrophobia in my youth, I find habitation in nature's scenic wonderland not only tranquil and satisfying, but essentially compulsory."

—M. Dale Baughman

1984. There was a fellow in my home county, Lomer Jones, whose trouble was that he couldn't keep anything to himself. Lomer seemed compelled to ferret out the wrongdoings of his neighbors and friends and then blab them all over the countryside. The fact that he always told the truth made matters worse.

On one occasion, however, he was properly chastised, when he met a talking turtle on the road. The turtle said, "Lomer, you talk too damn much!" Those words made Lomer jump right up and run for town.

He went to the local tavern and told the patrons all about the talking turtle. At first they only laughed at him but as Lomer became more convincing as he pleaded on and on, the whole crowd finally gave in and followed him. However, when they reached the old turtle, he wouldn't say a word. The disbelievers, mad because of the long walk and wasted time, shoved Lomer into a ditch and went back to town.

Lomer quickly scrambled from the ditch and stood up. The old turtle slowly blinked its red eyes. "Didn't I tell you before?" said the turtle, "you talk too damn much!"

1985. The quiet man in the crowd had grown tired of the boastful talk of the others. So, when there was a lull in the conversation, he began:

"This morning I went over to see a new machine we've got at our place, and it's astonishing how it works."

"And how does it work?" asked one.

"Well," was the reply, "by means of a pedal attachment a fulcrum lever converts a vertical reciprocal motion into a circular movement. The principal part of the machine is a huge disc that revolves in a vertical plane. Power is applied through the axis of the disc, and work is done on the periphery, where the hardest steel by mere impact may be reduced to any shape."

"What is this wonderful machine?" chorused the crowd.

"A grindstone."

Viewpoint

1986. The old saying about the grass being greener on the other side of the fence might be changed to "You don't see the thistles in the green grass from a distance."

1987. Two Greeks were watching their first football game. Said one to the other: "This is all American to me."

1988. A man's feet must be planted in his country, but his eyes should survey the world.
—GEORGE SANTAYANA

1989. A hen and a hog were out in the barnyard tending to their Sunday morning duties, when the morning breeze wafted the front page of the *Indianapolis Star* into the farm lot. The hen read the blazing headlines which said, "U.S. FACES BIG HAM AND EGG SHORTAGE."

The hen called to the hog, "Come on over, big boy, and see what the paper says." The hog read the headlines and replied, "So what?"

Said the hen, "We've got to do something."

The hog replied, "Listen, little girl, I don't see why you're so upset; it's just a production job for you; it's life or death for me."

1990. Whenever two people meet there are really six people present. There is each man as he sees himself, each man as the other person sees him, and each man as he really is.
—WILLIAM JAMES

1991. A farmer took his new hunting dog out for a "test run." Presently he shot a duck. The dog walked out on the water, retrieved the duck and brought it in. The farmer blinked, rubbed his eyes, and tried again, with the same result.

Incredulous, bewildered and completely flabbergasted, he invited a neighbor to go with him the following day. True to form, when either man hit a bird, the dog would walk on the water and retrieve it. The neighbor said nothing. The farmer said nothing. Finally, unable to hold in a moment longer, the owner of the dog blurted a query, "D-did y' notice anything unusual about my dog?"

The neighbor rubbed his chin reflectively, "Yeah," he said at length. "Yeah, come t' think of it, I did. The son-of-a-gun can't swim!"
—*Louisville Courier-Journal Magazine*

1992. A customer waiting for a job to be done on his car watched a mechanic change the oil in another car—not spilling a drop—check the radiator carefully, clean the windshield, wipe away the greasy finger marks, place a clean cloth over the upholstery, wash his hands thoroughly and drive the car slowly out to the street curb.

"Now there's a real mechanic," the customer observed.

"Oh," said the station manager, "that's his own car."

—Machinist

1993. The educated man is the one who refuses to view the world from the steeple of his own church.

—Missionary Tidings

1994. A reporter asked a Chinese delegate to the United Nations, "What strikes you as the oddest thing about Americans?"

His reply was, "I think it is the peculiar slant of their eyes."

1995. A big-league umpire once remarked that he could never understand how crowds in the grandstand, hundreds of feet from the plate, could see better and judge more accurately than he, when he was only seven feet away.

Another man commented that in life, too, we call strikes on a chap when we are too far away to understand. Perhaps, if we had a closer view of the man and his problems we would reverse our decisions.

—Information

1996. Driving in the country one day, a man saw an old fellow sitting on a fence rail, watching the automobiles go by. Stopping to talk, the traveler said, "I never could stand living out here. You don't see anything. You don't travel like I do. I'm going all the time."

The old man on the fence looked down at the stranger slowly and then drawled: "I can't see much difference in what I'm doing and what you're doing. I set on the fence and watch the autos go by and you set in your auto and watch the fences go by. It's just the way you look at things."

—Wall Street Journal

1997. A family stops before a show window filled with women's wearing apparel. The wife sees the beautiful dresses and notes the kind of material they are fashioned from; the husband sees the price tags; and the little son sees the wax dummies.

—Lowell Filmore, *Weekly Unity*

1998. After his first visit to Congress, a high school boy said this about the proceedings: "A man gets up and says nothing. Nobody listens—then everybody disagrees."

1999. "What funny names those Korean towns have," remarked an Illinois native from Teutopolis as he read a Tiskilwa newspaper while on his way to Somonauk.

2000.
I thought that foreign children
Lived far across the sea,
Until I got a letter from a boy in Italy.
"Dear little foreign friend," it said
As plainly as could be.
Now I wonder who is "foreign"—
The other child or me?

—Ethel Blair Jordan, *Phi Delta Kappan*

2001. The simple realization that there are other points of view is the beginning of wisdom. Understanding what they are is a great step. The final test is understanding why they are held.

—Charles M. Campbell, *Supervision*

2002. A boy who dwelled in the mountains was fascinated by a house on the opposite side of the valley. Each evening its windows were sheets of shining gold. Unable to resist the temptation, he made his way across the valley toward the house. But the path was rough and in exhaustion he lay down and slept.

Early the next morning he hurried to the house. Instead of sheets of gold, the windows were but ordinary glass. Disappointed and bitter, he turned toward home, then stopped in surprise. Across the valley, the house he lived in was a-gleam with windows of gold.

—*Rotarian*

2003. Age seems to be viewed as a relative thing by many people. Whether you're "old" or "young," and whether you accept the designations as a matter of course, depends to some extent on the line of work you're in. Richard Nixon at 43 is regarded as a "young" Vice-President. A female movie star of 43 is called "middle-aged."

333

A baseball player at 43 is called "old." At age 50 corporation executives are considered relatively young. But a coal miner is old when he is 50.

2004. A great deal of what we see depends upon what we are looking for.

2005. A penny will hide the biggest star in the universe, if you hold it close enough to your eye.

2006. Prejudices are rarely overcome by argument; not being founded on reason, they cannot be destroyed by logic.

2007. There is a fable about two buckets on their way to the well. One commented, "How dismal you look." "Ah," replied the other, "I was reflecting on the uselessness of our being filled, for we go away full, but we always come back empty."

"Dear me! How strange to look at it that way," said the other bucket. "I enjoy the thought that, however empty we come, we always go away full. Look on it in that light and you will be as cheerful as I am."

2008. Five men entered the same field. The geologist found various types of rock formations. The botanist found the many kinds of plants. The entomologist discovered butterflies, beetles, and other insects. The farmer found the variations in the soil. The poet saw the wind in the grasses and the warmth of the sun and the flight of the bird against the azure sky. Thus, each man found the thing he was looking for.

—Indiana Farmers Guide

Voice

2009. With an engine it's the tune; with your voice it's the tone. Is it a yell, sarcastic, drippy, monotonous?

2010. A social worker in a hospital says that there are 57 different ways in which patients say "Come in," when she knocks on their doors.

2011. When Mae West says, "Come up and see me sometime!" it is not what she says but the *tone* behind the words that have the real double meaning.

—ELMER WHEELER

2012. Ninety per cent of all the friction of daily life is caused by mere tone of voice. When a man speaks, his words convey his thoughts and his tone conveys his mood!

Will—Will Power

2013. "How did you keep from crying?" someone asked a little girl who had fallen and hurt her knee. She answered firmly, "I just said to myself, 'Stop that,' and made myself mind me."

2014. Three thousand years ago in the ancient country of Greece there lived a great oracle who never had given a wrong answer to any question. He came one day to a small town where there lived a little boy.

This little boy, sitting on the back step of his home, kept thinking that if he could ask just one question that would cause the great man to make a mistake, just this once he would be the littlest big shot in the little town.

He planned and thought and suddenly there came to him a plan which was fool-proof. Here is what he planned and said to himself: "I'll go out in the woods and catch a small bird, one small enough that I can hold safely concealed in my two hands. Then I'll go to the great man and ask him, 'Oh, great oracle, what hold I in my hands?' He of course will say I hold a bird. I will then say, 'Yes sir, but is it dead or alive?'

"Now if he says it is dead, I will but open my hands and the little bird will fly away. If he says it is alive, I will silently crush it. No matter what his answer, I will prove him wrong."

The little boy, happy with his plan, ran off into the woods and had soon caught a small bird, one he could safely conceal in his hands. He found the building where the great man was and soon was granted an audience. He stood before the great man, excited but confident, and said, "Oh, great oracle, what hold I in my hands?"

The great man smiled and said, "Little boy, you hold a bird in

335

your hands. "Yes sir," said the little boy, "but is it dead or alive?" The oracle was about to answer; then a look of great wisdom came into his eyes. Placing his hand on the little boy's head, he said, "Young man, the answer to that is in your hands."

2015. We are not sent into the world to do anything into which we cannot put our hearts. We have certain work to do for our bread, and that is to be done strenuously; other work to do for our delight, and that is done heartily—neither is to be done by halves, but with a will, and what is not worth this effort, is not to be done at all.

—JOHN RUSKIN

2016. Will Power: The ability, after you have used three-fourths of a can of paint and finished the job, to close the can and clean the brush, instead of painting something else that doesn't really need it.

—*Indiana Telephone News*

2017. A seventeen-year-old applied for a job with a road construction gang. He was rather slightly built and the boss eyed him critically. "Afraid you won't do, son," he said. "This is heavy work and you can't keep up with the heavier, older men." The youngster glanced at the crew leaning on their shovels. "Perhaps I can't do as much as these men *can* do," he replied, "but I certainly can do as much as they *will* do." He got the job.

—*Executives' Digest*

Willingness

2018. The world is full of willing people; some willing to work, the rest willing to let them.

2019.   We cannot gain the sweetness of success
    Just through a set of rules at our command,
    Since rules, however good, will never work
    Unless we lend a willing, eager hand.

—INEZ CLARK THORSON, *You Magazine*

Wisdom

2020. It is never wise to argue with a fool; onlookers never can discern which is which.

2021. I would indeed be a wise man if I could answer these questions which our five-year-old daughter, Dala, asked me:

> How big is big?
> What is the sky made of?
> What are you going to be when you grow up?
> How soft is an eyeball?
> Why doesn't Jesus kill the Devil?
>
> —M. DALE BAUGHMAN

2022. Wisdom is the scar tissue of intelligence.

—GENE GLEASON, *Catholic Digest*

2023. Will of your own is more likely to help you succeed than the will of a rich relative.

—*Indianapolis Times*

2024. Much wisdom often goes with fewest words.

—SOPHOCLES

2025. But to know that which before us lies in daily life is the prime wisdom.

—MILTON

2026. Knowledge can be memorized. Wisdom must think things through.

Wisdom is the something that enables us to use knowledge rightly.

Wisdom does not climb on the bandwagon. It does not follow the crowd.

Wisdom gives generously but it does not let money be taken away. Wisdom may buy but it does not let itself be "sold."

Wisdom resists group pressures, thinks for itself, and is reconciled to the use of its own judgment.

2027. The doorstep to the temple of wisdom is the knowledge of our own ignorance.

—SPURGEON

2028. Some people are like owls. They get the reputation for being wise just by hooting at everything.

—GUY WAGNER, *Education*

2029. Discretion-maxim of the native Haitians, as reported by a returning traveler: "Never insult an alligator till after you have crossed the river."

2030. A wise man uses foolishness to explain his wisdom; a foolish man uses wisdom to explain his foolishness.

2031. It doesn't matter how much money you have; everyone has to buy wisdom on the installment plan.

—*Grit*

2032. The proverbs tell us that the house of wisdom has seven pillars. In all humility I would like to offer these Biblical pillars: knowledge, integrity, and judgment; imagination and courage; tolerance and faith.

—E. B. FRED

2033. The fool wonders but the wise man asks.

—DISRAELI

2034. To be a questioner also shows a willingness to admit ignorance. To conceal ignorance is to imitate wisdom. To admit ignorance is to exhibit wisdom.

—ASHLEY MONTAGUE

2035.   A wise old owl sat in an oak.
The more he heard the less he spoke,
The less he spoke the more he heard.
Why aren't we like that old bird?

2036. If we are kind without being soft, if we are gracious without being sentimental, and if we are wise without being smart, we will be able to put at students' disposal that which God has given us by the accident of birth.

—DR. HOWARD THURMAN, Dean of Marsh Chapel,
Boston University

2037.   It taketh age to make a sage,
The wise no longer doubt it;
The older we grow the more we know
And the less we brag about it.

2038. Every man is a fool for at least five minutes a day. Wisdom consists in not exceeding the time limit.

2039. Common sense, in an uncommon degree, is what the world calls wisdom.

—COLERIDGE

2040. Not experience, but *thinking* about experience, gives wisdom.

2041.   If wisdom's ways you'd wisely seek,
Five things observe with care;
Of whom you speak,
To whom you speak,
And how and when and where.

2042. "Ve grow too soon oldt, und too late schmart."

2043. Who is wise? He that learns from everyone. Who is powerful? He that governs his passions. Who is rich? He that is content. Who is that? Nobody.

—BEN FRANKLIN

2044. When you assemble a number of men to have the advantage of their joint wisdom, you inevitably assemble with these men all their prejudices, their passions, their errors of opinion, their local interests and their selfish views.

—BEN FRANKLIN

Words

2045. Many a true word is spoken through false teeth.

2046. Words are like sunbeams—the more they are condensed, the deeper they burn.

2047. Words are the dress of thought, which should no more be presented in rags, tatters and dirt than your person should.

2048. Words are storybooks; words are adventurers; words are fun—no less so when appearing sometimes in formidable alphabetical order in volumes of sturdy binding and sober dress. Let's know the truth about our living language—and make it known.

—*National Parent-Teacher*

2049. The wife of a rising young tycoon hired her first interior decorator to fancy up her new menage. He showed her a whole spectrum of colors. She insisted she wanted "something different, something none of our friends will have." Finally the decorator choked, "Madam, there is no such color! It's just a pigment of your imagination!"

—TONY WEITZEL, *Chicago Daily News*

2050. Research by Dr. Wilfred Funk revealed the ten most expressive words in the English language:

The most bitter word is "Alone"; the most reverent, "Mother"; the most tragic, "Death"; the most beautiful, "Love"; the most cruel, "Revenge"; the most peaceful, "Tranquil"; the saddest, "Forgotten"; the warmest, "Friendship"; the coldest, "No"; the one bringing the most comfort, "Faith."

Work

2051. When you play, play with all your might, but when you work, don't play at all.

—THEODORE ROOSEVELT

2052. Did you hear of the guy who gave up his job because of illness? He got sick of it.

2053. Some fellows always reach for the stool when there is a piano to be moved.

2054.
If your nose is close
    To the grindstone rough,
And you hold it down there
    Long enough
In time you'll say
    There's no such thing
As brooks that babble
    And birds that sing.
These three will all your
    World compose:
Just you, the stone
    And your silly old nose.

—Author Unknown

2055. The man who removes a mountain begins by carrying away small stones.

—Chinese Proverb

2056.
You never see me watch the clock
    When work is still undone;
Let other fellows quit at five—
    I'll wait till 5:01.

—PHILIP LAZARUS

2057. Too many people stop looking for work when they get a job.

2058. Solomon should have taken a closer look at those ants. Or so contends Dr. R. G. Wheeler, University of North Dakota: "Ants spend a lot of time loafing. We get an impression of activity, but that's because there are so many ants, and all look alike."

—*Quote*

2059. I never did anything worth doing by accident, nor did any of my inventions come by accident; they came by work.

—THOMAS A. EDISON

2060.   I was early taught to work as well as play;
My life has been one long, happy holiday—
Full of work, and full of play—
I dropped the worry on the way—
And God was good to me every day.

—JOHN D. ROCKEFELLER

2061. Man must work. That is certain as the sun. But he may work grudgingly or he may work gratefully; he may work as a man, or he may work as a machine. There is no work so rude that he may not exalt it; no work so impassive that he may not breathe a soul into it; no work so dull that he may not enliven it.

—HENRY GILES, *Good Business*

2062. Nothing is really work unless you would rather be doing something else.

—SIR JAMES BARRIE

2063. Hard work means nothing to a hen. She just keeps on digging worms and laying eggs, regardless of what the business prognosticators say about the outlook for this or any other year.

If the ground is hard, she scratches harder. If it's dry, she digs deeper. If it's wet, she digs where it's dry. If she hits a rock, she digs around it. If she gets a few more hours of daylight, she gives up a few more eggs and digs a few hours longer. But she always digs up worms and turns them into hard-shelled profits. Did you ever see a pessimistic hen?

2064. There is no record of anybody ever being drowned in sweat.

—BURTON HILLIS, *Better Homes and Gardens*

2065. Consider the hammer.

A good one doesn't lose its head and fly off the handle. It finds the point and drives it home.

It looks on the other side and clinches the matter.

Occasionally, it makes mistakes, but it rectifies them.

It keeps pounding away until the job is done.

It is the only knocker in the world that does constructive work.

2066. Harry Houdini, the wizard whom shackles could not hold, once tied my handkerchief into two seemingly hard-and-fast knots, and then tugged—and the knots were not.

But there are no more Houdinis. The only way the average man can untie the knotty problems of life is to work like blazes, hope, play, love, laugh—and then work some more.

—JERRY FLEISHMAN, *Trailer Talk*

2067. Joining a club is like taking a stance at home plate; after that there has to be a swing and a follow through.

2068. People who think they don't like to work remind me of an officer I knew in the Navy. For four years he griped about everything connected with the Navy. Then when the time came to get out—he signed up for four more years! Don't wait until you retire to realize you like to work. Start enjoying your job today.

—JOHN LUTHER, *Economics Press Pamphlet*

2069. Creative, inventive, original work is grueling hard work. It involves a persistence and a love of work with which few men are gifted, and is seldom accomplished except under pressure. If there were no reward to be gained, very few would undertake it. In place of driving hard to get ahead, it is so much easier to relax and drift with the current.

—JACOB DOLSON COX, JR., *Material Human Progress*

Worry

2070. Grandpa and Grandma were too busy scratching for a living to need books on how to stop worrying.

—*Cincinnati Enquirer*

2071. Don't spoil today by worrying about tomorrow. The hills flatten out when we come to them.

—*Phi Delta Kappan*

2072. A doctor says little worries won't hurt anyone. Has he ever tried raising a large family?

2073. The patient told her doctor she was so worried that she had butterflies in her stomach.

"Take an aspirin," advised the doctor, "and the butterflies will go away."

Whereupon the lady moaned, "But I took an aspirin—they're playing ping-pong with it now!"

—*Wisconsin Telephone News*

2074. Worry is like a rocking chair. It gives you something to do, but it doesn't get you anywhere.

2075. A man worries about what the future will have in store, but a woman worries about what the stores will have in the future.

—ROBERT CUMMINGS

2076. When a Chicago policeman started to ticket a double-parked car, a man hurried up and explained that he always double parks when he visits his dentist. He likes to have something to worry about to keep his mind off the pain.

Youth

2077. We used to hear so much about youngsters running away from home to get married. In this day and time they get married and run back home.

—*Wisconsin Journal of Education*

2078. It may be that adults give entirely too much attention to preparing the path for our youth and much too little attention to preparing our youth for the path.

2079. Youth is a time when you can be a college track star during the day—but can't go to the corner drug store at night without the family car.

2080. At the age of 18, I was an accomplished ne'er do well, with little in the pocket and less in the head. Oh, I knew my "P's" all right (powder, picnics, passivity), but the "Q's" (quickness, queries, qualms) were to come much later.

2081. In the bright lexicon of youth there may be no such word as "Fail" but he soon learns a lot of dandy synonyms.

2082. Questions of peace are decided not by brave warriors locked in mortal combat, but by little chaps with high foreheads.
—*Ethical Outlook,* DR. MATTHEW SPETTER

2083. Patrick Henry said, "Give me liberty or give me death." His descendants just say, "Gimme."

2084. Money alone cannot cure delinquency. In our society, it is easy to forget that the whole course of life is determined, not by our material gains and losses, but by our spiritual values.
—OVETA CULP HOBBY

2085. When we say delinquency is increasing we really don't know what we are talking about. Useful data will be obtained only when we separate records of children in serious trouble. The statistics we have are like illness statistics we'd have if the health department couldn't distinguish between smallpox and chickenpox.
—DR. SOPHIA M. ROBISON

2086. Denunciation of the young is a necessary part of the hygiene of older people and greatly assists in the circulation of their blood.
—LOGAN PEARSALL SMITH

2087. The ambitious youth of today has only to be alert, study hard—and not get nervous in the isolation booth.
—IVERN BOYETT

2088. Some teen-agers regard home as the drive-in where pop pays for the hamburgers.
—NOEL WICAL

2089. Youth grows and develops largely by example. It seeks the esteem of those it respects for character and achievement. When this respect and example are mutual among groups coming together on common ground, the influence of one upon another is enormously multiplied.
—WALT DISNEY, *Indiana Freemason*

2090. School girls in England were warned to beware of the "Seven C's": "clothes, cinemas, cigarets, crooning, chocolate, candlelight, and chops."

2091. Youth is not a time of life—it is a state of mind. It is not a matter of red cheeks, red lips and supple knees. It is a temper of the will, a quality of the imagination, a vigor of the emotions; it is a freshness of the deep springs of life. Youth means a temperamental predominance of courage over timidity, of the appetite for adventure over a life of ease. This often exists in a man of 50 or more, than in a boy of 20. Nobody grows old by merely living a number of years; people grow old by deserting their ideals.

—Samuel Ullman

2092. A young man took his father's car without permission, picked up a pal, and went on a joy ride. Speeding up, he attempted to pass another car, his car landing in a ditch and he in the police station, cut and bruised, with his pal in the hospital.

Sitting on the edge of his cot, he thought of the car and his pal. He wondered if the car could be repaired, if his friend would recover.

Looking up he saw his father's face through the grating and exclaimed: "I don't know what you'll think of me but—" He was cut short by his father, who asked: "What do you think of yourself?— That's the question."

2093.   Ah, lucky lad, may Fortune not forsake you;
(I, too, when young, peeped into Paradise)
May Time, the Watchman, never overtake you;
Nor Caution dull the mischief in your eyes.

No matter what the whim of Fate denies,
No matter how the years may bump and blunder,
God in His mercy keep your shining eyes
Glued to the knothole of eternal wonder.

—Joseph Auslander

2094. Some people think the modern youngster's prayer seems to be: "Lead us not into temptation, but tell us where it is and we'll find it."

2095. It's foolish to worry about confused, miserable teenagers. Give them a few years and they'll turn out to be normal, miserable adults.

345

2096. A car being driven in reverse down a street in Coeur d'Alene, Idaho, was stopped by police. Said the teen-age driver, "I ran up too much mileage and now I'm unwinding some of it."

—FRANCES RODMAN

2097. There's likely to be a breakdown in communication between young ones and parents unless Pa and Ma learn teen talk.

This mother of a sub-teen-ager learned quickly, though.

"Mama," the young lady asked, "may I hit the flick?"

"Hit the flick?" mother repeated. "I'm afraid I don't read you."

"Oh, Mama," said the subject, "you mean you don't know? 'Hit the flick' just means 'go to a movie.'"

"So!" said Mama. "Well, you ask me again after you rub the tub, scour the shower, spread the bed and swish the dish."

—LEO AIKMAN, *Atlanta Constitution*

2098. Pat O'Brien, famous Hollywood actor, closed his address at a national convention of secondary school principals by reading the famous "Lounsbury Will," which was found on the body of a London pauper. The following reprint is a portion of the will along with some introductory remarks of the lawyer who probated the will.

If the court please, I would like to probate the will (holds up tattered scrap of paper) of the late George Lounsbury who died this past Tuesday in debtor's prison. Lounsbury was a pauper, yet he has left one of the richest wills I have ever come upon. There are several legal aspects as to the disposition of property which may interest the court. May I proceed?

"I, Charles Lounsbury, being of sound and disposing mind and memory, do hereby make and publish this, my last will and testament, in order, as justly may be, to distribute my interests in the world among succeeding men.

ITEM: I give good fathers and mothers, in trust for their children, all good little words of praise and encouragement, and all quaint pet names and endearments; and I charge said parents to use them justly, but generously, as the needs of their children shall require.

ITEM: I leave the children inclusively, but only for the term of their childhood, the flowers of the fields and the blossoms of the woods, and the right to play among them freely, according to

346

the custom of children, warning them, at the same time, against the thistle and the thorns. And I devise to the children the banks of the brooks and the golden sands beneath the water thereof, and the odors of the willow that dip therein, and the white clouds that float high over the giant trees. And I leave to the children the long, long days to be merry in a thousand ways, and the night and the moon, and the train of the Milky Way to wonder at, but subject, nevertheless, to the rights hereinafter given to lovers.

ITEM: I devise to boys, jointly, all the idle fields and commons, where ball may be played, all pleasant waters where one may swim, all snow-clad hills where one may fish, or where, when grim winter comes, one may skate, to have and to hold the same for the period of their boyhood. And I give to said boys each his own place at the fireside at night with all the pictures that may be seen in the burning wood, to enjoy without hindrance and without any encumbrance of care. . . .

ITEM: To young men, jointly, I devise and bequeath all boisterous inspiring sports of rivalry and I give to them the disdain of weakness and undaunted confidence in their own strength. Though they are rude, I leave to them the powers to make lasting friendships, and of possessing companions, and, to these exclusively, I give all merry songs and brave choruses to sing with lusty voices. . . ."

I leave it to the wisdom and discretion of the court to appoint a suitable executor for this man's estate. . . .

—*Bulletin, N.A.S.S.P.*

2099. He holds blueprints in his genes.
There are plans in his bones.
The old flames of a million savage
campfires flicker in his veins.
The future is alive in his blood. . . .

He's growing up.
He's heir to everything.
He's going to run the works.

—GORDON McCLOSKEY, *Youth Leaders' Digest*

2100. My little story is about Antipater, a man whose name is fairly well known, but whose history is not so well known. Antipater was, in the high jargon of today, Alexander the Great's number one boy —his most trusted general. Whenever the great conqueror went off to take over another chunk of the world, he always left Antipater at home to govern the Greek states. Antipater was a fine soldier. He was loyal and capable, but he did not have much imagination. The Greeks had a lot of imagination, so he had a lot of trouble with them. Of all the Greek states, the one that gave him the most trouble was the little state of Sparta. The citizens of this state were continually doing things for which he felt they should be punished. One time they must have done something particularly bad because he brought a rather large army and surrounded the city. After he surrounded the city, he sent his emissaries to the leaders of the Spartan people with this message: "If you will give me forty of your boys as hostages—boys whom I may take away with me to guarantee that you will be good—I will not lay waste to the city." He was a bit surprised and chagrined to find that his emissaries returned almost immediately with this message from the leaders of the Spartans: "You may have forty of our wisest and cleverest men, but you cannot have a single one of our boys."

I tell this story as a dramatic illustration of a very ancient fact that the future of any people is dependent not only upon their material resources and their industrial capacity but also it is even more determined by how they treat their youth. I think this premise needs no defense.

—Arthur F. Corey, *Bulletin, N.A.S.S.P.*

LIST OF SPECIAL INDEXES

SUBJECT INDEX

Subject Index

(Numbers in the index refer to selections in the text, not to page numbers)

Direction, *See also* objective, 316, 317, 828, 834
Disappointment, 895
Discipline, 139, 318-337, 1011, 1037, 1105, 1919
Discontent, 338-340
Discouragement, 341-343, 1704, 1775
Dissatisfaction, 1936
Dissension, 1615
Distraction, 1249
Doctor, 2072, 2073
Doubt, 963
Downtown coach, 1559
Driver education, 1062
Duty, 344, 345, 1218

E

Economist, 1652
Education, 346-411, 505, 657, 826, 830, 904, 979, 1204, 1213, 1333, 1764, 1908, 1993
Efficiency, 651, 1223
Eloquence, 1342
Emotions, 1841, 2090
Enemy, 1203, 1223
Energy, 1707
Engineer, 1275
English, 1060, 1202
Enthusiasm, 412-417, 1496
Entomologist, 2008
Ethics, 418-424, 1149
Equation, 1174
Evolution, 1875
Examination, 352, 425-434, 1085, 1095, 1163, 1663
Example, 435-441, 2089
Exercise, 1236, 1584
Expectation, 1960
Experience, 72, 441-447, 781, 1323, 1724, 1771, 1780, 2040
Experiment, 1678
Expert, 155, 258, 448-453, 839, 1411, 1663
Explanation, 1504
Expression, 1418, 1601

F

Facts, 454, 455, 594, 623, 1904
Failure, 3, 364, 655, 678, 912, 1147, 1704, 1711, 1721, 1831, 2081

Faith, 2050
Family-Family living, 456, 515, 2072
Fanatic, 1631
Fate, 2093
Father, 2092
Fear, 467-469
Fire drill, 1208
Fisherman, 870
Flattery, 470-471, 1477
Follower, 472, 473, 644
Food-Diet, 474-478, 1413
Fool, 2020, 2033, 2038
Football, 431, 437 1457, 1544, 1559, 1560, 1561, 1562, 1565-1575, 1601, 1625, 1626, 1629, 1642, 1644, 1648, 1649, 1688, 1711, 1728, 1750, 2007
Football coach, 1646
Force, 1937
Forgotten, 2050
Freedom, 479-482, 680, 1207
Friction, 2012
Friendliness, 1292
Friends, 1285
Friendship, 483-490, 2050
Fundamentals, 491-495, 1478, 1835
Future, 863, 873, 1283, 1798

G

General education, 1255
Genius, 661, 1253
Geologist, 1167, 2008
Geometry, 1181
Gifted child, 1056, 1205
Gifts-Giving, 496-498
Goal, 832
Golf, 73, 1476, 1490, 1576, 1576-1583, 1600, 1621, 1632, 1634, 1636, 1637, 1645, 1650
Good, 930
Good will, 1279
Gossip, 499-502
Grammar, 1682
Greatness, 1276
Grindstone, 1985, 2054
Group discussion, 529, 578
Grouping, 1071, 1096
Guidance, 503-506

S

Safety, 172, 793, 1173-1182
Salary, 1228, 1788, 1792, 1824, 1825, 1834, 1866, 1905
Salary raise, 1111, 1113
Salesman-Salesmanship, 583, 584, 745, 985, 1155, 1183-1187, 1494, 1741, 1797
Schedule, 1216
Scheduling, 1188, 1189
Scholarship-Scholarships, 1190, 1191
School, 142, 188, 394, 407, 491, 517, 610, 948, 953, 1022, 1043, 1070, 1086, 1171, 1188, 1192-1221
School Administration-Administrators, 256, 645, 966, 1018, 1023, 1025, 1166, 1222-1244, 1283, 1647, 1826, 1854
School Board, 1208, 1220, 1228, 1240, 1245-1247, 1866
School Building, 1246
School Custodian, 517
School Courses, 1217
School Fight, 1204
School Secretary, 1248, 1473
School Teacher, 1875
School Trip, 524
Science, 1250-1258
Scum, 1258
Secretary, 1515
Self, 1259-1271, 1799
Self-Admiration, 526
Self-Confidence, 85, 1267
Selfishness, 1280
Self-Importance, 1268
Self-Improvement, 1261
Self-Interest, 1260
Self-Reliance, 712
Self-Respect, 915, 1271, 2092
Sentence, 1682, 1798
Serenity, 1242
Service, 514, 706, 1019, 1272-1282
Simmons College, 1190
Skill, 907, 925, 1278, 1286
Slang, 2097
Small School, 1197
Sound, 1253
Spare Time, 1945

Speaking-Speech, 90, 201, 643, 794
Speakers-Speaking-Speech
  Brevity, 1376-1401
  Closers, 1527-1542
  General, 1287-1376
  Hecklers, 1520-1526
  Introductions, 1402-1420
  Openers, 1421-1501
  Relief Devices, Transitions, Recoveries, 1502-1519
Speaker's Notes, 1324, 1352
Specialization, 1283-1286, 1410
Spelling, 1549
Spiritual Values, 2084
Sports, 1074, 1543-1650
Stage Fright, 1339, 1341, 1345, 1361, 1403, 1433, 1456
Standards, 708
Statistics, 1307, 1651-1658, 2085
Story Telling, 1289, 1343, 1358
Strategy, 1659, 1660
Strength, 1493
Student Masterpieces, 1067, 1221, 1661-1673
Study, 214, 1163, 1167
Stunts, 1674-1686
Substitute, 1598, 1620, 1648
Success, 5, 246, 247, 364, 591, 673, 678, 832, 957, 1014, 1617, 1676, 1679, 1687-1747, 1831, 2019, 2023
Summer School, 1215
Superintendent, *See also* School Administrator, 645, 1208, 1220, 1229, 1232, 1234, 1238, 1244, 1249, 1293, 1347, 1389, 1800, 1822, 1823, 1850, 1883
Supervision-Supervisor, 1166, 1748-1750
Support, 1655
System, 1660

T

Tact, 1751-1753
Talent, 891
Talk, 1359, 1383
Tardy, 1165, 1791
Taxes, 1299, 1754-1757

AUTHOR AND SOURCE INDEX

Author and Source Index

(Numbers in the index refer to selections in the text, not to page numbers)

AUTHOR AND SOURCE INDEX

AUTHOR AND SOURCE INDEX

N

O

P

Q

R

AUTHOR AND SOURCE INDEX

INDEX TO NAMES AND PERSONALITIES
REFERRED TO IN THE TEXT

Index to Names and Personalities
Referred to in the Text

(Numbers in the index refer to selections in the text, not to page numbers)

M